THE ANATOMY OF TORT LAW

THE ANATOMY OF TORT LAW

PETER CANE

Corpus Christi College,
Oxford

·HART·
PUBLISHING

OXFORD

1997

Hart Publishing
Oxford
UK

Published in the United States by Hart Publishing

© Peter Cane 1997

Hart Publishing is a specialist legal publisher based in Oxford, England. To
order further copies of this book or to request a list of other publications please
write to:

Hart Publishing, 19 Whitehouse Road, Oxford, OX1 4PA
Telephone: +44 (0)1865 434459 or Fax: +44 (0)1865 794882
e-mail: hartpub@janep.demon.co.uk

Payment may be made by cheque payable to 'Hart Publishing' or by credit
card.

British Library Cataloguing in Publication Data
Data Available
ISBN 1–901362–08–6 (cloth)
1–901362–09–4 (cloth)

Typeset in 12pt Bembo
by SetAll, Abingdon
Printed in Great Britain on acid-free paper
by Bookcraft, Midsomer Norton

. . . ethics are confessedly a branch of academical learning, and Aristotle himself has said, speaking of the laws of his own country, that jurisprudence or the knowledge of those laws is the principal and most perfect branch of ethics.

William Blackstone, *Commentaries on the Laws of England*, Vol. 1, (1765–9), 27

The law and morality are inextricably interwoven. To a large extent the law is simply formulated and declared morality.

Smith New Court Securities Ltd v. *Scrimgeour Vickers (Asset Management) Ltd* [1996] 3 WLR 1051,1073, *per* Lord Steyn

PREFACE

THIS book is not an introduction for beginners or a comprehensive text. However, I hope that it will be accessible to anyone who has done a basic course on tort law, while at the same time offering stimulation to those whose knowledge and understanding of the subject is more advanced. The approach I take is a development of the mode of analysis I adopted in *Tort Law and Economic Interests*, 2nd edn (Oxford, 1996). My aim is to show that it is possible to think about the law of tort in an analytically rigorous way without being tied to the traditional textbook approach to the subject. For me, tort law is an exercise in applied ethics, and I believe that much illumination can be gained by seeking to understand the ethical principles to which it gives practical content.

I owe some major debts. The first is to the British Academy and the Leverhulme Trust whose generosity in awarding me a Senior Research Fellowship in the academic year 1996–7 made the completion of this book possible much sooner than the normal demands of teaching, examining and administration would have allowed. Secondly, in addition to providing me with a constant source of intellectual inspiration and companionship, Jane Stapleton read a draft of this book and, as always, made many penetrating and extremely helpful comments and criticisms

Thirdly, I want to thank Richard Hart and Jane Parker for agreeing to publish the book. I am delighted that it will be one of the first publications of Hart Publishing. I have known Richard for many years, and I am extremely grateful to him for the loyalty, friendship and encouragement which he has bestowed on me and on so many other authors. It is these qualities, even more than his commercial flair and his eye for quality, which make him a great publisher. And I owe much to Jane for her enthusiasm and warm friendship, as well as for playing her essential part in the production of this book with wisdom and quiet efficiency.

I am writing this preface in anticipation of taking up a Chair of Law in the Division of Philosophy and Law of the Research School of Social Sciences at the Australian National University in Canberra.

This book is, therefore, the last large piece of academic work which I shall complete in Oxford. I cannot let the occasion pass without saying how lucky I am to have been able to spend half my academic life in Oxford, particularly at Corpus. My arrival in Oxford as a graduate student in October, 1974 in a very real sense marked my intellectual birth. Those two years reading for the BCL were enormously exciting. To be able to return as a tutor was a dream come true. Oxford's unique social organization and teaching system, together with the intimacy and mutual respect of the Corpus academic community, have provided me with just the sort of environment I needed to develop as a lawyer. I cannot think how things might have turned out better. So this book is offered as a toast to Corpus Christi College and to Oxford.

PFC
Corpus Christi College
Oxford

April, 1997

TABLE OF CONTENTS

ABBREVIATIONS

AC	Appeals Cases
All ER	All England Reports
CICS	Criminal Injuries Compensation Scheme
D	defendant
EC	European Community
EU	European Union
FSR	Fleet Street Reports
ICR	Industrial Cases Reports
KB	King's Bench Division Reports (High Court)
LJ	Law Journal
LMCLQ	Lloyd's Maritime and Commercial Law Quarterly
LQR	Law Quarterly Review
LR	Law Review
MLR	Modern Law Review
NESS	necessary element of a sufficient set
New LJ	New Law Journal
OJLS	Oxford Journal of Legal Studies
P	plaintiff
P & CR	Property and Compensation Reports
QB	Queen's Bench Division Reports (High Court)
So Cal LR	Southern California Law Review
WLR	Weekly Law Reports

TABLE OF CASES

TABLE OF LEGISLATION

1 . DISMANTLING TORT LAW

INTRODUCTION

As its name implies, this book is about the structure of tort law. Its starting point is the proposition that the law of tort can be viewed as a system of ethical rules and principles of personal responsibility for conduct. This approach is in contrast to the traditional one of seeing tort law as made up of a number of discrete "torts", that is, legal formulae which can be used to obtain remedies from courts or as bargaining counters in out-of-court negotiations. I see tort law as a collection of causes of action (or "heads of liability") each made up of three main components: an interest protected by the law, some conduct which the law sanctions, and a remedy or sanction by which the interest is protected and the conduct is sanctioned. The structure of causes of action in tort is "correlative"; that is, every cause of action in tort is a two-sided affair made up of elements relating to the plaintiff and elements relating to the defendant. In Chapter 1, I explain the relationship between the traditional approach to the exposition of tort law and my "personal responsibility" approach; and I give an account of the basic structure of tort law in terms of correlativity, protected interests, sanctioned conduct and sanctions.

In Chapters 2, 3 and 4 respectively I offer an account of the sorts of conduct which tort law sanctions, the sorts of interests it protects and the sanctions by which it does the protecting and the sanctioning. In Chapter 5 I draw together the strands of the previous three chapters and show how the various interests protected and the various types of conduct sanctioned by tort law are combined into heads of liability, defined in terms of protected interests and sanctioned conduct, which trigger the various sanctions available in tort law. This chapter provides the reader with a whistle-stop tour of tort doctrine. It provides a range of new perspectives on a well-cultivated landscape. What I do in Chapters 2–5 is to break tort law up into its constituent building blocks and then put those blocks back together in a novel way which not only illuminates the inner workings of tort law but also lays the groundwork for a better understanding of the

relationship between tort law and other areas of the law, such as contract law and criminal law. Against the background of the idea of personal responsibility, this account offers fresh insight into, and greater
understanding of the significance of, many aspects of tort doctrine.

It is, of course, not only tort law which can be described in terms
of the ethics of personal responsibility, and it is not only tort law
which has a correlative structure. In this light, Chapter 6 tackles two
difficult questions raised by my approach: what, if anything, holds
together the body of law traditionally referred to as the law of tort
and gives it "unity"; and in what way, if any, is that body of law distinctively different from other bodies of law which are concerned
with personal responsibility (such as contract law). The basic argument of this chapter is that legal categories such as tort and contract
are useful, if at all, only for educational purposes and to facilitate
access to legal materials. This conclusion will not be very congenial
to those who wish, for whatever reason, to preserve sharp conceptual
divisions between different areas of civil law. Amongst other things,
it has important implications for the issue of concurrent liability and
for modes of analysis of the "law of obligations".

Finally, in Chapter 7, I explore the implications of my approach
for the relationship between the doctrines, rules and principles of tort
law on the one hand, and the functions and effects of the law on the
other. This relationship is complex because practising lawyers and
their clients often seek to use tort doctrine for pragmatic purposes
which may conflict with the principles of personal responsibility
which underlie that doctrine. The basic thesis of this chapter is that
the meaning and value of tort law viewed as a set of ethical rules and
principles of personal responsibility can be properly understood only
if account is also taken of its functions and effects. This is because
there is a symbiotic relationship between the rules and principles of
tort law and its functions and effects.

TORTS AS RECIPES

In this first chapter, then, I shall argue that the traditional approach to
tort law conceals its nature as a system of ethical principles of personal
responsibility. My claim is that organizing the law around the ideas of
correlativity, protected interests, sanctioned conduct and sanctions
provides a much deeper understanding of its inner logic than the traditional approach, and also a more satisfactory way of sorting out the
relationship between tort law and other legal categories. In my view,

the framework I offer provides, both for theoretical and practical purposes, a much better way of thinking about and organizing tort law than the traditional division of the law into "torts".

If you look at a typical text on the law of tort in any common law jurisdiction (that is, where the applicable law is, or is derived from or based on, English law), you will find the law discussed and expounded in terms of a number of "torts". These include the tort of negligence, the tort of nuisance, the tort of conversion, the tort of defamation, and so on. Indeed, one author has constructed an "alphabetical list of known torts" containing more than 70 entries.[1] This approach to expounding tort law I shall call the "common law approach". This approach is in notable contrast to that adopted in civil law jurisdictions (that is, where the law is derived from or based on Roman law). France provides, perhaps, the most extreme example of the civil law approach: there, much of the law of delict (or "tort") is derived from a few very general provisions in the *Code Civil*, such as Article 1382: "Every act whatever . . . which causes damage to another obliges him by whose fault the damage occurred to repair it".[2] This provision has two notable features: first, it is very general, and secondly, it bases liability directly on a principle of personal responsibility for damage caused by faulty conduct. The common law approach, by contrast, has at least two important characteristics relevant to the present discussion. First, and putting the point very crudely, whereas a French lawyer might see the process of deciding particular legal disputes as involving the application of broad general principles to particular facts, the common lawyer is more likely to think of that process in terms of determining whether a particular fact situation fits into a framework of rules and quite narrow principles which define the elements of "a tort". Secondly, the common lawyer tends to view the elements of particular torts as technical requirements of the law rather than as applications of ethical principles of personal responsibility concerned with what people ought or ought not to do, such as that people ought not to cause damage deliberately. The common lawyer's understanding of the law of tort consists largely of knowledge about the technical definitions of legal terms and concepts and about fact situations which have, in the past, been held to give rise to tort liability. The typical common lawyer would not (in a professional capacity, at least) think of the law

[1] B. Rudden (1991–2) 6/7 *Tulane Civil Law Forum* 105.
[2] See K. Zweigert and H. Kötz, *An Introduction to Comparative Law*, 2nd edn (Oxford, 1987), 656.

of tort as a set of ethical principles of personal responsibility, principles about how people ought and ought not to behave in their dealings with others.

The common law way of thinking about tort law can be traced
historically to the "forms of action" which were central to the "formulary system" of pleading cases before courts.[3] Under a formulary
system of litigation, an action can be started (and will succeed) only
if the facts of the plaintiff's case fit one of the formulae which the
courts recognize, or if the plaintiff can persuade the court to recognize a new formula. In the heyday of the English formulary system,
the courts would process a claim only if it could be and was appro-
priately "packaged". If a container (called a "writ") of the right shape
was not available, the claim would fail even if, had the court
processed the claim, it would have found the claim to be meritori-
ous. In short, under a formulary system, the way a claim is packaged
is as important as the claim's strength. Changing the metaphor, forms
of action were a bit like recipes – recipes for success in litigation. The
prime concern of the lawyer in a formulary system is to follow the
recipe faithfully.

The English formulary system was gradually replaced in the 19th
century by the modern system under which what matters (in theory,
anyway) is not how a complaint is packaged but whether the complaint is a good one. In other words, what is important is not the
"form" of the claim but rather whether it states a "good cause of
action". The forms of action have been replaced by causes of action.
A cause of action provides a court with a legally recognized ground
for granting a remedy to a claimant. This change from forms to causes
of action was of enormous importance in the history of the law and
of legal thought because it shifted attention away from the mechan-
ics and procedure of making legal claims (were they properly packaged?) to the substance and merits of claims.[4] Under a formulary
system it is impossible to understand the law without also understanding procedures for litigating, because claims have to be packaged
in a way which is recognized by the processing authorities, the
courts. By contrast, the typical modern text on the law of contract or
tort, for instance, contains almost nothing about procedural law
but is primarily concerned with the "*substance*" of the law or, in

---

[3] J.H. Baker, *An Introduction to English Legal History*, 3rd edn (London, 1990), ch. 4.
[4] There is one area in which a sort of formulary system still operates, namely that of applications for judicial review in public law. See generally P. Cane, *An Introduction to
Administrative Law*, 3rd edn (Oxford, 1996).

other words, with the grounds on which courts will award legal remedies.

Because, in practice, the procedures for making legal claims have subtle and complex effects on the substance of the law relevant to resolving such claims, this distinction between procedure and substance is, to a certain extent, misleading – but only to a certain extent. We can gain a great deal of useful knowledge about the law without knowing much, if anything, about the procedures for litigation. One important reason for this is that civil law (as opposed to criminal law), of which the law of tort is a "department", has both backward-looking functions and forward-looking functions. The backward-looking functions are concerned with the resolution of disputes and the provision of remedies. The procedures which were central to the formulary system were procedures for resolving disputes in the courts and for obtaining judicial remedies. Even under our modern, non-formulary system, a knowledge and understanding of relevant procedures for resolving legal disputes is important to success in making a legal claim. This is true whether the claim is heard by a court or, as is most commonly the case, it is resolved by an out-of-court settlement. For instance, if a legal claim is not made within a specified period (the "limitation period"), it will fail, however strong the substance of the claim might be; and one of the commonest causes of complaint against solicitors is delay beyond the limitation period in making legal claims.[5]

One of the forward-looking functions of civil law is to guide conduct. If people know the sorts of conduct the law allows and those it prohibits, or the interests which the law protects and those it does not, people can attempt to plan their lives in such a way as to minimize the chance of being involved in a legal dispute or of breaching the law. Knowledge of procedures for resolving disputes is quite unimportant if one's interest is in using the law in this prophylactic or precautionary way. Moreover, for most people most of the time, the law is much more important as a guide to conduct than as a set of rules for resolving disputes. Relatively speaking, only a tiny proportion of human conduct which is regulated or affected by law gives rise to legal disputes which become the subject of litigation or other formal modes of dispute resolution. For this reason alone, knowledge and understanding of the substance of the law is much more important than knowledge of the procedures of litigation.

[5] A lawyer who is guilty of such delay may be liable to pay damages to a client whose claim fails as a result.

The emergence of legal textbooks as we know them today was partly a result of the demise of the formulary system. This encouraged lawyers to think about the substantive principles underlying the forms of action and to organize causes of action according to these principles. One of the most important products of this new intellectual approach was the development of what is now often referred to as "the classical law of contract", that is, a set of rules and principles governing the formation and termination of contracts. Exposition of these rules and principles (concerned with offer and acceptance, consideration and so on) occupies a substantial part of most modern contract texts; and although the law recognizes specific contracts, such as contracts for the sale of goods and contracts of guarantee, which are governed by special sets of rules, these special rules are usually seen as applications or adaptations of the general principles of the law of contract to meet particular circumstances. No one doubts that we have a law of contract (singular) rather than (or, perhaps, in addition to) a law of contracts (plural).

However, although the forms of action were replaced by causes of action, the thinking underlying the formulary system continued to exert a powerful influence on the way textbook writers (and courts) thought about the law in general and tort law in particular. So, for instance, some of the old forms of action, such as trespass or nuisance, took on new life as causes of action: and today, texts on the law of tort still contain sections dealing with trespass and nuisance in their various manifestations. Furthermore, in certain respects, such causes of action are just as formulaic as the forms of action were. If some "element" of a modern cause of action "in tort" is not present in the plaintiff's claim, the plaintiff may lose even if some notion of fairness or justice would suggest that the plaintiff should win. For instance, since the days of the formulary system, it has been the law that in order to succeed in an action in nuisance, the plaintiff must have an "interest in land". This means, for example, that if a family has noisy neighbours, the only member of the family who can bring a nuisance action against the neighbours is the member who owns or rents their house, even if the whole family suffers equally from the noise. In some contexts, this rule is now thought by many to produce unsatisfactory results; but judges have had great difficulty in deciding whether to allow a person who does not have an interest in land to bring a nuisance action or whether, instead, the law should recognize a new tort which would not be encumbered with the "interest in land" requirement and which might be used to deal, for instance, with cases of "harassment" of people in their homes, whatever the nature of their interest in the property.[6]

On the other hand, abolition of the formulary system did have at least one effect of fundamental importance on the law of tort. This effect took some time to develop, reaching maturity in 1932 in the decision of the House of Lords in the famous case of *Donoghue* v. *Stevenson*,[7] which is commonly treated as having recognized the tort of negligence. This development exemplified the non-formulary mode of thinking about law in the sense that underlying it lay an ethical injunction of extremely wide potential scope – namely "take care not to injure your 'neighbours'".[8] As a legal principle, this injunction is hedged about with a complex web of qualifications and exceptions; but still, the foundation of the tort of negligence is not a set of specific rules and principles such as exemplified the forms of action, but an ethical principle of great generality. Furthermore, the tort of negligence operates in a very wide range of situations to provide remedies for carelessly caused injury. Nevertheless, despite the breadth of its operation, a plaintiff can succeed "in the tort of negligence" only by persuading the court that the "elements" of the tort are present in the claim. Common law courts typically do not decide "negligence cases" in tort by reasoning from general principles but by seeing whether the plaintiff's claim fits into a previously recognized pattern of liability; and, if it does not, by deciding whether a new pattern into which it would fit should be recognized. *Donoghue* v. *Stevenson* concerned the liability of a manufacturer of ginger beer to a woman who, it was alleged, suffered illness as a result of drinking a bottle of beer containing the decomposed remains of a snail. The leading judgment of Lord Atkin contained a very general principle (called the "neighbour principle") sanctioning[9] careless conduct, and much more specific principles dealing with the liability of manufacturers for defective products.

Ever since *Donoghue* v. *Stevenson* was decided, there has been debate about the status of the neighbour principle: is it a legal principle which can be used as the basis for deciding particular cases, or is it just an ethical and aspirational statement of little or no legal force? In the 1970s and 1980s in England some courts appeared to opt

---

[6] See further p. 72 below.

[7] [1932] AC 562.

[8] For discussion of the legal meaning of this word, see p. 125 below.

[9] The verb "to sanction" can mean either "to authorize or reward", or "to penalize". In this book it is used in the latter sense.

briefly for the former view, but now the latter approach is preferred. Courts in some other common law countries (such as New Zealand and Canada) still profess adherence to the former approach, but in practice tend to decide negligence cases in tort in much the same way as the English courts – that is by developing detailed rules and principles to deal with individual cases and resisting the idea that such rules and principles can be deduced in any straightforward way from a general principle such as "take care not to injure your neighbours".

Despite the abolition of the formulary system, the prevalent approach to tort law is still essentially formulaic. Under this approach, the modern torts are treated as formulae, or sets of technical legal rules which define the conditions for success in litigation: winning in a tort action depends largely on finding a formula which fits one's case. Causes of action in tort operate in a similar way to the forms of action – they regulate and shape the resolution of legal disputes by litigation and other modes of dispute settlement. However, causes of action in tort are also important in relation to the forward-looking functions of the law, because through them we organize the substantive law of tort liability into manageable portions. A lawyer advises a client whether planned action might attract tort liability by surveying the causes of action in tort and determining whether the proposed activity falls within any of them.[10] The mind of the tort lawyer, whether as litigator or adviser, tends to be dominated by the recipes for forensic success which the individual torts represent.

Does it matter whether or not we take a formulaic approach to the law of tort? Different legal actors might answer this question differently. A practising lawyer whose concern is to advise a client about what a court will do or to persuade a court to decide in the client's favour is well-advised to present the client's case in terms of the established formulae of tort law. For the practising lawyer whose main concern is to further his or her client's interests, a formulaic approach may not only be adequate but also, in most circumstances, the most economical and successful one. However, if our concern is to deepen our understanding of the structure and functions of the law of tort or of its relationship to other areas of the law, or if our concern is that tort law should develop in a just and rational way, we can gain much by analyzing the law not in terms of torts but in terms of a set of ethical principles of personal responsibility which can be found to

---

[10] A very good example of this sort of approach is J. Conaghan, "Gendered Harms and the Law of Tort: Remedying (Sexual) Harassment", (1996) 16 *OJLS* 407.

underlie the traditional torts. The formulaic approach makes it difficult to explain and understand tort law as a system of ethical precepts
about personal responsibility, and to think clearly about when tort
liability ought to be imposed as contrasted with when it has been or
might be imposed.

Besides the obvious value of making explicit the ethical nature of
tort law, several more mundane (and technical) reasons can be given
in favour of a non-formulaic approach. First, the coverage of torts
may overlap with one another in the sense that a claim which falls
"within" one tort (such as negligence) may also fall within another
tort (such as nuisance). Such overlaps are confusing and suggest that
the accepted distinctions between the overlapping torts do not accurately reflect the (ethical) principles underlying their scope and operation. Secondly, as we saw above in relation to the example of
nuisance and harassment, too close a concentration on the traditional
formulae may make it unnecessarily difficult to reform the law in
ways widely agreed to be desirable. Thirdly, the division of the law
into torts may conceal important organizing categories in the law. For
example, one of the main foci of the law of tort is personal injury and
illness; but there is no single tort which is concerned exclusively with
such misfortunes, and a number of torts can be "used" to obtain compensation for personal injuries. We can learn a great deal about tort
law by focusing on personal injuries (for instance) as an organizing
category. Fourthly, concentration on the formulae of tort law makes
it unduly difficult to understand the relationship between it and other
related areas of the law (such as the law of contract or restitution)
because these other areas are not, of course, organized around the
formulae of tort law. In fact, no other area of civil law is as formulaic
as tort law.[11] We are much more likely to be able to understand the
relationship between different but related areas of the law if we can
develop a common set of concepts and principles for analyzing them.

Fifthly, the area of operation of the tort of negligence is so wide
that it may be positively misleading to treat it as a single legal formula.
We may learn much more about liability for negligent conduct by
looking at the different interests which the law of negligence protects, such as the interest in personal health and safety, the interest that
tangible property not be damaged, and the interest in the preservation of intangible wealth. Indeed, on closer examination we find that

[11] Criminal law is highly formulaic. For an attempt to expound the "general part" of
criminal law or, in other words, to identify general principles underlying the plethora of
crimes, see Glanville Williams, *Criminal Law: The General Part* (London, 1964).

the tort of negligence protects various interests differently even though there are also features common to the protection it gives to the various interests.

Ironically, the tort of negligence also illustrates a pitfall which may be encountered in searching for ethical principles of personal responsibility underlying the formulae of the law of tort. One of the reasons why the tort of negligence conceals important differences in the way it protects various interests is that at bottom, the tort is based on an extremely general principle: take care not to harm your neighbours. Principles of this generality tell us little about the law because in order to be useful, they need to be heavily qualified and modified to deal with individual cases. There are many situations in which failure to take care not to harm others does not (and by general agreement should not) incur tort liability. The sort of principles which will help us to understand tort law are those which are general enough to explain a significant category of instances of liability (as opposed to single instances), but which are not so broad that they encompass categories which are importantly different from one another. To be useful, principles must be broad enough to enable us to spot legally relevant similarities between different fact situations, but narrow enough to enable us to spot legally relevant differences.

How, then, should we go about identifying such principles? In the next section, I shall explain how I intend to approach this task.

THE ANATOMY OF A TORT

The law of tort is part of a larger body of civil (as opposed to criminal) law sometimes called "the law of obligations". Other parts of the law of obligations are the law of contract, the law of restitution and the law of trusts. The law of obligations may be contrasted with the law of property. The law of property consists of rules (which we might call "constitutive rules") which establish (proprietary) rights and interests which the law of obligations protects by what might be called "protective rules". For example, tort law protects real property through the tort of trespass: to enter someone's land without their permission and without legal justification is to commit the tort of trespass to land. Property law defines who owns what land, and tort law protects the rights of the owner against unwanted intruders.

Although contract law and the law of trusts may be treated as part of the law of obligations, in fact these bodies of law contain both constitutive and protective rules. The law of contract not only establishes an obligation to keep contracts, but it also lays down rules about how contracts are formed or, in other words, about what constitutes a binding contractual undertaking which there is a legal obligation to fulfil. Similarly, the law of trusts not only establishes an obligation to comply with trusts, but it also contains the rules which determine whether a trust has been created. In fact, the interest of a beneficiary under a trust is a form of property, and the law of trusts is often treated as part of the law of property rather than as part of the law of obligations. By contrast, tort law and the law of restitution are purely protective – they establish obligations designed to protect interests created by constitutive rules of the law of property, trusts and contract or which arise in some other way.[12]

Confusingly, too, not all protective causes of action encompassed within the law of obligations are causes of action for breach of an obligation in any meaningful sense. For instance, liability resting on A to restore to B money paid by B to A as a result of an uninduced mistake (which is restitutionary liability) is not liability for breach of an obligation by A because A has, by definition, not done anything to cause the payment to be made. Again, a person may be vicariously liable for the tort of another, even if that person has breached no obligation, simply by virtue of being in a certain relationship with that person (such as that of employer-employee). Nevertheless, very many causes of action in the law of obligations are based on breaches of obligations, that is on action which a person ought not to have taken or on failure to take action which a person ought to have taken.

Both the law of obligations and the law of property are part of what we call "civil law" as opposed to criminal law. Civil law is a social institution by which we organize and interpret human conduct in a particular way. A central feature of civil (or, as it is sometimes called, "private")[13] law is "bilateralness" or (more euphoniously)

[12] The most important interest in this last category is the interest in personal health and safety, which each human being has by virtue of being human. The point made in the text – that tort law does not create the interests it protects – is not inconsistent with the argument made below (see pp. 18, 208) that causes of action in tort may themselves be viewed as a form of wealth. Even if such causes of action were treated as a form of property (see F.H. Lawson and B. Rudden, *The Law of Property*, 2nd edn (Oxford, 1982), 27–8), this would be by virtue of property law, not tort law.

[13] Private law may be contrasted with "public law". Private law is about relationships between citizens whereas public law is a about relationships between citizens and the state and between different "organs" of the state. In this sense, criminal law may be categorized as public law. But the main departments of public law are constitutional law and administrative law. Confusingly, however, private law rules, such as rules of contract or tort law, can apply to dealings between individuals and the state. For discussion of these difficult issues see P. Cane, *An Introduction to Administrative Law*, 3rd edn (Oxford, 1996), esp. chs 2 and 11–14.

"correlativity".[14] What this means in simple terms is that civil law organizes relationships between individuals on a one-to-one basis. In the law of obligations, for instance, one person's obligation corresponds ("is correlative") to another person's right. The rules of the law of tort, contract and so on are couched in terms of bilateral relationships between individuals, and that every cause of action in the law of obligations is two-sided. For example, tort law recognizes no concept of negligence "in the air". Tortious negligence is conduct which affects another in particular ways. This does not mean, of course, that there may not be tort actions (for instance) involving more than one plaintiff or more than one defendant or more than one of both, but only that for the purpose of determining the legal rights and obligations of these multiple parties, the law deals with them in twos – one plaintiff versus one defendant.

The idea of correlativity can be explained more graphically by contrasting a tort action for personal injuries suffered in a road accident with a claim for social security benefits made by a victim of a road accident who is, for instance, rendered incapable of work. In the tort action there will be two parties, the victim and the injurer. If the injurer is found liable, he or she will be ordered to pay damages to the plaintiff calculated by reference to the injuries suffered in the accident because of the interaction (the road accident) between the two parties. By contrast, when a road accident victim makes a successful claim for social security benefit, he or she will receive payment out of a fund, not from an individual; and typically not because of any interaction between the claimant and any other individual but simply because the claimant has certain financial needs which the State has decided to meet. Social security law is not based on the idea of correlativity.

[14] For a difficult and extremely sophisticated exposition of this idea see E. Weinrib, *The Idea of Private Law* (Cambridge, Mass, 1995), reviewed by Cane (1996) 16 *OJLS* 471. However, it should be noted that the sense in which I use the word "correlativity" is rather different from the sense in which Weinrib uses it. In the first place, he correlates "rights" and "obligations" *per se*, not the positions of the two parties. More importantly, his concept of correlativity is much stronger than mine in the sense that for him, obligations are a normative expression of, or in some way normatively inherent in, rights. In my analysis, correlativity only expresses the fact that causes of action in tort are two-sided. I do not, for instance, see any necessary connection between interests and conduct on the one hand and particular remedies on the other. Sanctions are chosen to protect interests and sanction conduct according to moral judgements which are not inherent in any of those concepts but reflect views about the value of the interest to be protected and the culpability of the conduct to be sanctioned.

This idea of correlativity provides the framework within which I will analyze the law of tort. Every cause of action in tort and, therefore, every principle of tort liability, has two basic (sets of) elements, one concerned with the position of one party to a bilateral human interaction (the "victim" of the tortious conduct) and the other concerned with the position of the other party to that interaction (the perpetrator of the tortious conduct, or the "injurer"). For the sake of convenience (and following a practice common amongst legal writers), I shall often refer to the victim as the plaintiff (P) and to the injurer as the defendant (D). It is important to remember, however, that tort law is not concerned only, or even primarily, with litigation, with court actions between plaintiffs and defendants. Its main function is to enable people to know how to organize their lives in such a way as to avoid becoming a party to litigation. Even when disputes arise to which the law of tort is relevant, very rarely do such disputes end in the commencement of litigation, let alone in a court hearing.

The aim of this "correlative analysis" is to understand and explain the law of tort as a system of ethical principles of personal responsibility or, in other words, a system of precepts about how people may, ought and ought not to behave in their dealings with others. This analysis of the law of tort will be built on three basic concepts: sanctioned conduct, protected interests and sanctions. Let us look briefly at each of these concepts. First, sanctioned conduct. Tort law is concerned with people's responsibility for their acts and omissions. And because it deals with interactions between people, it contains principles relevant not only to the conduct of injurers but also to the conduct of victims. For example, in the tort of negligence, not only is there a principle that people should take reasonable care not to injure others, but there is also a principle that people should take reasonable care for their own safety. Every cause of action in tort has elements concerned with the conduct of the interacting parties. For our purposes, a "sanction' can be defined as some legal consequence adverse to the perpetrator of the sanctioned conduct. In the case of conduct of injurers, the sanction will typically be a remedy, such as an order to pay damages to the victim. In the case of conduct of victims, the sanction will typically be refusal of a remedy or a reduction of damages.

Because tort law rests on the idea of correlativity, the only conduct sanctioned by it is conduct relevant to or part of some interaction between the two parties. This point can be neatly illustrated by the following example: suppose that a person with a serious criminal record of convictions for theft is injured as the result of a brawl in which that person was *not* taking part. If the victim applied for compensation under the Criminal Injuries Compensation Scheme (which is a government-run compensation scheme for victims of violent crime, funded by general taxation), his or her previous criminal record could be taken into account to justify awarding less compensation than might be awarded to a "purely innocent" victim.[15] By contrast, if the victim sued his or her attacker in tort, any past conduct of the victim would be relevant to the claim only if it had contributed in a relevant way to the injuries suffered as a result of the brawl.

The second basic component of the correlative analysis of the law of tort is "protected interests". For instance, tort law protects a person's interest in maintaining a good reputation, in being healthy in mind and body, in not having tangible property damaged, and so on. The law of tort protects people's interests by sanctioning conduct which interferes with or damages those interests. Just as tort law is concerned with the conduct of victims as well as that of injurers, it is, conversely, also concerned with the interests of injurers as well as those of victims. But whereas, in relation to victims, the law of tort offers positive protection to a wide range of tangible and intangible assets by granting remedies of various sorts, to injurers the law offers negative protection. This latter point requires some explanation. The liabilities imposed by tort law are not universal in scope; in other words, the law of tort does not sanction every act or omission which interferes with or damages some protected interest of the victim; nor are all legally recognized interests protected by tort law. Moreover, not all of the interests protected by the law of tort are protected from interference or damage as a result of all of the types of conduct which tort law sanctions. In other words, an interest may be protected from interference or damage by conduct of one type but not of another. The imposition of tort liability limits people's freedom of action in a significant way by making certain courses of action (or inaction) more costly than they would otherwise be. The imposition of tort liability on someone will also typically reduce that person's wealth because the effect of granting a judicial remedy will usually be to make the defendant worse off and the plaintiff better off. Because the imposition of tort liability on a person significantly impinges on that person's freedom of action and reduces their financial wealth, the

---

[15] P. Cane, *Atiyah's Accidents, Compensation and the Law*, 5th edn (London, 1993), 263–5.

law, to be fair, must strike a balance between the interests of victims and the interests of injurers. This it does negatively by limiting the definition of "protected interests" and of "sanctioned conduct" and by protecting certain interests only from interference or damage resulting from certain types of sanctioned conduct.

My approach to tort law which views it as a set of rules and principles of personal responsibility must be understood in the light of the points just made. Legal responsibility impinges on freedom to act or refrain from action, and it is imposed in order to protect people's freedom from interference with certain of their interests. The law strikes a balance between "freedom to" on the one hand, and "freedom from" on the other. One of the virtues of the analytical method I use in this book is that it makes clear that law in general and tort law in particular balances freedom against responsibility. So when I talk of "responsibility", I use the term as a shorthand reference to the balance struck in the law between freedom and responsibility.

The selection of sanctions (which form the third basic component of the correlative analysis of tort law) is important in balancing the interests of victims and injurers. As we will see, a variety of sanctions are available in tort law, but not all of these sanctions are necessarily available to sanction all the types of conduct which fall within the purview of tort law, nor are they all available to protect all the types of interests which fall within the purview of tort law. The sanctions attaching to causes of action in tort express and give effect to the balance struck by the law between the positions of the two parties to each cause of action. We cannot give a full account of the interests protected and the conduct sanctioned by tort law without also giving an account of how those interests are protected and that conduct is sanctioned because sanctions are the means by which tort law gives practical expression to the balance it strikes between responsibility and freedom. For this reason, sanctions look in two directions at once. This creates a tension which, as we will see in Chapter 4, has to be taken into account if we are to understand how particular sanctions relate, at one and the same time, to the interest being protected and the conduct being sanctioned.

CORRELATIVITY AND THE FORWARD-LOOKING FUNCTIONS OF TORT LAW

The fact that the basic structure of the law of tort is correlative and that the law of tort organizes human interactions bilaterally does not mean that in relation to any particular human interaction so analyzed, the relevant principles of tort law refer exclusively to the two parties involved. This is because (superior) courts have law-making powers. There are two sources of law in common law systems, Parliament and the courts. Parliament makes law in statutes while the courts make law by giving reasons for decisions in individual cases. In the typical tort action, two sorts of questions arise: questions of law and questions of fact. For instance, the question of whether D owed a duty of care to P and, if so, what that duty required of D, are questions of law, while the question of whether D actually breached a duty of care is a question of fact. Answers given by courts to questions of fact have relevance only for the parties in the dispute before the court. In other words, answers to questions of fact "do not create precedents".[16] By contrast, answers to questions of law are not only relevant to deciding the case in which the answer is given; they can also generate legal rules and principles which may be of relevance in deciding disputes between other parties. In other words, answers to questions of law create precedents – they make law. As a result, when a court answers a question of law in a tort case, it will be concerned not only with the impact of that answer on the dispute before it, but also with its impact on other similar disputes which may already have arisen or which may arise in the future. Therefore, the court will not be concerned with the parties to the dispute before it simply as individuals, but also as representatives (so to speak) of other people who are or who may in the future be in a similar position.

This precedential effect of court decisions is most obviously relevant when a court hears what is called a "test case". When, for instance, a large number of plaintiffs bring individual tort claims against a single defendant, one or more of those claims may be picked out as test cases because they raise issues which are common to a number of the claims being brought. A test case is put before the court explicitly for the purpose of eliciting from the court a decision which will resolve not only the test case but also all the other cases with which it shares common features. Another type of case in which the precedential relevance of court decisions is prominent is that in which a court is asked to decide "a preliminary point of law". In this type of case, parties agree, for the sake of saving time and money, not to investigate the facts of the claim fully until they have found out whether the claim has any chance of success as a matter of law. Some

[16] This does not mean, of course, that legal rules may not refer to facts, for many do. But they refer to facts in the abstract, as it were, and not in relation to particular litigants.

of the most important cases in the modern law of tort have been decided in this way. The most famous example is *Donoghue* v. *Stevenson*.[17] As noted earlier, in this case it was alleged that P had become ill as a result of drinking a bottle of ginger beer manufactured by D in which were the decomposed remains of a snail. These facts were never proved, but were assumed to be true in order to raise the legal issue of whether, in those circumstances, the manufacturer could be held liable in tort to the consumer. The case established a rule of law which forms one of the foundations of the common law of product liability, namely that a manufacturer owes a duty to take care not to cause personal injury to consumers by marketing products containing defects which the consumer has no reasonable chance of discovering. In laying down this rule of law, the House of Lords was concerned not only with Mrs Donoghue as an individual, but also as representative of consumers generally; and it was concerned not only with Stevenson as an individual but also as representative of manufacturers generally. Nevertheless, even in their guise as representatives, the court was concerned with their positions relative to one another.

If the facts of the case had ever been investigated by a court, in doing so the court would have been concerned with the parties as individuals, not as representatives: had Mrs Donoghue actually been made ill by the drink, and had the drink actually contained the remains of a snail because Stevenson had been careless? Once again, the court would have been concerned with the interaction between the two parties, but now with aspects of it which were relevant only to the two parties as individuals. In this book I am only concerned with the former aspect of tort law; that is, with those aspects of court decisions which concern parties to tort actions as representatives. One reason why it is important to stress this point is as follows. A distinction often used in discussing legal rules is that between corrective justice and distributive justice. Distributive justice concerns the way wealth and other benefits are distributed throughout society. So, for instance, most people in Britain (and many other countries) would say that a society in which the law allowed men and women to be paid differently for doing the same job was distributively unfair. Corrective justice, by contrast, concerns making good certain alterations to the distribution of wealth or benefits in society. So, for example, if D intentionally disables P from working, most people

[17] [1932] AC 562.

would say that it would be fair to require D to make good ("correct") the loss of income suffered by P by paying damages to P.

Some people say that the law of tort is best explained in terms of corrective justice. On this view, it is a set of rules concerned, and concerned only, with correcting disturbances to the distribution of resources in society which come about in certain ways. However, this account of the law of tort is adequate only if we concentrate on its function of dispute settlement (as opposed to its function of guiding conduct) and only if we treat court decisions as being relevant only to the actual parties to the dispute before the court. Once we take account of the fact that court decisions can create precedents which can be used to guide people's conduct and to decide disputes other than that before the court, we can see that the law of tort is also concerned with distributive justice.[18] Consider *Donoghue* v. *Stevenson* again. If we assume that before that case was decided, consumers in the position of Mrs Donoghue could not recover damages from manufacturers in the position of Stevenson, while after the decision they could, it becomes clear that one result of the case was to alter the distribution of resources in society by giving consumers a right of action against manufacturers which they did not have before. Of course, if the dispute between Donoghue and Stevenson had eventually been decided by a court in Donoghue's favour, the court would also have corrected the wrong done by Stevenson to Donoghue. But in fact, the importance of the case went far beyond the correction of this wrong; it changed the distribution of wealth in society in a significant way by deciding that in future, manufacturers would have to bear costs associated with the manufacturing process which, on the assumption we have made, were previously borne by consumers. When we make judgements about the fairness of rules of tort law, independently of their application to the facts of individual cases, we are commenting on whether the distribution of legal rights and obligations established by those rules is fair.

---

[18] There are many different theories about what makes a distribution of resources just. Perhaps the most famous modern theory of distributive justice is that of John Rawls, *A Theory of Justice* (Oxford, 1972). A very different account is that of Robert Nozick, *Anarchy, State and Utopia* (Oxford, 1974), esp. Part II. An approach which has been influential in relation to tort law is that properly operating free markets automatically generate a just distribution of resources: R.A. Posner, *The Economics of Justice* (London, 1981), esp. ch's 3 and 4. For a useful discussion of various aspects of and approaches to distributive justice see J.R. Lucas, *On Justice* (Oxford, 1980), ch's 8–14.

LEGISLATION AND CORRELATIVITY

The discussion so far has revolved around the common law of tort, that is around judge-made law. Although very many of the rules and principles of tort law are, indeed, derived from the judgments of courts, a significant proportion are also contained in legislation made by Parliament and other legislators authorized by Parliament to make law. Such statutory rules and principles can be analyzed in terms of the concept of correlativity in the same way as judge-made rules and principles. The correlativity of the law of tort is not a function of its source but of the fact that it is part of a body of law by which we organize and interpret human relationships and interactions in a particular way. As we saw earlier when discussing the Criminal Injuries Compensation Scheme, there are bodies of legal rules and principles which are related to tort law and which even perform similar legal and social functions to those performed by tort law, but which cannot be adequately described in terms of the concept of correlativity. Such bodies of law are, by definition, not part of tort law because correlativity is an intrinsic feature of that human social institution which we call "the law of tort". An important advantage of the mode of analysis adopted in this book is that it facilitates the integration of the common law of tort with relevant statutes and statutory provisions.

This is not to say that the relationship between judge-made and statutory law is straightforward, as we will see in Chapter 2 when we discuss tort liability for "Non-Compliance with Statutes". It is also true, of course, that in case of conflict, statute prevails over the common law, and the impact of statutory provisions on the law of tort may be to require established rules of common law to be abandoned or modified. This point raises a much larger issue which crops up at various point throughout the book, namely that of "institutional competence". The basic function of courts is dispute-settlement, while rule-making is incidental to and parasitic on that basic function. By contrast, the part played by the legislature in relation to tort law is the making of rules, not the settlement of disputes. Moreover, whereas the legitimacy of legislation is based largely on the legitimacy of the political process and only secondarily on the content of the legislation, a crucially important source of the legitimacy of any particular judge-made rule is the degree to which it is consistent and coherent with the whole body of related common law rules. For this reason, courts may sometimes be unwilling to decide tort cases in such a way as to generate a rule or principle which could be criticized as being too radical a break from or development of the existing body of common law. In such a case a court might say that if a particular rule is to be made, the legislature must do it. For this reason, the legislature has a distinctive role to play in developing the law even in areas, like tort law, which are very largely the product of judicial activity. Indeed, there are some areas of law discussed in this book, such as intellectual property law and anti-discrimination law, which are basically creations of the legislature.

There is a second aspect of this issue of institutional competence which deserves mention. Later in this chapter I will argue that one of the functions of the law and of lawmakers is to resolve ethical disagreements in society by laying down rules of conduct which, although not uncontroversial, represent a reasonable compromise between competing views which society can adopt as a publicly enforceable code of behaviour. If deciding a tort case in a particular way would require the court to make a rule which would alter or develop the existing common law in a way which the court feels would be highly controversial, it may say that if the rule is to be made, the legislature will have to do so. The legitimacy of judge-made law depends crucially on its content, and that legitimacy is likely to be threatened if new common law rules are highly controversial. A third aspect of the issue of institutional competence is this: one of the factors which courts take into account in deciding whether to change or develop the law in a particular way is the practical consequences of doing so. If a court feels that it knows too little about what the consequences of changing the law in a particular way would be, it may decline to do so. Not only are the executive and the legislature better equipped to find out about the likely consequences of particular laws and changes in the law, but it is politically more acceptable for them to propose and make laws the likely consequences of which are largely a matter for speculation.

Tort law, then, is a complex amalgam of judge-made and statutory law. Moreover, the courts' view of their institutional competence vis-a-vis the legislature may make them unwilling to develop or change the common law if the proposed change would be too radical a departure from the existing law, or might be very controversial, or if the court feels it knows too little about what the consequences of the change would be. These issues of institutional competence provide important background to understanding the relationship between statutory and judge-made rules in the law of tort, and I will advert to them at various points throughout the book. Because the legislature and the courts have different and complementary rule-making functions, it is clear that a full understanding of tort law depends on integrating common law and statute in our account of the law.

A SUMMARY SO FAR

I can summarize the discussion so far by saying that this book aims to analyze the law of tort not in terms of the traditional formulae of specific torts but in terms of the concept of correlativity and the ideas of sanctioned conduct, protected interests and sanctions. My first task (which I perform in Chapters 2–4) will be to "dismantle" the various head of tort liability into their component building blocks: protected interests, sanctioned conduct and sanctions. This is not to say, however, that I will not refer to the traditional formulae of the law of tort, because it is important for me to explain how the formulae relate to my analysis. Having dismantled tort law, I will then put it back together (in Chapter 5) in terms of combinations of protected interests, sanctioned conduct and sanctions. By approaching the law of tort in this novel way, we will be able to understand it better as a social and ethical institution and not just as a set of technical categories into which lawyers force social life and which they manipulate, often in mysterious ways. My analysis will also provide tools for understanding better how tort law interacts with other related areas of the law (see Chapter 6).

A LAW OF TORTS OR A LAW OF TORT?

Since the decision in *Donoghue* v. *Stevenson*, writers have often asked this question: is tort law just a heterogeneous collection of loosely related causes of action, or is it underpinned by one or a few general principles of liability? Is there a law of torts (plural), or do we have a law of tort (singular)? At one level, this is an easy question to answer. The prevalent view of tort law, which I have called the "traditional approach", sees it as a set of discrete torts which are related more by marriage than by blood, as it were. The approach I adopt in this book rejects this traditional view, but I do not attempt to argue that tort law is based on one or a few general principles of liability. Law in general and the law of tort in particular are social institutions, ways of organizing and interpreting social life. Life is an extremely diverse,

complex and messy affair. One of the functions of law as a social institution is to introduce some sort of order into social life. Not only is
social life complex, but human ethical principles (of which tort law is
a subset or an application) are also complex. We often hold, at one
and the same time, ethical principles which conflict with one
another, and such conflicts may make it difficult for us to decide what
is the right thing to do in particular situations. Although we use law
as a means of imposing order on our social lives and our ethical commitments, law is incapable of eliminating social messes or resolving all
ethical conflicts. Law to some extent reflects the messiness of our lives
and the diversity and mutual inconsistency of our aims and ethical
commitments.

For this reason, if for none other, the idea that we might find a
single overarching principle, or even a very few general principles,
which would explain or justify any large body of legal rules and principles (such as the law of tort) is unattractive. It does not follow, however, that we should not search for, or that we may not find, a set of
ethical principles which can help to explain and justify a large area of
the law such as tort law. These principles will be uncertain and unclear
in some respects, and they may conflict amongst themselves, but this
is to be expected and should not discourage us from the search. My
view is that we can and should make the attempt to break out of
thinking about the law of tort in terms of the formulae of trespass,
conversion, nuisance, negligence, defamation and the rest. We can
and should think of tort law in terms of a set of ethical rules and principles, organized around the concepts of correlativity, sanctioned conduct, protected interests and sanctions.

So much for the simple answer. At a deeper level, however, the
question raises very difficult issues about the role of classification and
categorization in the law. How should we divide the law up, and
what role should legal categories play in legal reasoning? These issues
are discussed in Chapter 6, and because it is difficult to understand
fully the conclusions reached there without seeing how the approach
I propose actually works, I shall not anticipate the discussion except
by addressing one of its aspects in the next section of this chapter.

BEYOND THE LAW OF TORT

The rejection of formularism which underlies this book in fact has
implications beyond the law of tort. The reason for this can be
explained by a simple example. Suppose you employ a solicitor to

conduct a court action for damages which has a very high chance of success, but that the solicitor negligently fails to start the action in time, as a result of which you recover no damages in that claim. When you employed the solicitor, you entered a contract under which the solicitor could be liable *in contract* for damage caused by careless performance of the contract. But you could also sue the solicitor *in tort* for such negligence. In other words, in this situation you could sue the solicitor either in contract or in tort for one and the same piece of negligent conduct. In technical terms, this is somewhat confusingly described by saying that you have "concurrent causes of action in contract and tort" against the lawyer. In practice, your choice whether to sue in contract or tort will depend on which cause of action is more advantageous to you – the two causes of action differ in certain ways which may, depending on the precise facts of your case, produce different results. Some of these differences can be adequately explained and justified, but some make very little sense. For instance, you may have longer to start a tort action than a contract action, but it is difficult to think of any good reason why this should be so in a case where the conduct sanctioned and the interest protected by your right to sue in contract are exactly the same as the conduct sanctioned and the interest protected by your right to sue in tort. Nevertheless, courts tend to take the view that since a cause of action in contract and a cause of action in tort are different things, a litigant should be free to choose one cause of action rather than the other (or, if you like, to use one formula rather than the other) even if no-one can think of a good justification or explanation for the advantage thereby gained. Indeed, in a recent important tort case[19] a leading judge in the House of Lords described a suggestion that litigants should only be allowed an advantage by choosing one formula rather than another if there was some good reason for it as like "crying for the moon".

Such exploitation of competing legal formulae can benefit practising lawyers and their clients by giving them tactical choices. On the other hand, for every litigant who gains by having such a choice, another litigant loses by being subject to the other litigant's choice. This is, to adapt a famous phrase, the "unacceptable side of formularism". Fortunately, within recognized departments of the law, such as tort and contract, courts tend to be keen to prevent litigants taking advantage of distinctions which are agreed to lack merit. But at the

[19] *Henderson* v. *Merrett Syndicates Ltd* [1995] 2 AC 145, 186, *per* Lord Goff.

boundaries between departments (such as tort and contract), arid formularism is still unfortunately frequently tolerated. One of the aims
of this book is to analyze tort law in terms which can also be used to
analyze other areas of the civil law of obligations. In this way I hope
to be able to make it easier to identify formularism at the boundaries
of departments of the law and to suggest ways of avoiding it.

TORT LAW AS A SET OF ETHICAL PRINCIPLES

The treatment of tort law as a complex set of ethical principles of personal responsibility (and freedom) which concern how people may,
ought or ought not to behave in their dealings with others may be
contrasted with what are often called "instrumental" approaches.
Instrumentalists view (tort) law as a means (or "instrument") for
achieving desired social goals. The social goals most commonly associated with tort law are compensation for injuries and losses, deterrence of harmful conduct, fair distribution of accident risks and costs
throughout society, and economic efficiency. An instrumentalist will
attempt to explain and justify the rules and principles of tort law as
means to a particular end, will criticize rules or principles which do
not contribute to the achievement of that end, and may classify them
as "mistakes". For the instrumentalist, tort law is best understood as
the means to chosen ends.

In this sense, my approach is not instrumentalist because I view
tort law as a set of principles about how people ought to behave
rather than as a means to an end. However, I do not deny that tort
law may in fact have certain effects (such as deterring harmful conduct); or that it may further certain desirable social goals. Nor do I
deny that tort law can be used as a means to an end. Moreover, viewing tort law instrumentally may provide valuable perspectives and
insights. However, I think that for most of its history the common
law of tort has not been viewed instrumentally by the judges and
lawyers who were primarily responsible for making it, but on the
contrary as a set of principles of personal responsibility. For this
reason, I believe that we are likely to understand the substance of tort
law best if we view it in the way it has typically been seen – as a set
of ethical principles about individual behaviour towards others.

Another, and perhaps stronger, reason not to explain tort law
instrumentally is that when we examine closely the goals most commonly attributed to tort law we find that tort law is in fact very inefficient at achieving them. This is one of the main reasons why, in the

area of liability for personal injuries, many people have argued that tort law should be replaced by some other compensation system. When we critically assess tort law as an instrument for compensating victims of personal injuries and for reducing the incidence of personal injuries, we find that it fails to achieve either goal very satisfactorily and, moreover, that it is a very expensive way of pursuing these goals. Also, many of the rules and principles of tort law are difficult to explain and justify in terms of the goals of compensation and injury reduction – they make more sense when viewed as ethical principles of personal responsibility.

I am not arguing that the actual operation of tort law can be understood without reference to its social effects or to the social goals which are attributed to it. Indeed, there is reason to think that the ethical principles embedded in tort law have been influenced and perhaps even distorted by the social ends for which tort law has been used. All I am arguing is that the best starting point for understanding the rules and principles of tort law is to view them in terms of the ethics of personal responsibility. These issues are explored further in Chapter 7.

THE RELATIONSHIP BETWEEN TORT LAW AND MORALITY

Tort law is a system of ethical rules and principles. So is morality. What, then, is the relationship between tort law on the one hand and, on the other, moral principles which deal with the same issues as tort law does? In the first place, it seems obvious that law and morality might conflict in certain respects, or at least not coincide. To act in accordance with law is not necessarily to meet the demands of morality. For instance, the law may not require a person to warn an unsuspecting victim of fraud that he or she is being "taken for a ride" by a third party; but commercial morality might make such a demand. The most famous judicial statement of this idea is that of Lord Atkin when he said, in *Donoghue* v. *Stevenson*,[20]

> "The liability for negligence . . . is no doubt based upon a general public sentiment of moral wrongdoing for which the offender must pay. But acts or omissions which any moral code would censure cannot in a practical world be treated so as to give a right to every person injured by them to demand relief. . . . The rule that you are to

[20] [1932] AC 562, 580.

love your neighbour becomes in law: You must not injure your
neighbour . . ."

Conversely, the law may require people to act in ways which their
moral principles forbid or to refrain from doing what their morality
demands. Morality may, therefore, provide a basis for evaluating and
criticizing the law.

Such use of morality as a critical standard assumes that morality is
in some sense prior or superior to law. But there are important ways
in which morality needs law.[21] First, law can be used to supplement
morality by giving concrete content to broad moral principles. For
instance, morality may tell us to drive carefully, but it does not specify precise speed limits. Many of our moral principles are too vague
to tell us what to do in specific situations, and law provides one
means of overcoming such vagueness.

Secondly, law may provide a means for mediating between conflicting moral views. People often genuinely and reasonably disagree
about the right way to behave. Resentment, and even social conflict,
can arise if people are free to act in accordance with divergent moral
principles (although, of course, people should be given as much freedom to follow their morality as is reasonably consistent with the freedom of others to do the same). The law, by establishing a standard of
conduct for everyone, may promote social cohesion, especially if the
law represents a reasonable compromise between conflicting moral
positions. When the law performs this mediating function, it is
bound to diverge to a greater or lesser extent from some people's
morality; and such divergence may, at one level, be a ground for justified criticism of the law and even for a refusal to comply with it. But
at another level, divergence between law and morality may be a
ground for approval of the law if it promotes social harmony. The fact
that a law is morally controversial does not make it a bad law.

These two functions of supplementing moral principles and mediating between divergent moral views are central to the social role of
law in general and of tort law in particular. The appropriate social criterion for judging the acceptability of particular rules and principles
of tort law is not whether they coincide with one's own (or anyone
else's) morality, but whether they represent a fair and reasonable
regime of personal responsibility for society to adopt and enforce
against its members, given the range of relevant moral views held by

---

[21] What follows is based on T. Honoré, "The Dependence of Morality on Law", (1993)
13 *OJLS* 1.

its citizens. This criterion is partly a matter of political morality; and, of course, reasonable people might disagree about whether or not it is met by particular rules and principles of law. In a democratic society, such disagreements are dealt with by setting up institutions – the legislature and the courts – to make rules of (tort) law. The legitimacy of rules of tort law made by such institutions partly depends on the acceptance of these institutions as being appropriate bodies to decide what are fair and reasonable rules and principles of personal responsibility for our society to adopt.

On the other hand, of course, the rules they make are open to legitimate criticism if it can be persuasively argued that those rules are not a fair and reasonable set of principles of personal responsibility for society to adopt. Such criticism may be based on the content of the rules themselves, and throughout this book I will seek to indicate the main objections raised against various aspects of tort law. Another important quality of a fair and reasonable system of legal rules is that it should be coherent and internally consistent; and, as we will see, tort law is far from ideal in this respect.

CONCLUSION

The structure of tort law as portrayed in the typical tort text was laid down over a century ago under the influence of the formulary system of litigating disputes before the courts. Much understanding can be gained, not only of tort law but of also of other areas of the civil law of obligations, by analyzing tort law not in terms of the discrete torts which we have inherited from the days of the formulary system but in terms of the concept of correlativity and the ideas of sanctioned conduct, protected interests and sanctions. Underlying this approach is the view that tort law is best seen as a system of ethical rules and principles of personal responsibility (and freedom) adopted by society as a publicly enforceable statement about how its citizens may, ought and ought not to behave in their dealings with one another. Against this background, it is now time to begin the task of dismantling tort law into its constituent building blocks of sanctioned conduct, protected interests and sanctions.

2. SANCTIONED CONDUCT

IN this chapter we will examine the concept of "sanctioned conduct" in tort law. What sorts of conduct can attract tort liability? And what sorts of conduct on the part of victims of tortious conduct can lead to refusal of a remedy or reduction of damages? Remember, however, that sanctioned conduct is only one part of the tort equation. Another part consists of protected interests, which are discussed in Chapter 3. A complete understanding of both sanctioned conduct and protected interests also requires an examination of the sanctions which tort law makes available. This appears in Chapter 4. Moreover, not all of the interests protected by tort law are protected against all of the types of sanctioned conduct discussed below, and so a full picture of tort law will only emerge once we have examined which interests are protected against which types of conduct. The relationship between protected interests and sanctioned conduct is examined in Chapter 5. In other words, this chapter and the next three chapters must be read cumulatively; the full pattern of tort law will not appear until all the layers of the design have been placed one on top of the other.

Inevitably, these chapters are to some extent descriptive of the current law. However, because the law will be viewed and described from a novel perspective, a fresh and illuminating understanding of many of its features will emerge. For example, we will see that the word "intention" is often used inaccurately when reference is made to "intentional torts". We will see that the concept of "strict liability" in tort law rests on three quite different bases; and that distinguishing between the different types of strict liability throws helpful light on the defence of contributory negligence in this context. I will argue that the suggestion that the objective test of negligence is out of step with ideas of responsibility outside the law rests on a misunderstanding; and I will explore the relationship between tort liability and luck.

I begin by examining sanctioned conduct rather than protected interests because of the intimate relationship between the notions of responsibility and conduct. However, in Chapter 5, when I reconstruct tort law in terms of protected interests, sanctioned conduct and sanctions, I will organize the discussion of causes of action in tort according to protected interests; and in Chapter 6 I will suggest that in determining the relevance of tort law to any particular set of facts, the best place to start is with protected interests. I think I can better explain the logic of my approach by beginning with conduct; but once explained, I think that application of the approach to concrete cases would best begin with interests, as would the project of giving a systematic account of causes of action in tort.

The examination of sanctioned conduct in this chapter is divided into two main sections: the first is concerned with conduct which attracts tort liability and the second is concerned with conduct (of the victim) which displaces or reduces tort liability.

LIABILITY-ATTRACTING CONDUCT

Voluntary Conduct

So far as the law of tort is concerned, the word "conduct" can refer either to acts or omissions. In general terms, tortious conduct may consist either of doing something which the law says ought not to have been done (an "act"), or failing to do something which the law says ought to have been done (an "omission"). The distinction between acts and omissions is an important and difficult one which is discussed further later in this chapter.

An act can attract tort liability only if it was "voluntary". An involuntary act is a bodily movement over which the person had no control. In extreme cases, we would probably not call an involuntary bodily movement an act at all. If A physically overpowered B and used B as a missile to knock C to the ground, we would not say that B had voluntarily knocked C over or even that B had knocked C over – rather that A had knocked C over using B. Similarly, if A's car collides with B's car and causes it to knock over C, a pedestrian, we would not say that B had voluntarily knocked C over, or even that B had knocked C over. As applied to these two examples, the idea of "voluntary act" contains a tautology – the event of B knocking C over, we might say, was not an act of B because it was involuntary.[1] In its refusal to impose liability on B in such cases, tort law reflects

---

[1] Note, however, that in another sense of "voluntary", namely "not (morally or legally) obligatory", a "non-voluntary" (that is, obligatory) act may certainly be an act: A.R. White, *Grounds of Liability* (Oxford, 1985), 30–31. The opposite of "voluntary" in the sense used in the text is "involuntary", not "non-voluntary".

basic extra-legal conceptions of what it means to be an autonomous and responsible human being.

More complex are cases in which the lack of control is the result of some infirmity or incapacity of the actor resulting, for instance, from age, illness or intoxication. In the first place, because involuntariness involves lack of control over bodily movements, many types of mental disability and malfunction (delusions, for instance) would not provide a ground of exemption from liability on the basis of involuntariness.[2] This is not to say that a mental condition might not provide a defence to a tort claim even if it did not deprive a person of control of their body. For example, in some situations, tort liability only attaches to "intentional" conduct, which is a form of voluntary conduct. A mental abnormality which might not prevent a person acting voluntarily might, nevertheless, prevent them acting intentionally. The only point being made here is that acts attributable to or affected by mental disability may often not be involuntary.

Secondly, tort law does not treat as involuntary bodily movements which are outside a person's control because of self-induced incapacity caused, for instance, by deliberate consumption of excessive amounts of alcohol or drugs. Thirdly, lack of control will be irrelevant if the person knew or ought to have known that they would or might not be able to control their movements. Fourthly, in tort law lack of control will render bodily movements involuntary only if it was "total". For instance, a car driver who, through no fault of their own, suffers a partial impairment, as opposed to a total loss, of consciousness after suffering a stroke or a heart attack while driving, cannot escape tort liability on the basis of "automatism" (that is, involuntariness).[3]

It is also necessary to distinguish involuntary bodily movements from "automatic" ones. Doing things automatically is a typical result of repetition of tasks and the acquisition of skill. An experienced driver, for example, will do many things automatically or "without thinking" or "inadvertently" which a learner would do deliberately and attentively. The crucial difference between involuntary acts and automatic acts is that the former are uncontrollable whereas the latter are controllable but not consciously controlled. Far from being exempt from tort liability, automatic behaviour is frequently the very essence of tortiously negligent conduct. The competent driver is one who knows when it is necessary to pay attention and when doing

---

[2] *Morriss v. Marsden* [1952] 1 All ER 925.
[3] *Roberts v. Ramsbottom* [1980] 1 All ER 7.

things automatically will be safe. From this perspective, negligence consisting of inadvertent conduct may be seen as unacceptable "automaticity". [4]

The notion of involuntariness is even more problematic in relation to omissions (as opposed to actions). Of course, a person who is unconscious can no more cause their body to move than prevent it from moving. However, much tortious conduct, especially negligent conduct, consists of failure to act; and in general (as we will see in detail later in this chapter), a person cannot avoid tort liability for failure to act by establishing that it was beyond their physical, mental or intellectual capacity to act, even if the lack of capacity was not self-induced but was the result, for instance, of their genetic inheritance. The basic rule of tort law is that people are liable for failure to measure up to certain standards of behaviour even if reaching the required standard was beyond their capacities at the relevant time, unless there is some special reason why they should be exempted from liability. Involuntariness, as narrowly defined above, may provide such a reason. But on the whole, tort law does not exempt people from liability simply because they suffer from the "bad luck" of lacking the capacity, through no fault of their own, to measure up to the standards of conduct the law establishes. The best rationale for this approach is that since everything a person does is affected to a greater or lesser extent by factors beyond their control ("luck"), exempting human beings from responsibility for any action which was not entirely within their control would destroy the sense of ourselves as rational, free agents which is central to our individuality and feelings of achievement and self-worth.[5] Moreover, because our positive achievements in life are also more or less affected by factors beyond our control ("good luck"), it would be morally reprehensible to accept the credit for them without being prepared to shoulder the blame for our failures, even though these are the result, more or less, of matters beyond our control ("bad luck"). Luck is an inescapable fact of life, and our ideas of personal responsibility to a large extent ignore it. It is only when a person's luck is abnormally good or bad that we are likely to take it into account in allocating praise or blame to them.

[4] See generally J. Killingley, "Some Ergonomic Challenges for Fault-Based Compensation Systems" in R. Baldwin (ed), *Law and Uncertainty: Risks and Legal Processes* (London, 1997), ch. 3.
[5] See further below under the heading "The Ethical Imperatives of Tort Law".

Deliberate Conduct

It is important to distinguish between "voluntary" conduct and "deliberate" conduct. Both acts and omissions can be deliberate. All deliberate conduct is voluntary, but conduct can be voluntary without being the result of deliberation. This is true of automatic or "inadvertent" conduct. Sometimes deliberation is a precondition of tort liability. It is, for instance, a requirement for the imposition of secondary liability for tortious conduct, that is liability for assisting, inducing, encouraging, authorizing or conspiring in the tortious conduct of another.[6] However, tort liability very often attaches to inadvertent conduct.

Intentional Conduct

It is also important to distinguish between "deliberate" conduct and "intentional" conduct.[7] To understand this distinction it is necessary to draw another between conduct and its consequences. A consequence is a state of affairs which results from or is caused by some prior state of affairs. One and the same state of affairs may be both a cause and a consequence depending on whether we view it in relation to what went before it or what went after it. In tort law, "deliberate" is a term applied to causes, while "intentional" is a word applied to consequences. Conduct is deliberate if it is done with deliberation; and so automatic conduct is not deliberate. Conduct is intentional if it is done with the intention (or "aim") of causing a particular consequence. All intentional conduct is deliberate, but not all deliberate conduct is intentional (with respect to its consequences). A person may, for instance, deliberately hit another and thereby cause the other's death without intending to kill that person. But a person who hits another intending to kill the other thereby could not claim to have hit without deliberation.

Failure to link intention with consequences can lead to mistakes in understanding tort law. For instance, it is sometimes said that trespass to land is an "intentional tort", by which is meant that a person can only be liable for trespass to land if the person "intended to trespass".

---

[6] D.J. Cooper, *Secondary Liability for Civil Wrongs*, Unpublished PhD Thesis, University of Cambridge, 1995. In addition, a person can be secondarily liable for tortious conduct only if they knew of the facts which made the conduct tortious (although, of course, they need not have appreciated that it was tortious).

[7] The following discussions of intentional, reckless and negligent conduct concern the use of these concepts in tort law. Such usage may not coincide with that in criminal law. See generally A. Ashworth, *Principles of Criminal Law*, 2nd edn (Oxford, 1995), 167–194.

On analysis, however, this statement is obviously untrue. Trespass involves entering the land of another without that other's consent or without some legal justification. Trespass to land is not an intentional tort because trespass can be committed simply by going onto another's land without the other's consent and without any legal justification. Trespass can be committed by a person who does not know and has no reason to know that the land belongs to another. Moreover, the definition of trespass refers only to an act of entry, and not to any consequences of entry such as inconvenience to the owner or damage to the land or to buildings on it. Even if we artificially treat the physical act of moving on to the land of another separately from the "consequence" of "entering" the land of another, it is still clear that trespass to land is not an intentional tort because it can be committed by a person who enters the land of another without knowing or having any reasonable means of knowing that the land belongs to another. Indeed, trespass can be committed not only by entering the land of another unintentionally, but even by doing so without deliberation. The only requirement is that the entry should be voluntary. If A physically overpowered B and pushed B onto C's land, B would not have trespassed onto C's land. But if B absent-mindedly wandered onto C's land without adverting to whether it was his own or not, B might have committed a trespass.

The typical formula for intentional tort liability is "doing X (the act) with the intention of causing Y (the consequence of the act)". For example, there can be no tort liability for interfering with another's trade or business unless the interference was done with the intention (or aim) of causing economic loss to the target of the interference (and unless the interference in fact caused such loss to the target).

Reckless Conduct

Distinguishable from intention is recklessness. Like intention, recklessness refers to the consequences of actions rather than to the actions themselves; and like intentional conduct, reckless conduct is necessarily deliberate. Whereas to intend a consequence is to aim at producing it, to be reckless as to a consequence is to know that one's action may produce it without caring whether it does or not. The reckless person does not do an action with the aim of producing a particular consequence, but rather with the awareness that it may produce a particular consequence, being indifferent as between the occurrence and the non-occurrence of the consequence. A person is reckless as to an outcome only if that person actually knew that there was a risk that his or her conduct would produce that outcome. A person who ought to have been, but was not in fact, aware of the risk is not reckless in relation to the outcome.

Although intention and recklessness are clearly distinguishable, in tort law they are treated as ethically equivalent. A requirement in tort law to prove (for instance) that D intended to injure P can be satisfied by proof that D was reckless as to whether D's conduct would injure P. This is probably because both intentional and reckless conduct necessarily involve deliberation. To aim at an outcome or to be indifferent as to its occurrence are both conscious states of mind which imply deliberation. Deliberate interference with another's interests is ethically distinguishable from non-deliberate interference whether the outcome was intended or only the object of indifference. Harming a person by deliberate conduct betokens a fundamental lack of respect for that person's individuality.

Fraudulent Conduct

Fraudulent conduct deserves brief separate mention because of its conceptual complexity. In tort law, the concept of fraud is used in relation to statements of fact under the head of liability called "deceit". A fraudulent statement is a false statement made deliberately and with the intention that someone should rely on it and suffer loss as a result. A person can make a false statement deliberately only if they did not honestly believe it to be true, either because they knew that it was false, or they knew that it might be false. This latter state of mind is sometimes referred to by the term "recklessness" in the sense of making a statement knowing but not caring that it might be false. However, it is better to use this term only with the meaning given to it in the previous section of this chapter, which refers to the risk that conduct will result in a particular outcome. Fraud is one of only a very few heads of tort liability which require knowledge of certain facts. Another is the "public law tort" of misfeasance in a public office, where knowledge that conduct is or might be *ultra vires* (and that it will or might injure the plaintiff) is an alternative to intention to injure as the basis of liability.[8] And another is interference with contract (which perhaps requires knowledge of the existence of the contract). Lack of honest belief in the truth of a statement (in this context called "malice") can also defeat a defence of fair comment or qualified privilege in the law of defamation.

[8] *Three Rivers DC v. Bank of England (No 3)* [1996] 3 All ER 558.

Motive

A person's motive for doing something is the reason why they do it or their purpose in doing it. To do something without a motive is to do it "for no reason". Like deliberation, motive is a mental state; although unlike deliberation, a motive may not be conscious. Motive is obviously different from recklessness. To say that someone acted with indifference to consequences tells us nothing about why they did it. But motive is also different from intention. My intention in hitting someone may be to hurt them, but my motive for doing so may be to impress a friend. This is not to say, however, that motive and intention may not coincide. It may be that a person's only reason for hitting another is to inflict injury on the other. Because motive and intention may coincide in this way, it is very easy to confuse the two. However, it is important not to do so. This is because the fact that someone does something with a bad motive does not necessarily make the action itself bad or the wrong thing to do. For instance, telling the truth is not in itself bad even if one's reason for telling the truth and one's intention in doing so is to destroy another's reputation and livelihood; and so bad motive ("malice") does not defeat a defence of justification ("truth") in the law of defamation. At the same time, a person's motives are clearly relevant to our ethical assessment of the way they have behaved.

The general rule in the law of tort is that the motive with which conduct was done is irrelevant to its tortiousness. On the one hand, if an interference with the interests of another would not, as such, be tortious, the fact that it was done out of a bad motive (with "malice") would not make it tortious. On the other hand, tortious interference with the rights of another cannot be excused by pleading a good motive. There may be room for dispute about whether tort law's general approach to motive is morally acceptable. It has been argued, for instance, that ". . . *all* the aspects of one's act must be rightful for the act to be right".[9] On this basis, a good motive could not excuse unlawful conduct, but a bad motive would render otherwise lawful conduct unlawful. However, my feeling is that people are not necessarily condemned for doing the right thing for the wrong reason. At any rate, the general rule of tort law is subject to a number of exceptions and qualifications, the most notable being found in the law of defamation, where bad motive can defeat a defence of fair comment

---

[9] J. Finnis, "Intention in Tort Law" in D.G. Owen (ed), *Philosophical Foundations of Tort Law* (Oxford, 1995), 238 (emphasis in original).

or qualified privilege. Without taking all the exceptions and qualifications into account, it is unwise to make any statement about the relationship between tort law and moral principles. It may be that reasonable people take different views about the relevance of motive to moral judgement of a person's conduct. If so, the fact that the law does not coincide with one of those views would not make it a bad law, because one of the most important functions of law is to mediate between different views on fundamental moral issues.

Negligent Conduct

Negligence as a Standard of Conduct

A fundamental difference in tort law between deliberation, intention and recklessness on the one hand and negligence on the other is that whereas the former concepts refer to states of mind, negligence refers to a standard of conduct. Tortious negligence is not a state of mind but rather a failure to reach a certain standard of conduct. There is no necessary relationship between states of mind and negligence. While involuntary conduct cannot attract liability in tort for negligence (or on any other basis), deliberate, intentional and reckless conduct alike may attract tort liability for negligence if the conduct satisfies the definition of negligence, which is in terms of failure to attain a certain standard. In this way, the concept of negligence in tort law is rather different from the non-legal concept of carelessness, which implies inadvertence or lack of deliberation.

Negligent Conduct and the Tort of Negligence

Negligence as a form of sanctioned conduct must be distinguished from the so-called "tort of negligence". The tort of negligence is a formula of tort liability consisting of three main elements: the existence of a duty of care, a breach of that duty, and damage caused by the breach. Negligence as a form of sanctioned conduct corresponds to the second of those elements. As a form of sanctioned conduct, however, negligence is also an element of certain other torts (that is, formulae of tort liability), such as trespass to the person causing personal injury. As was noted in Chapter 1,[10] such overlapping of elements between different torts suggests that the traditional division of tort law into separate torts does not accurately reflect the ethical underpinnings of tort liability and is the result of an anachronistically formulaic approach.

[10] See p. 22 above.

Negligence and Risk

Central to the concept of negligent conduct is the notion of "risk". The word "risk" refers to the "chance", or "possibility", or "probability", or "likelihood" (less than 100 per cent) that some undesirable event will occur in the future. Life is full of risks. Risks create uncertainty. Uncertainty is not a bad thing – without it life would be both boring (witness the attraction of gambling to many people) and frightening (imagine you knew it was inevitable that you would be seriously injured tomorrow no matter what you did). Underlying the concept of negligence is the assumption that a certain level of risk is an inevitable and, indeed, ethically acceptable concomitant of human life. Very few, if any, human activities are entirely riskless. Many risks could only be entirely eliminated by not engaging in the activity which generates them. We are often prepared to accept a certain degree of risk in order to secure the benefits that risky activities bring. Negligence consists of imposing an "unreasonable" level of risk, of engaging in an activity which generates an unacceptable degree of risk without taking reasonable precautions to prevent the risk materializing in an adverse event. The concept of negligence is not about eliminating risk but about reducing it to an acceptable level by taking reasonable precautions.

The Value of the Risky Activity

The first question to be asked in deciding whether a defendant has been negligent is whether the activity in which D was engaged was valuable enough (or whether its benefits were great enough) to render acceptable the risk which it created and which has materialized. For instance, in one case the question was whether the risks attaching to allowing left-hand drive vehicles on public roads were justified by the fact that there was a shortage of ambulances. Some activities, such as saving life and limb, may be thought to justify the taking of risks which less valuable activities might not. It is often said that the benefits of driving at, say, 30 miles an hour rather than 10 miles an hour so outweigh the risks that it is not negligent to drive at 30 miles an hour. But if an activity was considered not to be worth the risks attendant upon it, then it would be negligent to engage in that activity.

The value (or "benefit" or "utility") of activities is judged not in the light of the interests of the two parties to a tort claim but by reference to the interests of society at large. Some people argue that courts applying tort law should concern themselves only with the interaction of the two parties, and that they should ignore the wider social impact of that interaction. On this view, the only issue should be whether the injurer's activity unduly interfered with the interests of the victim; and it should be irrelevant whether and to what extent society at large benefits from the injurer's activity. The fact that society at large might benefit, it might be said, does not affect the impact of the injurer's conduct on the victim. In my view, there are at least two good reasons to reject this approach. First, it seems clear that ideas of responsibility and blame outside the law are sensitive to social context. We *are* happy for drivers of emergency vehicles to take risks (such as driving on the wrong side of the road or running red lights) which we would criticize other drivers for taking. Secondly, the approach seems to ignore the fact (discussed in Chapter 1) that tort law is concerned not only with resolving bilateral disputes about past events, but also with providing general guidance to citizens about how to lead their lives. The same rules have to function both as solvents of particular bilateral disputes about the past and as general guides to future conduct. Tort law could not perform the latter function effectively if it ignored the social context of the lives of those subject to it. Tort law rightly does not treat individuals as "islands unto themselves" but as social creatures. Tort law is not just about correcting past injustice to individuals but also about creating a good future for society and those who live in it. It is certainly arguable that a tort law which is sensitive to the social context of people's lives is better than would be a tort law which ignored it.

Was the Risk Foreseeable?

Once it has been decided that given the risks of the defendant's activity, it was not negligent to engage in the activity in the first place, the next question is whether the risk which has materialized was foreseeable. It is not negligent to fail to take precautions against an unforeseeable risk. A foreseeable risk is one which a person ought to have foreseen. By contrast with negligence, a person can intend an uncertain future event or be reckless in relation to an uncertain future event only if they actually foresaw the risk of that event. A person cannot intend or be indifferent to an outcome if they were not consciously aware of the risk of that outcome occurring as a result of their conduct; but a person can be negligent in relation to an uncertain outcome even if they were not consciously aware of the risk of its occurrence, provided they ought to have been. In tort law, this point is made by saying that foreseeability is an "objective", not a "subjective" concept. The relevant question in relation to negligence is not whether a person was actually ("subjectively") aware of a risk but whether they ought ("objectively") to have been aware of it. Not only may a person fail to foresee a risk which the law says they ought to have foreseen; but a person may also, conversely, foresee a risk which the law would not require them to have foreseen.

What risks does tort law require people to foresee? Foresight is a function of knowledge, and the relevant questions are: at the time when it is alleged that the defendant ought to have taken precautions against the risk, did anyone[11] have the knowledge required to foresee it? If so, ought the defendant to have had that knowledge? The first question is an empirical one, but the second question can be answered only by making a value-judgement. The concept which tort law uses in answering this second question is that of "reasonableness". The defendant ought to have had the necessary knowledge if a reasonable person in the defendant's position would have had it. This concept of reasonableness is discussed below.

Reasonable Care

Assuming that it was not negligent on the part of the defendant to engage in the activity in the first place, and that the risk which has materialized was foreseeable in the above sense, the next question is whether the defendant took reasonable care or precautions to reduce or eliminate the risk. Failure to take reasonable care may consist either in doing something unreasonable or failing to do something reasonable; that is, in an act or an omission. Is there anything which D should have done (but did not do) to reduce or eliminate the risk? Alternatively, did D conduct the activity in a way which created an unacceptable risk? To answer these questions we must first define what is an acceptable risk. This involves making an assessment of the relative weight of three factors. They are the probability that the risk will materialize if no precautions are taken to prevent it, the likely seriousness of the adverse effect on the plaintiff if it does materialize, and the cost and difficulty of reducing the risk to any particular level.

In theory, at least, the probability and likely seriousness of many risks could be ascertained with some degree of statistical precision, as could the cost of reducing them to a particular level or eliminating

---

[11] But this is a vague term. It probably does not mean "anyone in the world", but something like "anyone situated similarly to the defendant" (whatever "similarly" is taken to mean).

them. In practice, however, many risks are unquantifiable or their magnitude is contested; and there may frequently be irresolvable disagreement about the cost of reducing risks to a particular level or eliminating them. As a result, courts often determine the acceptability of a risk in an impressionistic and imprecise way. To this extent, judgements of acceptability of risk may be value-laden: a risk will be seen as unacceptable if it is one against which the court thinks precautions should have been taken. Even if reasonably precise and agreed mathematical values could be given to the three factors of probability, seriousness and cost, their relative weight and the ultimate question of acceptability is inevitably a matter of judgement. Like decisions about the value of particular activities, decisions about the acceptability of particular risks are ultimately based on the decision-maker's view of what constitutes the good society. It should be noted, too, that although the three factors listed above represent the formal structure of reasoning about unacceptable risk, in practice the three factors are often not explicitly referred to. The court will often simply make an unanalysed pronouncement that the risk was a serious one against which certain precautions ought to have been taken.

Having decided how unacceptable the risk was, the next question is whether the defendant took "reasonable precautions" or "reasonable care" to reduce it to an acceptable level or to eliminate it. The most difficult part of the concept of reasonable care (as well as of the concept of reasonable knowledge mentioned already) is the idea of "reasonableness". The word implies a value-judgement about which honest and fair people may legitimately disagree. It follows that particular judgements of reasonableness by courts may be controversial. That, of course, does not make them bad, but it inevitably puts judges in the position of having to make decisions which may be ethically and socially controversial. This has to be accepted.

Whether any precautions taken in a particular case were reasonable has to be judged in the light of all the circumstances of that case. However, there are also certain relevant legal principles which apply to all cases of negligence. Here are the most important:

1. Once it is decided that it was not negligent to engage in an activity simply because a particular risk attached to it, it would not be reasonable to expect the person conducting the activity to have taken such costly or difficult precautions that the activity would have had to cease.

2. Reasonableness is an "objective" (as opposed to a "subjective")

standard – the test is not whether the defendant thought any precautions taken were reasonable, but whether the court thinks so.

3. Tort law explicitly recognizes two degrees of unreasonableness. There is no accepted terminology to describe the two degrees, but I will call them "ordinary unreasonableness" and "extraordinary unreasonableness". Ordinarily unreasonable conduct is conduct which, in the court's view, would be thought unreasonable by the generality of people suitably qualified to have an opinion on the matter, even if some such people would think it reasonable. Extraordinarily unreasonable conduct is conduct which, in the court's view, would be thought unreasonable by all those suitably qualified to have an opinion on the matter: if a suitably qualified body of opinion, however small, would think the conduct reasonable, it would not be extraordinarily unreasonable. As a general rule, conduct will fail the test of reasonableness if it is ordinarily unreasonable. However, in certain cases, conduct will fail the test of reasonableness only if it is extraordinarily unreasonable.

The two main categories of case in which the latter test applies are actions against medical practitioners (and, perhaps, members of the other long-established professions, such as lawyers), and certain actions against public authorities such as county councils.[12] Such leniency to doctors and other professionals is designed to give them freedom to experiment with unorthodox but potentially beneficial practices. It is also based on a belief that being held liable for negligence is likely to have a particularly damaging effect on the reputation and livelihood of professionals. This approach is highly controversial. The leniency to public authorities is based on a desire not to overburden the public purse with orders to pay damages, and the idea that government needs considerable freedom to act (or to refrain from action) in the public interest even if such conduct injures individual citizens. In fact, this is only one of a number of techniques which are used to protect public authorities from tort liability. Others are discussed later in this chapter and elsewhere in this book.

The notion of "those suitably qualified to have an opinion on the matter" is a vague one. Suppose, for example, that most doctors would describe some medical procedure as "reasonable". It would not follow that the procedure was reasonable for the purposes of tort law because a court might take the view that doctors were not the only people suitably qualified to have an opinion on the matter. If the

---

[12] This is discussed further below under the heading "Non-compliance with Statutes".

court felt that opinion among doctors was out of step with opinion in society more widely, it might be prepared to say that compliance by a doctor with standards of conduct accepted by doctors generally to be reasonable was not reasonable for the purposes of tort law. This point is commonly put in terms that while compliance with common practice will normally be reasonable, and failure to comply with common practice will normally be unreasonable, common practice is not necessarily conclusive of what is reasonable or unreasonable conduct. Reasonableness is not a question of what people actually do but of what courts think is a reasonable standard of conduct for society to enforce against its citizens through the mechanism of tort law. What people actually do provides a good starting point for this inquiry, but it is only a starting point. The courts have a constitutional responsibility to establish standards of conduct for society.

4. In judging whether a person's conduct was reasonable, age is to be ignored unless the person was too young yet to have developed the mental and social skills imparted by education and experience which are necessary to have an adult appreciation of risk. This rule is based on a unitary conception of adulthood which, while perhaps scientifically contestable, seems ethically sound. Adults who cannot take reasonable precautions should not engage in risky activities; but if they do, they cannot complain if they are required to bear the consequences.

5. In judging whether a person's conduct was reasonable, the degree of their personal skill or experience in relation to the risky activity is irrelevant unless, perhaps, the defendant actively led the plaintiff to think that he or she was more than typically skilled or experienced. The pragmatic justification for this rule is that it would be exceedingly difficult to operate a system of variable standards of care. Ethically, the rule might seem harsh on defendants; but as between the two parties, it seems fair that the risk of lack of skill or experience should rest on the actor rather than the victim, especially since any failure by the latter to take reasonable care of their own interests can be sanctioned as "contributory negligence" or "voluntary assumption of risk", which are defences discussed below. The idea of correlativity, which underpins tort law, requires a person's conduct to be judged not in isolation but relative to the interests of another; and interests are to be assessed, not in isolation but relative to the freedom of action of another. It is true, of course, that desirable skills and experience can only be acquired over time, and that society has an interest in their acquisition. However, the law's judge-

ment is that society's interest should be qualified for the sake of the interests of injured individuals.

6. As a general rule, in judging reasonableness the defendant's financial resources and physical and mental abilities are ignored. We have seen that one factor relevant to deciding whether a risk is unacceptable is how difficult and costly it would be to guard against it. Once the court has decided that given the probability and seriousness of the risk, certain precautions would not have been too costly or difficult, the question of whether the defendant was able or could have afforded to take them is irrelevant. The ethical principle underlying this rule is the same as that considered in paragraph 4 above, namely that people ought to acknowledge their limitations and mould their activities accordingly. Those who cannot afford to take necessary precautions against the risks of an activity should not engage in the activity; but if they do, they cannot complain if they are required to bear the consequences.

There are, however, two situations in which tort law takes account of resources and abilities namely, when a landowner is sued for injury suffered by a trespasser arising out of some danger on the land, and where a landowner is sued for damage suffered by a neighbour as a result of neglect by the landowner of the state of the land. In these two contexts, landowners are not expected to take precautions beyond their resources. The first of these exceptions is usually justified on the basis that trespassers are, in some sense, undeserving; and the second rests on an old idea that landowners should be free to do what they want with their land, even to the point of letting it deteriorate.

7. For more than 100 years, the standard of reasonable care was typically referred to in terms of the "reasonable *man*" or "the *man* on the Clapham omnibus" or some expression conveying a similar social context. Increasingly, this terminology is being replaced by "the reasonable person" or simply "reasonable care". In recent years, some scholars have argued not only that use of the word "man" is an anachronistic linguistic convention, but also that the standard of conduct which it refers to is male-oriented; in other words, that the rationality of the law of negligence is based on a male way of viewing the world to the exclusion of a different female perspective: what men consider to be reasonable behaviour, women might not consider reasonable, and vice-versa.[13] This argument would be quite difficult

<hr>

[13] For an excellent general discussion see J. Conaghan, "Tort Law and the Feminist Critique of Reason" in A. Bottomley (ed), *Feminist Perspectives on the Foundational Subjects of Law* (London, 1996).

to substantiate convincingly; but assuming that it is true, there is little agreement as to what ought to be done about it. One approach is that gender should be taken into account in deciding whether a person acted reasonably. A quite different approach is that we should aim at a gender-neutral notion of reasonableness. These two contrasting approaches turn on different views about the role of gender in human behaviour. Both, however, share the view that notions of reasonableness are affected (if not determined) either by biology or culture or both, and more or less reject the idea that there can be ethical values and principles of near-universal validity. Once this view is accepted, the question inevitably arises as to whether, in judging reasonableness, the law ought not to require that explicit account be taken of all sorts of factors, such as race and religion, rather than that such factors should be ignored, leaving judges free silently to give effect to their own views (or prejudices).

In Chapter 1 I argued that legitimate disagreement about detailed matters of ethics is to be expected, and that one of the functions of the law is to mediate between different ethical views and to lay down rules and principles which, although controversial, can be defended as a sound basis for organizing social life. In this light, the fact that tort law does not comply with everyone's notions of reasonableness would not, in itself, be a ground of criticism. But if it were true that tort law consistently favoured the interests and values of one group in society at the expense of others, this would suggest that tort law was not successfully mediating ethical disagreements but rather generating the very resentment which such mediation is meant to prevent. There may be insoluble disagreements in society about what "reasonable conduct" in particular situations is. The task of tort law is to adopt standards of reasonableness which, although they may not be uncontroversial, can be defended as socially fair. This should not be impossible, because many people accept laws with which they do not personally agree as a price of living in a society with laws which, on the whole, treat them fairly.

8. Subject to the qualifications discussed in the above paragraphs, in judging reasonableness the relevant point of view is that of a person in the position of the defendant or, in other words, with the same characteristics as the defendant and in the same situation as the defendant. This means, for instance, that professionals are judged by the standards of their profession; that GPs are judged by the standard of GPs, not of consultants; that the conduct of a person faced with an emergency is not judged as if there had been time for calm reflection,

and so on. Put in very abstract terms, the test of reasonableness is based on the idea that certain factors are ethically relevant to deciding whether a person has acted reasonably or not and that certain other factors are not. To this extent, it mirrors non-legal morality.

Conduct Neither Intentional or Negligent

Tort law sometimes sanctions conduct which was neither intentional, (reckless) or negligent. Indeed, it may sometimes sanction conduct which was neither intentional, nor negligent nor even deliberate, as when a person enters land without the owner's consent or legal justification but in complete and not unjustified ignorance that it belongs to someone else. We might call such inadvertent conduct "accidental"; however, in tort law, the word "accidental" is used as the negation of "negligent", not of "deliberate" (remember that inadvertence is not part of the definition of negligence). Liability for conduct of these types is called "strict". Defining strict liability in this negative way tells us little about its basis. In fact, tort law recognizes several quite distinct types of strict liability.

Conduct-based strict liability

First, strict liability may attach simply to the voluntary doing of a specified act, most notably interference with or exploitation of another's property without their consent or legal justification. For example, a person can be liable for taking another's property and treating it as their own even if they did not know and had no reason to know that the property was not theirs (as when a person is duped into buying a stolen car), and even if they did not deliberately take it (as when a person inadvertently takes a pen from a customer desk in a bank). This form of strict liability typifies the use of tort law to protect property rights. It expresses the very high value which we put on real and personal property and the importance attached to making it easy for people to recover their property by recourse to law so as to discourage possibly-violent self-help. The institution of private property is fundamental to our society, and a powerful way of expressing the distinction between what is mine and what is yours is through such a rule of strict liability. This form of strict liability is also found in the law of defamation[14] – the wrong of defamation consists of publishing a statement which would tend to damage a person's reputation amongst "right-thinking people" or to cause that person to

[14] Statutory torts may also fall into this category – for instance, discrimination under the Sex Discrimination Act 1975 and the Race Relations Act 1976.

be shunned by such people. The basic rule (subject to limited qualifications) is that a person can be liable for defamation even if they did
not know and had no reason to suspect that they were publishing a
defamatory statement or even that the defamed person existed. Once
again, strict liability here expresses the very high value put on reputation, although many would question this valuation now that freedom of expression is thought so important.

Relationship-based strict liability

A second type of strict liability is based on the fact that the person
liable is in a particular relationship with a tortfeasor. This is "vicarious liability". Vicarious liability is liability for the tortious conduct of
another which is imposed on the basis that the person vicariously
liable is in a certain relationship with the tortfeasor (that is, the person who committed the tortious conduct). The main relationship
which attracts vicarious liability is that of employer and employee –
employers are vicariously liable for tortious conduct of their employees committed in the course of their employment and affecting third
parties. The employer may be vicariously liable even if the employer
did not intend the tortious conduct to be committed, was not negligent in letting it happen and did not know and could not have
known that it was happening; even if the employer had forbidden the
conduct; and even if the conduct of the employee attracted strict tort
liability.

The law of vicarious liability is complex, and this complexity has
defeated many attempts to justify it in all its details. Two types of
argument should be noted here.[15] The first seeks to find a justification in some principle of personal responsibility. So it has been suggested that those who engage in activities for profit should bear the
costs of tortious conduct arising out of that activity.[16] The second
type of argument seeks to justify vicarious liability in terms of efficient loss distribution. Arguments of the latter type rest on the
assumption that the prime function of tort law is to compensate victims of tortious conduct. Vicarious liability furthers this aim by
increasing the chance that the victim will be compensated: in general,
employers are likely to be in a better position than employees to pay

[15] Another important type of argument sees vicarious liability as providing incentives for
accident avoidance. See G. Schwartz, "The Hidden and Fundamental Issue of Employer
Vicarious Liability" (1996) 69 So Cal LR 1739, 1755–67.
[16] J. Stapleton, Product Liability (London, 1994), ch. 8. This argument would justify the
imposition of strict liability in a wide range of situations in which it is currently not imposed.

tort damages or to insure against tort liability. Under this approach, the ethical principle supporting vicarious liability is not one of personal responsibility for an outcome, but is of the type which supports social welfare systems: from each according to wealth, to each according to need. Under this social welfare principle it may be said that one person ought to provide financial support to meet another's need even though the former is in no way personally responsible for the fact that latter is in need. In the jargon of political theory, the social welfare principle is not a principle of "corrective justice" but one of "distributive justice"; that is, it is a principle about how resources ought to be distributed in society, not a principle about correcting the results of unfair dealings between individuals.

A full assessment of these contrasting approaches would require a detailed exposition of the law of vicarious liability and a close examination of the arguments which would be out of place in this book. Only two points need to be made. The first is that the "social welfare" argument cannot explain why vicarious liability is more or less limited in its application to the employer-employee relationship and why tort law is not generally based on social welfarist principles. Secondly, once we seek to justify tort law in terms of efficient compensation, we find that it falls very far short of the ideal of an efficient compensation system. These points are discussed in more detail in Chapter 7.

Outcome-based strict liability

The third type of strict liability in tort law is based on the idea of risk creation. To explain this form of liability it is necessary to introduce the concepts of "actionability *per se*" and "causation". To say that conduct is "actionable *per se*" means that there can be liability for the conduct even if no-one suffered any physical, mental or financial injury, loss, damage or harm as a result of the conduct. For instance, entering another's land without their consent and without legal justification may be tortious even if the landowner suffers no injury, damage or harm beyond the mere fact of the entry. The act of entry is itself tortious regardless of its consequences. Publishing a defamatory statement is also actionable *per se*. A plaintiff may succeed in a defamation action even if P cannot prove that anyone actually thought less of P as a result of the publication of the statement or that the publication damaged P's reputation. If it is clear that P's reputation was not damaged, P may be awarded only "nominal" or even "contemptuous" damages.[17] However, P may be awarded substantial

---

[17] Concerning these types of damages, see p. 102 below.

damages to compensate for damage to reputation even in the absence of proof that anyone thought less of P as a result of the defamatory publication. In effect, the law presumes that in the normal course of events, damage to reputation follows from the publication of a defamatory statement.[18]

By contrast, other forms of tort liability will arise only if it can be proved that P suffered some physical, mental, financial or other injury, loss, damage or harm as a result of the tortious conduct. In such cases, it is said that injury (or "loss", "damage" or "harm") is "the gist of the action". In such cases, an element of the plaintiff's case will be that D's conduct caused the injury. The concept of causation is complex and is discussed in Chapter 5. The relevant point here is that outcome-based strict liability, unlike the other two forms of strict liability, rests upon a causal connection between some conduct which attracts the liability and some injury, loss, damage or harm actually suffered by the victim.

The elements of outcome-based strict liability are the conduct by D of an activity which creates a risk of injury, the materialization of that risk, and injury caused to P by the materialization of the risk. The liability is strict because D can be liable even if D did not intend to cause injury to P, even if D was not reckless as to P's injury, even if D was not negligent in creating the risk and even if D did not cause it to materialize. An example of such liability is, perhaps, that of distributors of defective products under the Consumer Protection Act 1987 (Part I). A distributor of a defective product may be sued under the Act by a person who suffers injury as a result of the defect if, when asked, the distributor does not identify the producer of the product, even though the distributor did not know and had no reason to know that the product was defective and was in no sense responsible for the defect. In this case, the risky activity is the distribution of (defective) products; and because of the causal connection between the defect and the injury, there is necessarily a (weak) causal connection between distribution of the product and the injury to the

---

[18] According to another view (held by Jane Stapleton), damages for defamation compensate not for injury to reputation but for the risk of such injury arising from the publication of defamatory statements, just as an injunction may issue to restrain threatened trespass to land. However, in a trespass action, substantial compensatory damages are only available in respect of injury actually suffered, whereas according to this interpretation of defamation liability, substantial compensatory damages (as well as injunctions in certain cases) are available as of right merely on the basis of a threat to reputation. If this interpretation is correct, reputation is even better protected by tort law than real property, and better protected than any other interest.

recipient of the product from the distributor. The remarkable thing about this example is that it is only in a weak sense (if at all) that we would say that the distributor created the risk of injury. For this reason, it may be better to see the distributor's liability as effectively vicarious; or as a hybrid of relationship-based and outcome-based strict liability.

Outcome-based strict liability is, in fact, very rare in tort law, especially in judge-made tort law. Under the so-called "rule in *Rylands* v. *Fletcher*" a landowner can be held liable for the escape from its land of things likely to cause damage if they escape, which the landowner has accumulated on the land for its own purposes and in the course of a non-natural use of the land. On the face of it, this principle looks like a principle of outcome-based strict liability: the risky activity is accumulation of dangerous things for a non-natural purpose, and the principle contains no requirement of intention, recklessness or negligence. However, the rule has been interpreted in such a way as to weaken its claim to be a rule of strict liability. The term "non-natural" has been given a meaning close to "negligent"; it has been held that there can be liability under the rule only in relation to "foreseeable" damage; and although P need not prove that the escape was the result of either deliberate or negligent conduct by the landowner, the landowner will not be liable if the escape can be shown to have been the result of a natural event or human conduct which was not foreseeable by D.

The Ethical Imperatives of Tort Law

The rarity of outcome-based strict liability in tort law is a result of adherence to a principle usually put in terms that there should be "no liability without fault". This adage needs a little explanation. It is only applied to tort law, and only to that part of tort law which is concerned with liability for physical, mental and financial injury and damage. It is not thought, for instance, to cast doubt upon conduct-based strict liability (as, for instance, in the tort of conversion). "Fault" refers to intention and negligence. The basis for the adage is usually taken to be the idea that outcome-based strict liability is in some sense inconsistent with non-legal morality in holding people responsible for outcomes which they did not intend and which they could not have avoided. However, it is by no means clear that outside the law people are never held responsible for such outcomes. It has been argued, for instance, that we are sometimes prepared to hold a person responsible for an outcome which that person caused but which they neither intended nor could have avoided, provided the person is of "full age and capacity", so to speak.[19] The basic idea of "outcome responsibility" is that risk-taking is part of ordinary human life, and that when we take risks, sometimes things turn out well and sometimes they turn out badly. Since we take the benefit when things turn out well, we should also take responsibility when things turn out badly, even if we could have done nothing to prevent the bad outcome. A major problem with this argument is that it would support a regime of tort liability in which the general rule of liability for outcomes was strict liability.[20] In other words, it does not explain why we sometimes hold people responsible only for outcomes which they intended or could have avoided, whereas in other cases we hold people responsible for outcomes which they did not intend and could not have avoided.

One suggested criterion for the imposition of outcome-based (as well as relationship-based) strict liability is profit-making: a person who stands to make a financial profit from an activity should bear the risk that the activity will cause harm to others.[21] This is a normatively attractive proposal, but it does not accurately reflect the current state of tort law. Another suggestion is that outcome-based strict liability attaches to the conduct of activities which are "specially dangerous to others".[22] A major problem with this suggestion lies in the difficulty of defining "specially dangerous activities", because the dangerousness of most activities is related as much to the way they are carried on as to their intrinsic nature. In practice, arguments for outcome-based and relationship-based strict liability are often not founded on ideas of personal responsibility at all but on a desire to make it easier for the injured to obtain tort compensation or to encourage entrepreneurs to make their activities safer.

Some people have found not only strict liability but also negligence liability ethically problematic. We have seen that the test of reasonableness in negligence is objective. Reasonable precautions are precautions which the reasonable person would have taken regardless of whether they are precautions which the person whose conduct is under scrutiny could have taken. This test allows that people may be held liable in negligence for doing things which they could not per-

---

[19] T. Honoré, "Responsibility and Luck: The Moral Basis of Strict Liability" (1988) 104 LQR 530.

[20] J. Stapleton, *Product Liability* (above n.16), 185.

[21] Ibid.

[22] Honoré, op. cit. n. 19 above.

sonally have avoided doing at the relevant time and for failing to do things which they could not personally have done at the relevant time, not because of any moral fault on their part but just because they had the ("moral") bad luck to be born lacking the skill or capacity to meet the standard of conduct which the law considers to be reasonable. On reflection, however, the objectivity of legal fault appears not to be inconsistent with extra-legal ethical principles. The good or bad luck of being born with certain characteristics is an ineradicable feature of the human condition. Morality requires us to do what we can to correct deficiencies in our personalities and capacities which are apt to produce blameworthy conduct. It also requires us not to undertake tasks which we know or ought to realize we are not capable of performing without injuring others. Both of these moral obligations may justify holding a person responsible for conduct which, at a particular point of time, they could not have avoided. But moral censure may even attach to conduct which is the result of incorrigible personal characteristics or of forgivable ignorance of our limitations. Everything we do (or fail to do) is affected to a greater or lesser extent by "lucky" factors beyond our control, including our personal endowments. If people could disclaim responsibility for their conduct, either in law or outside it, simply by pointing to the role of luck in their endowments and capacities, the whole concept of personal responsibility, on which our sense of ourselves and others as rational and free agents depends, would dissolve. It is only when a person's natural endowments fall below a minimum level that we are prepared to allow luck to affect our judgements about the person's responsibility for their conduct. Just as it is ethically acceptable for people to claim personal credit for conduct which is partly a product of their good luck in having a certain personality and certain capacities, [23] so people must accept responsibility for conduct which is partly a product of bad luck in having a certain personality and certain capacities.

Tort law, then, is a complex mixture of principles of personal responsibility for conduct (whether intentional, reckless or negligent) and personal responsibility for outcomes (strict liability). Different ethical imperatives underlie these two forms of responsibility. That

---

[23] But an important element of the virtue of humility is to recognize and not to claim personal credit for elements of exceptional luck in our achievements. Concerning the relationship between tort liability and luck, see further P. Cane, "Retribution, Proportionality and Moral Luck in Tort Law" in P. Cane and J. Stapleton (eds), *The Comparative Law of Torts: Essays in Honour of John G. Fleming* (Oxford, forthcoming 1998).

underlying conduct-responsibility is not to engage in the liability-attracting conduct; and that underlying outcome-responsibility is to compensate for adverse outcomes of the relevant activity. Viewed in this way, tort liability based on outcome-responsibility is a sort of tax on activities which attract such liability rather than a penalty for engaging in it. Liability based on conduct-responsibility, by contrast, implies a disapproval of the liability-attracting conduct which does not attach to outcome-responsibility.

On the other hand, the disapproval implied by the imposition of tort liability based on conduct-responsibility is not as strong as that implied by the imposition of criminal liability. This has led some people to view "conduct-based tort liability" as also being a sort of tax. In extreme versions of this view, the moral imperative underpinning tort liability for intentional harm would be either to desist from causing intentional harm or pay damages to the victim. Similarly, the moral imperative underpinning negligence liability would be to desist from negligent conduct or pay damages to the victim. Most people, perhaps, would find this idea repugnant in relation to intentional harms even if not in relation to negligence. It is arguable, however, that both applications misrepresent tort law. The ethical imperative of conduct-based tort liability is not to engage in the sanctioned conduct, and conduct-based tort sanctions are a form of penalty, not a form of tax. Of course, it is true that the moral stigma attaching to conduct-based tort liability is not as great as that attaching to criminal liability. Nevertheless, the moral stigma attaching to such tort liability is greater than that (if any) which attaches to outcome-based tort liability.

Non-compliance with Statutes

The question to be considered here is when non-compliance with a statutory provision can attract tort liability. In the first place, breach of a statutory provision may amount to a tort quite independently of the statute. For example, rape is an offence under the Sexual Offences (Amendment) Act 1976; but a rapist would also commit the tort of trespass to the person (battery). Secondly, in cases of negligence, breach of a legislative provision may provide evidence of negligence. For instance, breach of traffic regulations (imposing a speed restriction, for instance) may support an argument that the defendant did not take reasonable care. The rule in this type of case is that although compliance with a statute may help a defendant sued for negligence, and although breach of a statute may assist an argument that the defendant was negligent, neither compliance with nor breach of a statute is conclusive of the issue of negligence.

Thirdly, some statutes create what may be called "statutory torts". For example, certain breaches of the Sex Discrimination Act 1975 can, by virtue of the statute, give rise to liability to pay damages which is, in effect, tort liability.[24] Infringements of statutory intellectual property rights, such as patents and trade marks, are also statutory torts. Section 27 of the Housing Act 1988 makes harassment of a tenant by a landlord a wrong for which damages can be recovered.[25] Part I of the Consumer Protection Act 1987 creates a regime of liability for injury and damage caused by defective products; and the Defective Premises Act 1972 creates liability for the provision of substandard dwellings. The Misrepresentation Act 1967 creates liability for negligent misrepresentations which induce contracts. All of these statutes created new liabilities which had not previously existed. On the other hand, some statutes, such as the Occupier's Liability Acts of 1957 and 1984, replace pre-existing common law grounds of liability, while others modify or qualify them. Occasionally a statute may abolish an existing common law ground of liability. For instance, the Torts (Interference with Goods) Act 1977 abolished the "tort of detinue". Tort law is a complex web of statutory and non-statutory rules and principles. While the legislature enacts statutory rules of tort law, the courts interpret them and fit them into the larger body of tort law. In doing this, they start from the position that a statute will not be taken to have altered the common law unless it clearly says so. But to the extent that a statute clearly conflicts with the pre-existing common law, the common law must give way. The courts designed and continue to tend the garden of tort law. The legislature, however, owns the garden, and may supply flowers and trees which the gardener must plant and tend according to the owner's instructions. Still, the owner leaves many aspects of the gardening to the discretion of the gardener.

This discretion is nowhere clearer than in relation to the many statutory provisions which impose duties or prohibitions on individuals but say nothing about whether breach of the provision can give rise to an action for damages. There is a formula of tort liability called the "tort of breach of statutory duty" which is concerned with such provisions, and it provides us with a fourth way in which noncompliance with a statute can attract tort liability. The rules of this

[24] See P. Cane, *Tort Law and Economic Interests*, 2nd edn (Oxford, 1996), 157.
[25] Ibid, 34.

tort are concerned with two issues: first, when will breach of a statutory provision which is silent on the issue be "actionable in tort";
and secondly, if breach of the provision is actionable in tort, is the
standard of liability a form of strict liability or is it based on fault of
some sort? In theory, the answer to both of these questions depends
on the precise terms of the relevant statutory provision and their
proper interpretation. In practice, however, very many statutory provisions give little or no guidance as to how these two questions are
to be answered, and courts are left to answer them in accordance with
their own ethical sense and consistently with non-statutory principles
of tort law. To continue the gardening image, such statutory provisions are like plants which the owner leaves in the potting shed and
which the gardener must decide to plant or not according to what the
gardener thinks is the owner's wish in the matter. The general point
is that tort liability is only one way of enforcing duties and prohibitions, and the courts (rightly) do not assume that it is always the correct or best means of enforcement.

The legal position is more complicated in relation to statutory provisions which do not impose duties or prohibitions but which confer
powers (or "discretions") – such as, for instance, a power to take into
care children thought to be in physical danger. The difference
between a duty and a power is that a power confers a greater or lesser
element of choice about questions such as whether to act, or about
what to do, or about when to do it. The main beneficiaries of statutory powers are government bodies and non-government bodies
which are, in effect, delegates of the government. The question to be
considered here is when tort liability can arise out of the exercise of
a statutory power. The first point to make in answer to this question
is that there is a formula of tort liability called "misfeasance in a public office". This tort, as its name indicates, can only be committed by
a "public official"; and there is a body of law (which we need not
consider here) which defines what this term means. "Misfeasance"
means abuse or excess of power. All statutory powers have limits.
Some of these limits are defined by the statutory provisions which
create the power, and some are imposed by the courts under common law rules such as one which requires a person to be given a fair
hearing before a statutory power is exercised against him. To trans-
gress the limits of a statutory power is to exceed or abuse it. A person can be held liable for misfeasance in a public office only if the
person acted "maliciously". In this context, the word "maliciously"
bears one of two meanings. A person acts maliciously if they commit

an act of "misfeasance" either with the intention of inflicting injury or damage on another, or knowing that they are exceeding or abusing a statutory power (that is, deliberately) in the knowledge that P will or might be injured thereby. Difficulty of proving malice reduces the practical utility of this head of tort liability.

Secondly, if a person negligently injures another as a result of exercising a statutory power, the person may have committed tortious negligence. The relevant law is uncertain,[26] but it seems clear that exercise of a statutory power will be able to give rise to tort liability for negligence only if the imposition of liability would be "compatible" with the scheme and purposes of the statute in question. Unfortunately, the courts have as yet given only vague guidance as to the meaning of "compatible". It also seems clear (as noted earlier) that in certain cases, the test of "unreasonable conduct" in actions for negligence against public authorities is that of "extraordinary unreasonableness": did the defendant act so unreasonably that no reasonable authority could have so acted? What is less clear is which are these "certain cases". Suppose a local authority social worker is involved in a car accident while on her way to visit a child thought to be in danger of being abused by a parent, and injures a pedestrian. The local authority which employed her would be liable for any tort she committed because at the time of the accident she was fulfilling, on behalf of the authority, a task which the authority was authorized by statute to perform (that is, care for children in danger). In such a case, the test of whether the social worker had driven negligently or not would surely be the test of "ordinary unreasonableness". Suppose, however, that the social worker decides not to take the child into care, and soon afterwards the child is badly beaten by its parent. In that case, the test of negligence would, it seems, be that of "extraordinary unreasonableness". The difference between these two cases is expressed in a variety of ways. One of the most common is to say that in deciding whether to take the child into care, the social worker was performing a "policy" or "planning" function, whereas in driving her car she was performing an "operational function", even though both functions were an integral part of exercising the authority's statutory powers as a social welfare agency. The main function of this distinction is to preserve for public authorities a wide area of discretion in which they are free to take risks without incurring tort liability. The distinction places the risk of many

[26] The leading cases are X v. *Bedfordshire CC* [1995] 2 AC 633 and *Stovin* v. *Wise* [1996] 3 WLR 388.

governmental activities on individual citizens who may be harmed by the exercise of public powers rather than on the general body of tax-payers. In some contexts, this approach is highly controversial.

The third important point about liability for exercise of statutory powers is that there is no formula of tort liability (analogous to liab-ility for breach of statutory duty) covering abuse or excess of a stat-utory power. This fact may be explicable largely in historical terms: in the late nineteenth century when modern tort law was develop-ing, perhaps the predominant function of statute was to regulate var-ious social and economic activities by imposing duties and prohibitions on those engaged in them. It was in the twentieth cen-tury, with the enormous expansion of the welfare state, that statutes also became a crucial source of governmental power. By this time, however, the courts had become much less willing to invent new heads of tort liability. There is some reason to think that English courts may, in the foreseeable future and as a result of certain devel-opments in European Community law, allow that tort liability might arise out of abusing or exceeding statutory powers as such.

These developments in European Community law deserve some explanation. An important legal and political issue in the EU is how to ensure that governments of Member States comply with EC law. Sanctions are the key, and over the years the European Court of Justice (ECJ) has developed a number of rules under which individ-uals can sue governments for damage suffered as a result of breaches of EC law. The position now reached is that if a person suffers dam-age as a result of a serious breach by an organ of government of a Member State of a rule of EC law designed to protect individual rights, the person may recover damages from that State.[27] The con-cept of being "designed to protect individual rights" is analogous to the concept in English law of damages liability being compatible with a statutory provision. Whether a breach of EC law is "serious" depends on a number of factors including whether the breach was deliberate or not, the clarity of the rule allegedly broken and the amount of discretion which that rule gave to Members States in deciding what to do. A State can be liable under this principle even if the breach of EC law was not "malicious". This new "Eurotort" of "serious breach of EC law" is analogous to the tort of breach of stat-utory duty, but its scope is not limited to rules which impose duties or prohibitions on Member States: it extends to rules which confer

---

[27] The seminal case is *R* v. *Secretary of State for Transport, ex parte Factortame (No. 4)* (known as "*Factortame No. 4*" or "*Brasserie du Pecheur*") [1996] 2 WLR 506.

powers and, hence, to conduct of Member States which exceeds or abuses the powers of Member States under EC law. Furthermore (as just noted), unlike liability for misfeasance in a public office in English law, this liability is not limited to "malicious" conduct. Also, it seems clear that it is only relevant to the performance of "policy" or "planning" functions, as defined earlier.

Obviously, this head of liability only applies to breaches of EC law. However, past experience in other areas suggests that once a principle of liability becomes accepted in EC law, pressure soon mounts for it to be recognized in English law. It is possible, therefore, that in the not-too-distant future, English law might also recognize a head of tort liability along the lines of "serious breach of a statutory provision" (whether imposing a duty or prohibition or conferring a power) designed to protect individuals (by giving them a right to claim damages).

Illegal Conduct

Illegal conduct is conduct "contrary to law". Tortious conduct satisfies this description. Tortiousness is only one form of illegality (or "unlawfulness"). Breach of contract and breach of the criminal law are other forms. In some cases, in order to be tortious under a particular heading of tort liability, the law says that conduct must also be unlawful in some sense other than "tortious under that head"; or, in other words, the conduct must be "independently unlawful". Tort liability for non-compliance with statutory provisions, which we have just examined, is liability for independently unlawful conduct. In that context, tort liability functions as an additional sanction to whatever sanction (if any) the statute attaches to the non-compliance. In some cases, by contrast, independent unlawfulness operates as a constraint on the scope of tort liability. A good example is tort liability for interference with contract. Suppose that D causes C not to comply with a contract between C and P, and as a result P suffers damage or loss. Under certain conditions, (the details do not matter for present purposes), D may be liable to P in tort. In some (but not all) cases, one of those conditions is that what D did was independently unlawful. For example, suppose D prevents C from performing a contract with P to paint P's portrait by deliberately breaking C's arm. The condition of independent unlawfulness would be satisfied in this case because D's conduct in breaking C's arm would probably be both criminal and tortious independently of the fact that it led to C being unable to perform the contract for P.

An important justification for the requirement of independent unlawfulness in relation to liability for interference with contract is that the disabling of people from performing their contracts is often the result of ordinary market competition between rival producers and suppliers of goods and services. To render ordinary competition tortious would seriously hamper the operation of the market economy which is basic to the operation of our society. The courts use the idea of independent unlawfulness in certain circumstances as a way of drawing the line between legitimate and illegitimate competition.

Causality

As noted earlier, under many heads of tort liability, conduct will be sanctioned only if it can be said to have been a cause of some injury, loss, damage or harm suffered by the victim. Thus, having the status of a cause can be seen, in many cases, as one of the requirements for conduct to be sanctioned by tort law.[28] However, it is perhaps better to treat causation as an aspect of the required relationship between sanctioned conduct and protected interests. For this reason, it is dealt with in Chapter 5 below.

CONDUCT GIVING RISE TO A DEFENCE

As a result of its correlative structure, tort law is concerned with the conduct of plaintiffs as well as of defendants. This concern partly finds expression in certain defences to tort liability which relate to the conduct of the plaintiff/victim, and it is with such defences that this section is concerned.

Negligence

Negligent conduct on the part of the victim ("contributory negligence") may provide a defence against tort liability. Whereas liability-attracting negligence consists in failure to take reasonable care for the interests of another, contributory negligence consists of failure to take care for one's own interests. The concept of unreasonable conduct underlying contributory negligence is essentially similar to that underlying liability-attracting negligence. For instance, contributory negligence is an objective concept depending on what the reasonable

---

[28] Besides doing harm, there are other forms of causality which may attract tort liability, such as failing to prevent harm occurring (nonfeasance), authorizing, assisting or inducing the commission of a tort (secondary liability) and providing the opportunity for tortious behaviour (as in Stansbie v. Troman [1948] 2 KB 48).

person would have done in the victim's position. However, the law allows people to take less care for their own interests than it requires people to take care for the interests of others. In technical terms, this means that in judging the reasonableness of the precautions a person takes to protect their own interests, the law makes more allowance for age, resources and physical and mental capacity than in the case of liability-attracting negligence. Both in allowing a defence of contributory negligence and in applying the test of reasonableness leniently in that context, the law seems consistent with widely-held moral principles. Freedom of action would be unacceptably limited if, as a general rule, either a person could be held responsible for another's failure to protect their own interests, or people were expected to be as careful of their own interests as of the interests of others.

In ethical terms, it is fairly obvious why contributory negligence should be defence to a claim for negligence. Less clear is whether it is, or should be, a defence to liability based on intention or to strict liability. Although contributory negligence is a statutory defence,[29] the statute is not drafted in such a way as to resolve this issue. If a person intends to harm another, it does not seem fair to allow that person to argue that the victim did not take sufficient care to protect himself or herself from being harmed. The idea that a person might have "deserved what they got" because they took insufficient precautions to avoid it may be acceptable as a judgement of the victim relative to other (hypothetical) victims. But if we take correlativity seriously as the basis of tort law, the important question concerns the relative ethical positions of the plaintiff and the defendant, not their positions relative to other hypothetical plaintiffs or defendants respectively.

So far as strict liability is concerned, the defence is made available in certain instances by statute. [30] As a matter of principle, it may be argued that if fault is irrelevant to the issue of whether D's conduct attracts liability, it should also be irrelevant to the issue of whether P's conduct gives rise to a defence. However, the conclusion does not really follow from the premise either logically or ethically, and the strength of the argument may depend, in part, on the sort of strict liability in issue. In relation to outcome-based strict liability, we might think it fair both to require victims to take reasonable care for

[29] See Law Reform (Contributory Negligence) Act 1945
[30] E.g. Consumer Protection Act 1987, ss. 6(4),(5) (a defence to liability for defective product, even if strict).

their own safety and not to allow injurers to plead as a defence the negligence of anyone other than the plaintiff. This sort of approach is reflected in the fact that statutes which impose outcome-based strict liability not infrequently also allow contributory negligence to be pleaded as a defence.[31] It also seems fair enough that a defendant who is vicariously liable should be allowed to take advantage of a defence of contributory negligence which was available to the tort-feasor. By contrast, in relation to conduct-based strict liability, the primary role of which is to protect property rights (and analogous interests, such as reputation), the law has consistently followed the principle that people should not be expected to take care of their own property: the fact that I am careless of my property may make me an unworthy owner, but it does not make the property any less mine. Such an uncompromising attitude to the protection of property may also be thought essential to the smooth running of a market economy.

The principle underlying the defence of contributory negligence is that people should take reasonable care for themselves as well as for others. This principle finds expression in tort law not only in this defence to tort liability but also in rules about when tort liability can arise in the first place. Such rules figure prominently in the law governing liability for purely economic loss. For instance, financial loss suffered as a result of relying on the accuracy of a statement made by the defendant to the plaintiff will arise only if it was reasonable for the plaintiff to rely on the statement as being accurate. Thus, it would not normally be reasonable to rely on advice about a serious business matter which was given off-the-cuff in a social context; and in certain circumstances, it may not be reasonable for a person to rely on another's advice without getting a second opinion.

Consent

As a general principle, a person cannot complain in tort about anything to which they have consented. For example, there can be no liability for trespass to land if the owner consented to the entry; and it is a defence to an action for defamation that the person to whom the statement refers consented to its publication. Consent need not be expressed in words but can be "inferred" from conduct. Like deliberation, consent is a state of mind; and unlike negligence, it is a

---

[31] E.g. Consumer Protection Act 1987, ss. 6(4),(5). Concerning conduct-based strict liability see Torts (Interference with Goods) Act 1977, s11(1) (contributory negligence not a defence to an action for conversion).

subjective concept – the relevant question is not whether the reasonable person would have consented but whether the victim in fact consented. However, consent will provide a defence only if the victim was not "forced" by the defendant to consent. The test of whether consent was forced is ultimately an objective one: did the victim consent to the tort because the defendant threatened that if (s)he did not, (s)he would suffer some negative consequence which the court thinks it would not be reasonable to expect the victim to accept as the price of avoiding the tort.

Consent will provide a defence only if the consent related to the tortious conduct and was given before the tortious conduct occurred. This may explain why a defendant in a nuisance action cannot plead that the nuisance existed before the plaintiff came into the area ("coming to the nuisance is no defence"): it cannot be inferred merely from the fact that a person comes into proximity with a nuisance-creating activity that the person consented to the (continuance of the) unreasonable use of land.

In relation to negligence, the defence of consent is usually expressed in terms of the Latin maxim "*volenti non fit injuria*" or its English translation "voluntary assumption of risk". It has often been argued that the notion of consent-in-advance is inconsistent with the legal concept of negligence because it is impossible fully to appreciate in advance the risks attendant upon lack of reasonable care. This argument depends partly on the incorrect assumption that legal negligence implies inadvertence: in cases where negligence liability attaches to deliberate conduct, there is no logical difficulty in the idea of prospective consent. If I freely allow myself to be driven at night in a car which the driver has told me has no lights, I may be said to have voluntarily assumed the risk of being injured in an accident attributable to absence of lights. Similarly, if I freely agree to be a passenger in an aircraft piloted by a person whom I know to have consumed 20 units of alcohol in a few hours, I may be said to have voluntarily assumed the risk of being injured in an accident attributable to the pilot's drunkenness.[32] In these cases I may be said, by my conduct, to have consented to a lack of reasonable care on the part of another. This conclusion would, perhaps, be widely accepted outside the law; but for reasons we will explore in the Chapter 4,[33] it has proved controversial within it.

[32] See *Morris* v. *Murray* [1991] 2 QB 6.
[33] See p. 121 below.

Illegality

Earlier we examined the relationship between tort liability and "independent illegality".[34] In that discussion "illegal" was defined to mean unlawful in any sense other than "tortious" under the head of tort liability in question. The question to be discussed here concerns the effect on tort liability of the fact that the victim was acting illegally at the time of the defendant's tortious conduct. The most important meaning of "illegally" in this context is "in breach of the criminal law". It is, in fact, not uncommonly the case that victims of torts are guilty of acting illegally in this sense. For instance, many victims of road accidents are in breach of traffic regulations at the time the accident occurs. Such illegal conduct on the part of the victim might amount to contributory negligence. But independently of that, the issue is whether the fact that the victim was acting illegally ought to provide the injurer with a defence. On the one hand, it might be thought that a person who acts illegally hardly deserves much sympathy from the law. On the other hand, many technically illegal acts might not be thought very culpable. Moreover, suppose the illegal behaviour in no way contributed to the accident or to the plaintiff's injuries; should the *mere* fact that a victim was acting illegally affect their rights under tort law?

In fact, tort law adopts the morally defensible position of only allowing defendants to plead illegality as a defence if the victim's illegal conduct contributed in some significant way to bringing about the situation for which the defendant is held responsible. Tort law is not concerned with sanctioning conduct as such. This is the province of the criminal law, the focus of which is on punishment. Criminal law will sanction conduct which creates risks of adverse outcomes even if the risk never materializes. Tort law, by contrast, will only sanction risky conduct if the risk materializes. The primary concern of tort law is not to punish risky conduct but to make good the adverse effects of risky conduct. Of course, requiring someone to make good the adverse consequences of their risky conduct may be seen as a form of punishment for that conduct; and in fact, criminal courts have powers to award compensation to victims of crimes, and civil courts have limited powers to impose punishments on tortfeasors. Nevertheless, the focus of tort law and criminal law are different: criminal law is primarily concerned with risky conduct as such whereas tort law is concerned with the adverse consequences of risky

---

[34] See p. 57 above.

conduct. An unsuccessful attempt to commit a crime may be a crime. There is no such thing as an "attempted tort". This difference of approach between criminal law and tort law may go some way to explaining why, under the Criminal Injuries Compensation Scheme, compensation may be reduced in the light of the applicant's past (illegal) behaviour even if it bore no causal relationship to the injuries for which compensation is sought.

So far as culpability is concerned, the approach of the courts is influenced by the idea that whereas the prime function of the criminal law is punishment, the prime function of tort law is the protection and vindication of individual's interests, typically by compensating for injury suffered. This function would be unacceptably compromised if "contributory illegality" on the part of the plaintiff, however venial, provided a defence. While the lack of a clear definition of the required degree of culpability renders the law inevitably somewhat uncertain, the courts' approach to this question might be thought to reflect common extra-legal judgements about personal responsibility and desert.

ACTS AND OMISSIONS

So far the discussion of tort liability has been couched primarily in terms of "conduct". As I said earlier, this term covers both "acts" and "omissions" or, as it is sometimes put, "misfeasance" and "nonfeasance". Both misfeasance and nonfeasance can be tortious. For instance, suppose that A digs a hole in the unlit path leading from the gate of A's house to its front door, and that B falls into it at night and is injured. We would say that by the *act* of digging the hole, A caused B's injury – if A had not dug the hole, B would not have been injured. Suppose, alternatively, that the path became pot-holed by the elements and C tripped in a hole at night. In this case we might say that A caused C's injury by *omitting* to repair the path: if A had kept the path in good repair, C would not have been injured. Put another way, we might say that whereas A caused B's injury, A failed to prevent C's injury.

There is no doubt that outside the law, the distinction between acts and omissions is recognized and has ethical force. Sometimes, we may judge a person less harshly for failing to prevent injury than for bringing it about.[35] The thug who beats someone up may be judged

[35] See T. Honoré, "Are Omissions Less Culpable?" in P. Cane and J. Stapleton (eds), *Essays for Patrick Atiyah* (Oxford, 1991), 31–52.

more responsible for the person's injuries than the victim's (or the thug's) companion who makes no attempt to thwart the attack. But this is by no means universally so. A parent who harms their child by failing to feed it even though they could afford to is unlikely to be thought less culpable than a parent who causes the same harm by serving their child poisoned food. A passer-by who ignores an abandoned baby may be judged no less harshly than the parent who abandoned it. And just as omissions may attract as much moral censure as acts, so omissions may attract the same legal sanctions as acts. In the famous case of *Donoghue* v. *Stevenson*[36] Lord Atkin said that the religious injunction to love one's neighbour is translated by tort law into the principle that one must take care not to injure one's neighbour. He did not mean by this that tort law does not impose liability for omissions. Indeed, the legal definition of negligent conduct is couched negatively in terms of a failure to take reasonable care; and a failure of reasonable care can consist either in doing something the reasonable person would not do or *not* doing something the reasonable person would do. The most important point to be made here is that liability for omissions is by no means unknown in morals or in tort law.

Our attitude to omissions, both within law and outside it, depends on a number of factors including the status and situation of the person who fails to act, the costs of acting (both to the actor and to others), the status and situation of the person who would benefit from action, and the nature and size of that benefit. Perhaps all that can be said in general terms is that "acts . . . are often worse than omissions . . . because they create the . . . harms and risks of harm which omissions fail to remedy".[37] In technical legal terms, the difference between acts and omissions is expressed in a number of ways. At the level of duty, for instance, liability for failure to protect a person from harm is more likely to be imposed if the person on whom it is imposed has been paid for the protection, whereas liability for causing harm is very often imposed regardless of payment. At the level of breach of duty, the distinction between misfeasance and nonfeasance finds expression in value-judgements in individual cases about whether any precautions against the risk that harm would occur were reasonable.

---

[36] [1932] AC 562, 580.
[37] Above n.35, 33.

CONCLUSION

There is a great deal more that could be said about the concept of "sanctioned conduct" in tort law; and a lot more will be said about it in the course of this book. The aim of this chapter has been to describe the blocks out of which the concept is built rather than the details of how they are assembled. Many of these building blocks are also used in constructing the concept of sanctioned conduct in other areas of the law of obligations, such as contract and restitution. This chapter is, therefore, important to an understanding of the anatomy of not only tort law but also of other areas of civil law. The relevance of this point will become clearer later in the book.

3. PROTECTED INTERESTS

In this chapter we examine the concept of "protected interest" in tort law. As in the case of "sanctioned conduct", a full understanding of the concept of "protected interest" cannot be had independently of a consideration of the sanctions available in tort law, or, indeed, of the concept of causation. These topics are discussed in later chapters of the book. Because of its correlative structure, tort law is concerned with the interests of defendants as well as those of plaintiffs, just as it is concerned with the conduct of both. Furthermore, because the rules and principles of tort are of general application, and because tort law is a *publicly enforceable* set of ethical rules and principles of personal responsibility, wider social interests are relevant to defining the scope of tort liability. In the first part of this chapter we examine the concept of protected interests from the point of view of plaintiffs, and in the second part, under the heading of "Countervailing Interests" we examine the topic from the point of defendants and of society more widely. From the perspective of plaintiffs, an "interest" is a "resource" or an "asset"; for instance, a "right" under a contract, or "claim" to or right over some tangible thing, such as one's body or a plot of land, or some intangible thing such as a trademark.

An interest in this first sense should be distinguished from interests in the sense of advantageous objectives or states of affairs: everyone has an interest in freedom of action, and the public has an interest in good government. The two uses of the word "interest" are obviously related. One of the reasons why we recognize interests in the former sense is in order to further interests in the latter sense. In tort law, however, there is an important tension between the two types of interest because it is this latter sense which is relevant in the discussion of protected interests in the second part of the chapter from the perspective of defendants and of society more widely. In this second sense, protected interests play an important role in limiting the incidence and scope of tort liability. In tort law, interests in the first sense are the object of positive protection in the form of the imposition of tort liability, whereas interests in the second sense are the object of negative protection by the setting of limits to tort liability.

As we will see, tort law offers protection of various degrees and sorts to a wide variety of interests. The aim of this chapter is to describe these interests rather than to examine the degrees and sorts of protection offered by tort law. These latter topics are covered in later chapters. First, then, let us turn to interests in the sense of "assets" or "resources". The main types recognized by tort law are personal interests (for instance, in health, reputation and liberty), property interests, contractual interests, non-contractual expectancies, trade values and "wealth".

INTERESTS IN ONE'S PERSON

Physical Interests

Tort law recognizes that every human being has an interest in good health and in being whole in body and mind. However, it also insists that any life is better than none, and so does not allow "wrongful life" actions in which a child seeks to recover from a doctor damages for having been born disabled as a result of negligent failure by the doctor to alert its mother to the risk of the child being born disabled, thus depriving her of the chance to seek a therapeutic abortion. *A fortiori*, tort law does not allow actions by healthy children complaining of having been born as a result of a failed abortion or sterilization. Somewhat inconsistently, however, the law is prepared to award parents in both types of case damages representing the financial cost of rearing a disabled or unwanted child (as the case may be), and for associated non-pecuniary losses.

In theory, tort law does not distinguish between disease (such as cancer) and ill-health (such as bronchitis) on the one hand, and traumatic injuries (such as cuts and bruises or the loss of a limb) on the other. In practice, however, it is much easier to obtain a tort remedy in respect of the latter than the former.[1]

Tort law does distinguish formally between injury to the body (including the brain) and injury to the mind. At bottom this distinction is based on a particular understanding of what we mean by words such as "injury", "disease" and "ill-health". Such words are used to describe undesirable deviations from norms of health and the capacity for physical and mental activity. Within these norms, different people vary in the state of their health and in their physical and mental capacities. The law's distinction between physical injuries and

---

[1] See generally J. Stapleton, *Disease and the Compensation Debate* (Oxford, 1986).

mental injuries reflects a view that the accepted range of normality of physical health and capacity is narrower than that of mental health and capacity. Moreover, many abnormal mental states are extreme versions of mental states which most people would consider normal. By contrast, most diseases and many physical disabilities are perceived as being qualitatively different from (and worse than) normality, and not just quantitatively so. Another reason why the law distinguishes between body and mind may be that in general, it is less easy for the external observer to verify a person's mental state than their physical condition, both because the physical operation of the brain is hard to observe and because we know relatively little about the relationship between that and mental states. Finally, the distinction probably reflects a common feeling that people can reasonably be expected to put up with mental problems more than with physical problems.

Tort law distinguishes two types of mental suffering. One is actionable only if the plaintiff has suffered some other type of actionable injury as well; and the other may be actionable even if that is the only injury that a person has suffered. Mental suffering of the first type which is a concomitant of physical injury is commonly called "pain and suffering"; and mental suffering of this type which is a concomitant of other types of actionable injury is commonly called "anxiety and inconvenience". Mental suffering of the second type is commonly called "nervous shock". A more accurate alternative phrase is "medically recognized psychiatric illness". This latter phrase pinpoints the crucial difference between the two types of mental suffering: the second type is suffering recognized by the medical profession as ill-health or injury, whereas the first type need not be beyond the limits of what are accepted as normal mental reactions to external events or stimuli. The term "nervous shock" reflects the facts of cases in which, in the early twentieth century, liability for mental suffering was first allowed: these were cases in which people suffered a "shock" as a result of being involved in or witnessing horrific accidents. Now psychiatric injury may, in certain cases, form the basis of a tort action even if it is not the result of a shock in this sense.[2] Tort law, then, takes two quite different approaches to mental suffering. It will react to mental suffering standing alone only if it is medically recognized as abnormal; whereas, if mental suffering is a concomitant of some other actionably injury, tort law will react to it even though the plaintiff's mental state cannot be described as abnormal.

---

[2] *Walker* v. *Northumberland CC* [1995] ICR 702.

Nervous shock is itself divided into two types: that which is a direct result of a tort and that which is an indirect result of a tort. An example of "direct nervous shock" would be "stress-induced" psychiatric illness resulting from an excessive workload imposed on an employee by an employer.[3] Another example would be psychiatric illness suffered by the occupant of a car as a result of being involved in a road accident; or by a rescuer as a result of helping at the scene of an accident. If D's tort created a foreseeable risk that P would suffer bodily (as opposed to mental) injury, D can be held liable for direct nervous shock suffered by P even if it was so abnormal a reaction to the tort that it could be described as "unforeseeable", and even if, in fact, P suffered no bodily injury.[4] Victims of direct nervous shock are called "primary victims". Indirect nervous shock is shock suffered as a result of witnessing (even passively) the plight of primary victims, as happened to many of the people involved in the Hillsborough stadium disaster (a serious fire in 1991 at a football stadium in the North of England which left many dead).[5] Victims of indirect nervous shock are called "secondary victims". The liability to secondary victims of a tortfeasor liable for the plight of a primary victim is hedged about with limitations. First, the secondary victim's mental suffering must have been the result of suffering a "shock" in a colloquial sense. This means, for instance, that a secondary victim could not sue in respect of psychiatric illness resulting from having cared over a long period of time for an injured person. Secondly, the secondary victim's mental suffering must not have been so abnormal that it was not reasonably foreseeable. Thirdly, the secondary victim must (as a general rule) have been in a relationship of "love and affection" with the primary victim. Some relationships (such as parent and child) are assumed to be relationships of love and affection, but others (such as aunt and nephew) will only qualify as such if the plaintiff can prove that there were close ties of love and affection with the primary victim. Thirdly, the secondary victim must have witnessed the shocking incident or its aftermath personally; shock suffered as a result of receiving merely verbal reports is not actionable, although watching live TV coverage of an incident might count as personal observation. There is no precise definition of "aftermath", but it is

---

[3] *Walker* v. *Northumberland CC* [1995] ICR 702; *Frost* v. *Chief Constable of South Yorks Police* [1996] *New LJ* 1651.

[4] *Page* v. *Smith* [1996] AC 155.

[5] *Alcock* v. *Chief Constable of South Yorkshire* [1992] 1 AC 310.

said to require a fairly high degree of temporal and physical proximity to the incident.

Because these limitations on liability to secondary victims operate despite the fact that the person has suffered a recognizable psychiatric illness as a result of a tort, two explanations for their existence, couched in terms of the approach to tort law being taken in this book, deserve consideration. The first is that secondary victims who do not satisfy the criteria of liability are in some ethical sense undeserving of the protection of tort law; and the second is that to impose liability in favour of such victims would in some ethical sense be unfair to tortfeasors. The first explanation may be dismissed as being inconsistent with modern ethical ideas (backed up by science) that mental suffering is no more nor less likely than physical suffering to be the sufferer's "own fault". The second explanation perhaps rests on some idea that tort law should not impose liabilities "disproportionate to" the ethical gravity of the tort.[6] However, this idea is too vague to provide a satisfactory justification for a set of rules as complex as those dealing with secondary victims. In fact, it may be that the rules are motivated by an even more vague and unreasoned view that "tort liability has to stop somewhere".

At all events, many people find the current legal regime in this area unsatisfactory and even repugnant. How can we justify a rule which requires mentally traumatized people to go to court and prove that they have strong feelings of love and affection towards another? But how ought the law to be changed? One approach might be to abolish liability to secondary victims or even to all victims of nervous shock standing alone.[7] Diametrically opposed is an approach which would allow any victim of reasonably foreseeable nervous shock to recover.[8] Various intermediate positions involving reform of some of the rules about secondary victims but not others could be imagined and might appeal to some people. Since commonly-held moral principles are not detailed enough to generate a set of rules to deal with

---

[6] One of the fears expressed by the courts is that the number of secondary victims in any one incident may be "indeterminate". This fear of indeterminacy of the number of potential victims also features in cases concerned with liability for negligently inflicted economic loss. However, it is not used as a ground for denying or limiting liability for bodily injury, for instance. In my view, the fear is actually that liability will be indeterminate *and large*, and it is a function of some idea of disproportion. Because we think it more important to compensate for bodily injury than for mental injury or purely economic loss, we are more willing to impose large liabilities in respect of the former than the latter.

[7] J. Stapleton, "In Restraint of Tort", in P. Birks (ed), *Frontiers of Liability* (Oxford, 1994), 95-6.

[8] N.J. Mullaney and P.R. Handford, *Tort Liability for Psychiatric Damage* (Sydney, 1993).

the complex issues with which mental suffering confronts the law, the courts must develop a set of rules which are widely (even if not universally) accepted as a good basis for the use of state force against individuals. Many would argue that the current rules about tort liability for nervous shock do not satisfy this criterion.

Dignitary Interests

Tort law protects people not only from bodily and mental injury but also from attacks on their "dignity" and on those aspects of their life and personality which define their individuality. For example, depriving a person of their liberty may be tortious. Unwanted physical contact may be tortious even though it causes no bodily injury if, for instance, it is of an intimate nature. Invading a person's privacy by entering their land without their consent may be tortious. These last two examples illustrate an important difficulty in using tort law to protect dignitary interests. This difficulty arises from the fact that law in general, and tort law in particular, tends to reflect conditions in society at large, and it typically takes some time to respond to changes in social conditions. For much of its history, tort law was mainly concerned with protecting people from physical injury and from interference with their tangible property. The only dignitary interests to which tort law offered significant protection were personal liberty and reputation (considered below). Social demand for legal protection against invasions of privacy and sexual harassment, for instance, are quite recent. In the absence of action by the legislature, the courts have found it difficult (because of the legacy of formularism) to develop tort law to provide such protection. For instance, "invasion of privacy" is not, as such, recognized as a head of tort liability. This is not to say that tort law does not protect privacy, because heads of tort liability such as unauthorized entry of land (trespass) or unreasonable interference with the use of land (nuisance) can sometimes be used effectively to protect a person's privacy.[9] Again, various heads of tort liability may offer some protection against sexual and other forms of harassment.[10] However, to the extent that existing heads of tort liability were not developed in order to provide protection to the particular interest in question, such protection as they do provide may not be very effective.

[9] See D.J. Seipp, "English Judicial Recognition of a Right to Privacy" (1983) 3 *OJLS* 325.

[10] J. Conaghan, "Gendered Harms and the Law of Tort: Remedying Sexual Harassment" (1996) 16 *OJLS* 407.

A good illustration of the difficulty which modern courts have in adapting the law of tort to meet changing social needs is provided by their response to the problem of stalking. Stalking may not cause bodily injury or a recognized psychiatric illness and it may involve no intrusion onto the victim's land. In one case,[11] the stalker repeatedly telephoned the victim. Such conduct could amount to a nuisance, but since this head of tortious liability was developed to protect landowners, and since the victim did not own the house she lived in but was only an occupant, the court was confronted with the question of whether the victim should be allowed to sue in nuisance. The alternative canvassed in the case was to develop a head of tort liability specifically designed to deal with stalking and other forms of "harassment" (that is, infliction of emotional distress). The unease which judges feel when faced with the prospect of creating a new head of tort liability is illustrated by another case[12] in which, rather than formally recognize harassment as tortious, the Court of Appeal was prepared to order a stalker to desist without holding that he had committed any legal wrong at all. Such difficulties are a result of the formulary approach to tort law discussed in the first chapter.

Another (particularly striking) example of the shortcomings of the formulary approach is provided by a case[13] in which a celebrity was badly injured in an accident. Journalists, ignoring a "restricted visiting" sign on the door of his hospital room, photographed him in bed and "interviewed" him. A rather lurid story was subsequently published about him in their newspaper. The court thought that the journalists were guilty of a gross invasion of privacy, but the only basis in tort law which could be found for a decision in the plaintiff's favour was "injurious falsehood". On this basis, what the defendants had done wrong was not invading the plaintiff's privacy but rather implying in their article that P's consent to its publication had been obtained. This, it was said, damaged P's professional reputation by suggesting that he would do "anything for money".

These episodes also illustrate very important points about the relationship between judge-made and statutory law which I discussed in Chapter 1 in terms of "institutional competence". The legislature is free to identify particular conduct and attach tortious liability to it simply as a response to perceived social need.[14] On the other hand,

---

[11] *Khorasandjian* v. *Bush* [1993] QB 727. See further pp. 81–2 below.

[12] *Burris* v. *Azadani* [1995] 1 WLR 1372.

[13] *Kaye* v. *Robertson* [1991] FSR 62.

[14] There is now a statutory tort of harassment: Protection from Harassment Act 1997, s. 3

the courts are constrained in changing and developing the law of tort to meet changing social conditions by at least two powerful factors:[15] the first is a sense that they lack political legitimacy; the second (which is related to the first) is the fact that the courts (rightly) feel that they must develop the law in a way which is consistent with existing law (both judge-made and statutory) so as to maintain the common law as a reasonably coherent and consistent body of principles. The continuity and consistency of the common law to some extent makes up for the courts' lack of political legitimacy. The legitimacy of the common law is based largely on ideas of rationality, consistency and continuity, and not on political acceptability. However, the formulary approach to tort law limits the creative abilities of the courts to the point where they may not feel able to protect people's interests even in cases where doing so would receive very wide support in society at large.

So much for privacy. Now let us turn to reputation. As noted earlier, tort law has for centuries protected reputation. This it does chiefly through liability for defamation.[16] A person's reputation is what other people think of the person as opposed to the person's pride or sense of self-worth. A defamatory statement is one which would tend to lead "right-thinking people" to think less of its subject or lead them to "shun or avoid" that person. Notice the use of the words "would tend" in this definition: one of the most curious aspects of the law of defamation is that it imposes liability not for damaging a person's reputation but for making a statement which the court thinks could damage the person's reputation. The plaintiff in a defamation action need present no evidence that his or her reputation was actually damaged. Conceptually, this is probably a result of viewing reputation as a form of property, and defamation as an interference with that property. An important feature of tortious liability for interference with property is that it is actionable without proof of any actual damage to the property. One result of this state of affairs is that defamation plaintiffs are often viewed as "gold-diggers", more interested in their hurt feelings and their bank-balance than with any

---

[15] A third important constraint on judicial law-making arises from the fact that it is parasitic upon dispute resolution. Courts can tackle social problems only if and to the extent that the problem is presented to them in the form of a dispute. For this reason, it is difficult for the courts to deal with large issues comprehensively.

[16] Another head of tort liability which may be used to protect reputation is malicious falsehood. "Malicious (or "injurious") falsehood" protects commercial reputation (i.e. "goodwill"), not personal reputation.

negative impact on their reputation. Indeed, the accusation is sometimes made that a defamation action is being used as a source of pub-
licity and to enhance the plaintiff's future prospects rather than to
recover lost esteem. In other words, although defamation is formally
concerned with reputation, the rule that proof of damage to reputation is not necessary means that in practice, defamation claims are
often more concerned with things other than reputation.

Another important dignitary interest protected by the law is freedom from being discriminated against on grounds of sex or race (but
not, in England, religion). The Sex Discrimination Act 1975 and the
Race Relations Act 1976 establish heads of tort liability which protect
financial interests (for instance, by providing remedies for discrimination in the labour market), but also allow a person to recover damages for the fact of having been discriminated against. This is a good
example of an area of the law which has been created by the legislature and grafted onto the body of existing tort law.

Civil and Political Interests

One of the major legal developments of the twentieth century has
been the widespread adoption of "bills of rights" embodying, above
all, civil and political rights such as freedom of speech, freedom of
movement and association, and personal liberty, which are fundamental to active citizenship. The only one of the main civil liberties
protected by modern bills of rights which the common law of tort
has traditionally protected is personal liberty. Wrongful arrest and
wrongful imprisonment are heads of tort liability which, for centuries, have been used to counter abuse of public (and private) power.
Interference with freedom of speech or with freedom of movement
and association have never, as such, been heads of tort liability.
Indeed, in the late nineteenth century the jurist A.V. Dicey said that
in his view, one of the strengths of English law was that it "protected"
such liberties negatively by leaving people free to do anything
which was not specifically sanctioned. Thus, for instance, the English
are free to say what they like so long as it is not defamatory or in
breach of any other legal restriction on speech. Similarly, the English
are free to move about and associate as they wish provided they do
not commit trespass, nuisance or any other legal wrong. With the
exception of liberty, personal freedoms constitute a constraint on tort
liability rather than a focus of its attention. In the guise of
"Countervailing Interests", they are discussed further at the end of
this chapter.

PROPERTY INTERESTS

Property

One of the most important functions of tort law is to protect interests in tangible and intangible property. Property law creates property interests and tort law protects them. Not all the sorts of interests people can have in relation to property are property interests. Most importantly, a person can have a contractual right to use property without having a property interest "in" that property. Contractual interests are considered later. Tangible property is either "real" or "personal". Real property is land and things attached to it. Personal property (also called "chattels") is moveable. Intangible property is anything which lacks a physical form and over which the law grants people property rights. Examples include patents, trademarks and other "intellectual property rights" and debts.

In order to explain the role of tort law in protecting property rights, it is necessary to introduce the distinction between common law and equity. For many centuries in England there were two distinct sets of courts – common law courts and equity courts. The equity courts developed out of a medieval practice of litigants, who were dissatisfied with some judgment of one of the King's courts, petitioning the Lord Chancellor to take some action against the successful party to force him to act equitably in relation to the petitioner. The rules of "equity" administered by the equity courts were seen as glosses on the body of common law administered by the King's courts which were designed to make good what were seen as inadequacies or injustices in the common law. Perhaps the most important invention of the equity courts was the "trust". Put crudely, the trust is a device which allows an owner (the "settlor") to transfer ownership of property (the "trust property") to another (the "trustee") subject to a condition that the trustee manage it for the benefit of ("in trust for") a third party (the "beneficiary"). Whereas the common law courts would treat the property as being solely the property of the trustee, equity was prepared to enforce the condition in favour of the beneficiary. The way a trust worked was described in terms that while the trustee was the "legal owner" of the trust property, the beneficiary was the "equitable owner". In other words, the trustee had a legal property interest in the trust property while the beneficiary had an equitable property interest. Both tangible and intangible property could be put "into trust", but the "equitable property" belonging to the beneficiary was always intangible – it was, in effect, a right to enforce the terms of the trust against the trustee in a court of equity.

Tort law is a set of rules which was developed by the common law courts. In the formative years of the common law, only tangible things were recognized as being possible subjects of common law property rights. For this reason, much of the judge-made law of tort only protects interests in tangible property which is capable of being "possessed". The common law heads of tort liability known as "trespass" and "conversion" do not protect "ownership" as such, but rather actual possession of and the right to possess property. Most heads of tort liability which protect property interests in intangible property have been created by statute. Prominent amongst statutory intangible property is "intellectual property" – patents, trademarks, copyright and design rights. As the name implies, "intellectual property" refers to the products of intellectual effort, and the prime function of intellectual property rights is to facilitate control of the commercial exploitation of such products by the property owner. Infringements of intellectual property rights are not normally discussed in the context of the law of tort, but they are, in effect, statutory torts. The basic conceptual and ethical principles underlying the law relating to infringements of intellectual property rights are essentially similar to those underlying the common law property torts. This can be seen clearly by considering trademarks.

Registration of a trademark is a means of preventing unauthorized use of names, symbols, signatures and so on which identify a person as connected with the provision of particular goods or services with a view to attracting and retaining customers. The statutory tort of infringement of a trademark effectively protects what is called the "goodwill" of a business by protecting a mark which attracts business to its owner. However, goodwill is also protected by the head of common law tort liability called "passing off", which is sometimes described as "the law of unregistered marks". The essence of the tort of passing off (as traditionally defined) is a misrepresentation by D (resulting from the use of a "mark") that P is the source of goods or services marketed by D. Goodwill, for the purposes of the law of passing off, is treated as a form of property; whereas in the law of trademarks, the mark is the property. Nevertheless, both infringement of a trade mark and passing off are torts which protect property, even though one is statutory and the other non-statutory. As it happens, the common law never developed heads of tort liability dealing with the subject matter of the copyright and patents legislation; but these statutory heads of liability for infringement of copyright and patents share characteristics with common law heads of tort liability for unauthorized exploitation of another's property (notably conversion and trespass).

To recap: the common law and the equity courts developed different sorts of property rights. Equitable property rights are interests under trusts, whereas property rights developed by the common law courts are mostly interests in tangible things. Common law (as contrasted with equitable) property rights in intangibles are largely the product of statute.

Because the law of tort was developed by the common law courts, so long as those courts and the equity courts continued to exist as separate sets of courts with separate personnel, procedures, remedies and rules of liability, tort law could play no part in protecting equitable property rights. In the course of the nineteenth century, the two sets of courts were amalgamated into one, and the distinction between them is preserved only in a purely administrative distinction between the Queen's Bench and Chancery Divisions of the High Court. However, the two bodies of law, common law and equity, which the two sets of courts made and administered have remained stubbornly separate to a surprising degree, and it is still the case that tort law does not protect equitable property rights. In other words, breaches of trust and other interferences with equitable property rights are not treated as torts. They tend to be called "equitable wrongs". Nevertheless, the basic building blocks of liability for interference with equitable property rights are the same as the basic building blocks of liability for interference with common law property rights; and even if we treat them as different forms of liability, there is much to be gained from comparing and contrasting them. The relationship between "common law property torts" and "equitable property wrongs" will be examined further in Chapter 6 below.

The concept of "property" is a very tricky one. In one sense, property is things. But not all things are property in the legal sense. In this sense, for instance, the air we breathe is not anyone's property, and in a society where slavery is prohibited, living human beings are not property. To say that something is property in the legal sense is to say that people can have certain rights and obligations in relation to it which are recognized as "incidents (that is, legal characteristics) of property". Legal property is of two types: common law and equitable. The incidents of common law property are different from the incidents of equitable property. As a general rule, any type of common law property can be "put into" (i.e. made the subject of) a trust. Because tort law is a major legal tool for protecting common law property rights, discussion about the scope of existing tortious protection of property rights and about whether new heads of tort law should be developed to protect property rights is often, at bottom, discussion about whether a particular type of thing ought to be recognized as common law property. For example, there is a long-running debate about whether there can be tort liability for "breach of confidence"; and this debate has turned, to some extent at least, on whether confidential information is property. Again, there has been a long debate about whether the tort of passing off should cover the unauthorized use by D for financial gain of a photograph of P taken and owned by D: the law is unwilling to recognize that people can have property rights in images of themselves (as opposed to the paper or other tangible medium on which the image is printed).[17]

Interference with Property

Tort law protects property from various forms of interference. In this section I will discuss the following types of interference: misappropriation, unauthorized exploitation, interference with use and enjoyment and infliction of damage. From one point of view, these forms may be seen as varieties of sanctioned conduct. However, because each form of interference mirrors one of the incidents of property, I have chosen to treat them as aspects of the protected property interest.

Misappropriation

This form of interference can be committed only in relation to property which is capable of being possessed, that is, tangible property. Some intangible property is embodied in tangible property. For example, the value of a cheque for £100 is intangible property belonging to the owner of the cheque; but this value is embodied in the piece of paper which constitutes the cheque. Such intangible property is called "documentary" intangible property. So far as tort law is concerned, it is possible to misappropriate the piece of paper constituting the cheque, but not the £100 value. Misappropriation involves taking another's property away from them, or taking possession of another's property in circumstances where the other was either in possession of the property or had a right to take possession

---

[17] Computer-generated images present even greater challenges to the law.

of it immediately. But conduct will amount to misappropriation only if it is inconsistent with that other person's interest in the property. For example, one person may use another's pen without misappropriating it.

Possession is different from occupation or custody. A person can have possession of property at point in time T even if they do not have custody of it or are not in occupation of it at T; and conversely, the person in occupation or having custody of property is not, *ipso facto*, in possession of it. The essence of possession is control over the use of property. Tort law does not protect ownership of property ("title to" property) as such but rather that aspect of ownership which is captured in the concept of possession, namely the right to control the physical use of property. For example, for the duration of a lease of real property, the lessor does not have a right to possession of the property and so can be liable in tort for dispossessing the tenant. Similarly, for the duration of the hiring, the owner of a chattel does not have a right to possession of it and so can be liable in tort for repossessing it. Hiring out a chattel is a type of "bailment"; and so is lending. By means of bailment, an owner of a chattel can transfer possession of it to another for a limited purpose such as use or repair or safe-keeping. Both the transferor (the "bailor") and the transferee (the "bailee") have a property interest in the chattel. That of the bailor is based on ownership and that of the bailee on possession.

These examples illustrate two points of fundamental importance about property interests. The first is that there are different types of property interest, of which possession is only one. Secondly, several people can have (different types of) property interests in one and the same piece of property at one and the same time. In law, the concept of property is a complex amalgam of various rights and obligations in relation to things. Different people may have different rights in one and the same thing. This idea is central to the institution of the trust which, as we have seen, involves distinguishing between common law and equitable property interests.

In terms of the law of tort, misappropriating real property amounts to trespass. The action for regaining possession of real property is called the "action for possession". A colloquial term for misappropriation of real property is "squatting". The head of tort liability concerned with misappropriation of chattels is called "conversion". Conversion may also constitute some criminal offence such as theft.

Unauthorized Exploitation

A second form of tortious interference with property is unauthorized exploitation falling short of misappropriation. To exploit property is to make use of it for one's benefit. Examples of exploitation of real property include using land for access or for parking or for tipping waste; invasions of airspace by signs or the jibs of cranes; and the placing of scaffolding on adjoining land to facilitate building work. "Joyriding" would be an example of exploitation of a chattel. The head of tort liability most commonly used to impose liability for exploitation is trespass – either trespass to land or trespass to goods.

So far as tort law is concerned, although intangible property cannot be misappropriated, it can be exploited. Infringement of statutory intellectual property rights typically amounts to exploitation in this sense. Passing off also involves exploitation of property, in this case the goodwill of a business. There might be an argument for treating unauthorized disclosure of confidential information as exploitation of property and breach of confidence as a tort. However, the most commonly accepted view is that breach of confidence is breach of an obligation of confidence which arises either out of a contract or out of some "equitable" idea of "trust"[18] or "good faith". On this view, breach of confidence is either a breach of contract or an equitable wrong, but not a tort. Adopting this view, the English Law Commission some years ago recommended that a new statutory tort of breach of confidence should be created.[19]

This discussion of breach of confidence illustrates a point of fundamental importance to this book. This is that there may be different legal techniques or categories which can be used to protect one and the same asset or resource. One way of protecting confidential information would be to recognize it as property and to treat unauthorized disclosure and use of it as tortious. The law currently does not do this but uses either the law of contract or principles developed by the courts of equity to protect confidences. Tort law protects certain interests in certain ways, as does the law of contract and as do principles of equity. The distinctiveness of each of these techniques (tort, contract and equity) resides in fact that each offers a different pattern of protection

[18] The word "trust" is used both to describe the institution of the trust which involves the ownership and management of property by one person for the benefit of another; and also in a sense close to its non-legal sense, as in the phrase "I trust you to do the right thing". In the text at this point, the word is used in this second sense. Only if confidential information were recognized as property could it be made the subject of a trust in the former sense.

[19] Law Com No. 110 (1981).

(in terms of interests protected, conduct sanctioned and sanctions). To some extent these patterns may overlap; that is, two or more legal techniques may offer protection to one and the same interest against one and the same type of conduct. In Chapter 1[20] I argued that such "concurrency" of protection offered plaintiffs undesirable opportunities for exploitation of differences between the protection offered by the concurrent regimes of rules. The basic principle for which I would argue is that there should be only one set of rules for protecting any particular interest against a particular type of conduct, and not several sets offering slightly different protection between which the plaintiff can choose to the disadvantage of the defendant.

Interference with Use and Enjoyment

A third form of interference with property interests is interference with the use and enjoyment of property. There is no head of tort liability concerned exclusively with use and enjoyment of chattels; but depriving someone of the use of a chattel, for instance, might be actionable as a trespass or conversion. The main head of tort liability which sanctions interference with the use and enjoyment of real property is private nuisance.[21] A private nuisance is an unreasonable interference with the use and enjoyment of land. Typical examples are noisy neighbours and factory emissions. Such interference may result in damage to the land itself, financial loss (as in the case of a hotel blighted by noise), or "amenity damage". "Amenity" refers to the pleasure and enjoyment which people get out of their property: most people's enjoyment of life would be reduced by excessive noise, for instance. Some aspects of the enjoyment of land are not protected. In particular, blocking a view cannot be a nuisance; and it has recently been held that interference with TV transmission by the construction of a building cannot be a nuisance.[22]

A claim in respect of a private nuisance can be made only by a person with a property interest in the land. Effectively, this restricts such claims to owners or lessees. For instance, occupants, such as members

---

[20] See p. 22 above.

[21] Trespass also plays a part: see p. 142 below. Public nuisance is also a head of tort liability. Public nuisance is unreasonable interference with the rights of the public. A typical example is obstruction of the highway. Public nuisance does not protect any property interest of the plaintiff even when it relates to interference with the use of land – individual members of the public have no property rights in public land. If a person suffers "special damage" as a result of a public nuisance, damages may be recoverable in tort. Such tort liability typically protects contractual interests and expectancies, and wealth.

[22] *Hunter* v. *Canary Wharf Ltd* [1997] 2 WLR, 684.

of an owner's or lessee's family, cannot bring an action even if their
use and enjoyment of the property is just as affected as that of the
owner or lessee. This rule is a function of the fact that nuisance is seen
as interference with property rights rather than as interference with
use and enjoyment as such. Recently, the Court of Appeal attempted
to adapt the tort of private nuisance to deal with stalking by remov-
ing the interest-in-land requirement, but this development has since
been reversed by the House of Lords.[23]

Infliction of Damage

A fourth form of interference with property interests is the infliction
of damage. In the case of tangible property, the damage in question
is physical; and it includes destruction or loss. It is also possible to
"damage" intangible property in the sense of reducing its value. For
instance, one actionable form of infringement of a trademark is called
"dilution". The power of a trademark is to attract people to buy the
goods or services of the mark owner. If an identifying mark is used
widely enough, it may lose its drawing power. This has happened in
the case of the word "hoover", which in popular usage has become
a synonym for "vacuum cleaner" rather than the identifying name of
a vacuum cleaner made by one particular manufacturer. Whereas
exploitation of a trademark involves taking advantage of the drawing
power of the mark, damaging it by dilution consists of reducing its
drawing power. A common law head of tort liability which is concerned with damage to intangible property is injurious (or "malicious") falsehood. Injurious falsehood is, in effect, commercial
defamation. The property in question is goodwill, and the damage is
reducing the plaintiff's power to attract customers by making a false
statement about a person's goods, services, business or occupation.

As a general rule, only a person with a property interest (that is,
ownership or possession) in the damaged property can sue in respect
of that damage. However, there are exceptional cases in which a
person without such an interest may sue in respect of damage to
tangible property.[24] In such cases, any monetary compensation
recovered by the plaintiff on account of the damage is considered to
be "held on trust" by the plaintiff for the owner and must be paid
over to the owner on request and, in the meantime, administered for
the owner's benefit.

---

[23] *Hunter* v. *Canary Wharf Ltd*; n. 22 above.
[24] See P. Cane, *Tort Law and Economic Interests*, 2nd edn (Oxford, 1996), 93, fn. 427.

Contractual Rights

By contractual rights I refer to rights under existing contracts (as opposed to the chance of making a contract in the future).[25] Typically, a contract is a constitutive[26] arrangement for transferring resources (property or services) from one person to another in a way a court will recognize as effective and enforceable. However, contract is not the only way of transferring resources in a legally enforceable way. For instance, a gift is recognized by the law as effective to transfer assets from one person to another. Perhaps more importantly, a trust is an arrangement for (creating and) transferring equitable (or "beneficial") rights in property (an asset) from one person to another. It is not necessary at this point to discuss what makes a transfer of assets contractual. Most of the legal rules which can be used to protect contractual rights are treated as part of the law of contract. However, there are some rules of tort law which provide such protection. Tort law may protect a contracting party against conduct detrimental to the party's rights under the contract done by the other contracting party ("breach of contract"), or done by a "third party", that is, someone not a party to the contract.

Third Party Interference with Contractual Rights

In considering third party liability, it is necessary to distinguish between contractual rights in relation to property (that is, rights under contracts relating to the use of property) and other contractual interests. We have already seen that in general, tort law only protects (property) interests "in" property (that is, ownership, possession and rights to possession). Contractual interests in relation to property generally fall outside the scope of tort law. There is, however, some authority for the proposition that if D, knowing that P has a contractual right in relation to certain *tangible* property, interferes with that right (for instance, by making it impossible for the other contracting party to perform the contract) with the intention of injuring P, D may be liable in tort to P under the head of liability called "interference with contract". It must be admitted that the law in this

[25] A contractual option (or "right") to make a contract in the future is a contractual right in this sense.
[26] As to the meaning of this word, see p. 10 above.

area is very unclear and uncertain; but it is worth mentioning because it illustrates a very important difference between the approach of tort law to property interests on the one hand and contractual interests on the other. As will see further in Chapter 5, in many cases D can be "strictly" liable in tort to P for interference with a property interest even if D did not know that P had a property interest in the property, and even if D interfered with that interest inadvertently. This is true, for instance, in relation to misappropriation of chattels and land. One of the ways in which tort law marks a difference between (property) interests in property and contractual interests in relation to property and recognizes the relatively greater importance of the former is by using strict liability in some cases to protect the former but not the latter.

The factor of knowledge deserves a little more examination in relation to chattels. The basic function of common law property rules is to distinguish between "what is mine and what is yours". It would be a very strange idea of property according to which things were only mine if you knew they were mine. In fact, common law rules of property law which turn on knowledge are exceptional. For instance, if I buy stolen goods, the basic rule of the common law is *nemo dat quod non habet*: a transferee of property gets no better title than the transferor had. Exceptions to this rule in favour of purchasers who did not know that the goods did not belong to the seller are relatively few;[27] and all the exceptions require that the transferee paid for the property. In equity, by contrast, the doctrine of *bona fide* purchase for value is much more commonly available as a defence to a person who acquires trust property in ignorance of the equitable property interest of the beneficiary in it. This fact may be related to the function of equitable property rights. This is not to mark the distinction between what is mine and what is yours, but rather to ensure that the trustee acts in the interests of the beneficiary. In other words, equitable property interests are a protection against unconscionable conduct.[28] A person who acquires trust property, having paid for it and without knowing of the interest of the beneficiary, cannot be said to have acted unconscionably. In this respect, the law treats equitable property interests more like contractual interests than common law property interests. We will return to equitable property interests in Chapter 6.

[27] R. Goode, *Commercial Law*, 2nd edn, (London, 1995), 461, 470, 474, 476.
[28] *Westdeutsche Landesbank Girozentrale* v. *Islington LBC* [1996] 2 WLR 802, 828–9 *per* Lord Browne-Wilkinson.

By contrast with contractual interests in tangible property, contractual interests in relation to (that is, contractual rights to exploit) intangible statutory intellectual property (called "licences") are, on the whole, as well protected from infringement by third parties (as opposed to the owner) as the property rights of the owner. The reason for this is clear enough: the whole point of according statutory protection to intellectual property is to enable its owner to control its commercial exploitation. The protection of intellectual property against unauthorized exploitation would be very difficult and cumbersome if authorized users were not able to protect the property against third-party interference.

So much for third party infringement of contractual rights in property. Now we must consider third party infringement of rights under contracts not concerned with the use of property (such as contracts for the sale of goods or the provision of services). The trigger of liability for interference with contract is action by D which results in non-performance by C of a contract between C and P causing financial loss to P. D's action might consist of inducing C not to comply with the contract by persuasion or threats ("intimidation"), or D might disable C from complying with the contract. There is some authority for the view that the non-performance need not consist of a breach of contract actionable at the suit of P against C.[29] A contrary view says that liability for inducing non-performance with a contract is a form of secondary liability, and that there can be no secondary liability unless there is primary liability, in this case for breach of contract. On the other hand, it is said, liability for disabling a person from performing a contract is not secondary liability but rather primary liability for causing non-performance; and under this head there can be liability for causing non-actionable non-performance of a contract provided it resulted from unlawful conduct on D's part and D intended to inflict injury on P. [30]

The pragmatic justification for liability for interference with contracts is that a market economy cannot operate properly unless people can rely on contracts being performed. The ethical justification is that people should respect contracts, whether their own or other people's.

---

[29] *Torquay Hotel Ltd* v. *Cousins* [1969] 2 Ch 106.

[30] D.J. Cooper, *Secondary Liability for Civil Wrongs*, Unpublished PhD Thesis, University of Cambridge, 1995.

Tort Liability for Breach of Contract

Finally, we must consider tort liability for breach of contract. Conduct which amounts to a breach of contract may also amount to a tort. In particular, negligent breaches of contract may also be actionable as tortious negligence. It is clearly not the law that any and every negligent breach of contract will be actionable in tort. For instance, many breaches of contract consist of nonfeasance, and nonfeasance is less likely to attract tort liability than misfeasance, even if it can be called negligent. The typical breach of contract which is also actionable in tort is negligent misfeasance in the performance of services. In such cases, the plaintiff's interest in the performance of the contract is the same whether P's action is one for breach of contract or for tortious negligence; and yet the rules of liability in contract may produce a different result from those in tort. As has been argued earlier, such "concurrent liability" is, in principle, objectionable to the extent that it allows plaintiffs to choose to their advantage (and the defendant's disadvantage) between different regimes of liability rules. The point is explained in more detail in Chapter 6.

Contractual Expectancies

By the term "contractual expectancies" I refer to opportunities to make advantageous contracts in the future; that is, to make financial (or other) gains by contracting.[31] Liability for misstatements which induce a person to enter a contract protects a person's interest in not making a contract in the mistaken belief that it will be more advantageous than it in fact turns out to be. Tort liability for misstatement may arise under common law heads such as deceit and negligence; and under statutes such as the Misrepresentation Act 1967 and the Financial Services Act 1986. Tort liability for contract-inducing misstatements may attach to the other party to the contract or to a third party.

Tort law also provides remedies in respect of independently unlawful[32] conduct done with the intention of interfering with a person's opportunities for contracting under heads such as "intimidation" and "(unlawful means) conspiracy". The purpose of such interference will typically be to bring it about that the plaintiff does

---

[31] Note that the term "expectancy" does not refer to an expectation, either subjective or objective, of being able to make a contract but to the concept of the opportunity to make a contract.

[32] See p. 57 above as to the meaning of this term.

not contract with a third party or to secure that the plaintiff contracts with the defendant, or both. In the cases, such conduct is often called "interference with business" or "interference with trade". On one view,[33] unlawful means conspiracy is a form of secondary liability so that the unlawful means used would have to be actionable in their own right (independently of the conspiracy) because there can be no secondary liability without primary liability. Another view is that unlawful means conspiracy is a form of primary liability for agreement between two or more persons to injure another. On this latter view, agreement to do an unlawful act might be tortious even if the act itself could not form the basis of a civil action but was, for instance, only a breach of the criminal law. The latter view might seem more consistent with the fact that under the head called "lawful means conspiracy" there can be liability for lawful conduct done with the intention of interfering with business. What makes lawful means conspiracy wrongful is said to be the simple fact of agreement between two or more parties to injure another. In cases of interference with trade not involving conspiracy, the unlawful means need not be independently actionable – if this were necessary, the tort liability for using such means would be more or less superfluous.

A rather different form of liability for interference with the opportunity to contract can arise under statutes such as the Sex Discrimination Act 1975 and the Race Relations Act 1976, one of the aims of which is to allow civil actions in respect of refusals to contract with a person because of their sex or race. Such liability represents an inroad on the basic principle of the common law of freedom of contract, namely that people are free to contract or to refuse to contract with whom they will. It provides a neat illustration of the correlative structure of tort law: by the recognition of an interest in not being discriminated against in the search for advantageous contractual opportunities, the legislature has imposed a limitation on a long-recognized and well-established aspect of freedom of action.

NON-CONTRACTUAL EXPECTANCIES

Tort law may also protect opportunities of receiving financial gain in the future by means other than entering an advantageous contract. For example, if a provision in a will giving a legacy to an intended beneficiary is legally invalid because of some defect in the will

---

[33] Cooper, *Secondary Liability for Civil Wrongs* (above n.30).

resulting from the negligence of a legal adviser, the beneficiary may sue the adviser in tort and recover the value of the intended legacy. The precise scope of this protection is not clear – for instance, whether it only applies to legacies under wills or whether it extends to other non-contractual expectancies lost because of professional negligence.

More important, perhaps, is the protection given to family members deprived of continuing financial support as a result of the death of another member of the family. Under the Fatal Accidents Act 1976 "dependants" of a person who has been wrongfully killed have a cause of action in respect of loss of (actual and) future financial support from that person. "Wrongful death actions" are discussed in more detail in Chapter 5.

TRADE VALUES

I have said that statutory intellectual property rights receive similar protection to that which the common law of tort accords to certain non-statutory property rights. The Copyright, Designs and Patents Act 1988 and the Registered Designs Act 1949 also create certain non-property rights (such as the "moral rights" of a copyright owner, and "rights in performances") which are supported by causes of action analogous to tort actions. The conduct sanctioned by such actions is breach of statutory prohibitions, and the right protected is essentially similar to that protected by statutory intellectual property rights, namely the power to control the exploitation of the products of intellectual effort.

WEALTH AND THE CONCEPT OF FINANCIAL LOSS

Property rights and contractual rights are wealth-producing assets; and in a market economy, the opportunity (freedom) to make contracts is the chief legal technique for wealth creation. A person's wealth is the sum of their financial assets minus their financial liabilities. One way in which tort law protects wealth is by protecting wealth-creating assets; and one of the ways it does *this* is by making good financial loss (that is, reductions of wealth) caused by certain sorts of interferences with wealth-creating assets. Protecting wealth-creating assets from interference is a way of protecting wealth.

Tort law also provides some protection to wealth in its own right – the "capital" which a person's wealth-generating assets represent and produce. In other words, sometimes tort law makes good financial loss, reductions of wealth, without reference to any asset which represents or generated that wealth. For instance, in the tort of deceit, a fraudster may be held liable for having induced another to give money away; and in certain circumstances, a plaintiff may recover tort damages as a result of paying more than its value for a substandard service or item of property.

In fact, this residual category of cases in which tort law protects the interest in wealth as such is very small. Most heads of tort liability protect one or other of the interests discussed above.

THE REQUIREMENT OF DAMAGE

The distinction just drawn between interference with an interest and the infliction of loss is important for another reason as well. This is that under some heads of tort liability but not others, "damage is the gist of the plaintiff's action". This means that unless the plaintiff has suffered some loss, harm or damage (whether financial or not) as a result of the defendant's conduct, the plaintiff has not been the victim of a tort. Heads of tortious liability of which damage is *not* the gist are said to be actionable *"per se"*. Under such heads, a person may have suffered a tort even if no loss, damage or harm has resulted to that person from the defendant's conduct.

In cases of tort liability without damage, the gist of the tort is interference with a right or interest of the plaintiff. What is actionable is the interference as such ("*per se*"). Instances of *per se* tort liability include misappropriation of land and chattels and certain types of unauthorized exploitation of tangible and intangible property. Defamation is actionable *per se* in the sense that substantial damages for injury to reputation may be recovered even though P does not have to (and could not) prove damage to reputation as a result of the defamatory publication.[34]

One of the most important ramifications of the concept of actionability *per se* relates to remedies. Clearly if P has suffered no loss, there will be nothing for the law to make good. What it can do, however, is to order D not to interfere any more with the plaintiff's interest. Such orders are measures of prevention for the future rather than of correction of the past. Preventive orders may be available under heads of tort liability of which damage is the gist; but in such cases

---

[34] See pp. 47–8 above.

what a preventive order will be directed against is the infliction of loss in the future rather than against interference with some asset or interest of the plaintiff. An order designed to prevent future infliction of loss will only be made if there is a quite high probability that loss will be inflicted if the order is not made.

Another important ramification of the distinction between actionability *per se* and liability of which damage is the gist is that in some cases, in order to establish tort liability, P will have to establish that there was a causal link between the defendant's conduct and some loss, damage or harm suffered by the plaintiff. It does not follow that causation is never an issue in a case based on a head of tort liability which is actionable *per se*. Actionability *per se* only means that P may be entitled to a tort remedy even if P has suffered no loss as result of the tortious conduct. But even under heads of liability actionable *per se*, if P claims to have suffered loss as a result of the tortious conduct (for instance, if P alleges not only that D has entered P's land without P's consent but also that D has damaged P's buildings) and wants that loss made good, P will have to establish a causal connection between that loss and D's tortious conduct. The requirement of causation is examined in detail in Chapter 5.

The point made in this section deserves to be restated. Some of the interests discussed in this chapter are protected by tort law only to the extent that interference with the interest inflicts some loss, damage or harm on the interest-holder; whereas other interests are protected even from interferences which cause no loss, damage or harm beyond the very interference itself.

A HIERARCHY OF INTERESTS

As has been hinted at various points in the above discussion, and as we will see in greater detail in Chapter 5, the various interests examined in this chapter are protected in various different ways by tort law. In a number of respects, the protection given to some interests will be found to be "stronger" than that given to others. This implies that tort law values some interests more highly than others, and this hierarchy of interests is part of the ethical structure of tort law, because the stronger the protection, the greater the limitation imposed on the freedom of action of the person who has interfered with the interest.

COUNTERVAILING INTERESTS

Just as tort law may sanction conduct of the victim of a tort as well as of the tortfeasor, so tort law protects some interests of tortfeasors at the expense of the interests of victims. Tort law also protects some "public" interests at the expense of the interests of tort victims. Such protection does not deny the importance of the victim's interest, but only that some interest of the tortfeasor or of the public may be more important. Of course, in defining the scope of tort liability, the law always has to balance the interest of potential victims in protection against the interest of potential defendants in freedom to act or to refrain from action, and of the public in preserving this freedom. Such a balancing operation is at least implicit in all decisions about the scope of legal liability. My concern here, however, is with rules and principles of tort law which explicitly appeal to interests other than those of potential tort victims and give them some sort of protection. Ironically, perhaps, such explicit protection of countervailing interests also asserts the value of the victim's interest by accepting that it is prima facie worthy of protection which can be justifiably denied only by express appeal to some countervailing interest.

Public Interests

The protection given to some countervailing public interests takes the form of providing D with a defence to a claim in respect of tortious conduct. An important source of such defences are statutory provisions, which may "authorize" conduct which would otherwise be tortious. Common law public interest defences (truth, absolute and qualified privilege, and fair comment) play an important part in relation to defamation in protecting freedom of speech and information. There are also defences to claims for wrongful arrest and imprisonment to assist in the maintenance of law and order.

Other countervailing public interests are protected not by defences but by immunities. Whereas defences typically focus on the tortfeasor's conduct, immunities typically attach to the defendant's status. And whereas a defence only becomes relevant after the defendant's conduct has been adjudged tortious, an immunity prevents a person's conduct being subjected to scrutiny in a tort action. For instance, participants in court proceedings (judges, advocates, witnesses, litigants) enjoy an immunity from tort liability in respect of things said and done by them in those proceedings. MPs enjoy absolute privilege in the law of defamation in respect of things said in "proceedings in Parliament". Public bodies (such as regulatory agencies) may enjoy statutory immunity from tort liability for negligence, and there is a complex body of judge-made law designed to immunize "policy" decisions of public bodies from tort liability.[35] Because immunities give protection not only from being held liable but also being sued, they are only used to protect public interests.

How does the protection of public interests in tort law relate to the basic thesis of this book that tort law is best viewed as a set of ethical principles of *personal* responsibility? It will be recalled that a similar question arose in Chapter 2 in the discussion of the relevance of the social value of conduct to decisions about its reasonableness. The basic answer must be that human beings are social animals, and our notions of personal responsibility take that into account. Although some of our interactions with other people have few if any social ramifications (and in that sense are purely private), many of our dealings with others can only be properly understood in their social context. More particularly, an individual's personal responsibility for conduct can be affected by the social significance of that conduct. Suppose, for instance, that a newspaper publishes a true but damaging story about a prominent political figure. Surely we would want to say that the newspaper's "personal" responsibility for the damage was affected by the fact that the public has a legitimate interest in knowing the truth about its politicians. In publishing the truth, the newspaper is acting, as it were, on behalf of the public. A person who inflicts injury on another in circumstances where the injury-causing conduct was justified by a legitimate public interest should not be held legally responsible for that injury. Public interest can modify personal responsibility.

Private Interests

Defences designed to protect private interests of potential tortfeasors include self-defence (an answer to liability for intentional infliction of personal injury), defence of property (a defence to liability for deliberate entry onto land and intentional infliction of personal injury), necessity (an answer to a claim for intentional or negligent damage to property), and justification (an answer to liability for intentional infliction of economic loss to the effect that the defendant's motive was to protect his or her own legitimate financial interests).

[35] See p. 55 above.

There is another very important personal countervailing interest recognized by tort law, namely freedom of contract. The basic rule is that a person is free to contract with another in such a way as to limit or exclude potential liability of that person in tort (or, indeed, under any other head of civil liability). This freedom has been considerably modified by statute. For example, under the Unfair Contract Terms Act 1977, a term in a contract which purports to exclude or restrict liability for negligently-caused personal injury is ineffective; and such a clause purporting to exclude liability for any other type of damage negligently caused is only effective to the extent that it is "reasonable". Again, there are provisions in the Defective Premises Act 1972 and Part I of the Consumer Protection Act 1987 which render ineffective contractual provisions purporting to exclude liability under those Acts for defective premises and defective products respectively. The main thrust of all of these provisions is to protect private individuals against the superior bargaining power of businesses. In relation to liability for negligence on the roads, the prohibition on contractual exclusion contained in the Road Traffic Act 1988 is an adjunct to the requirement that such liability be the subject of compulsory liability insurance.

It is also well established that tort liability may, in certain circumstances, be excluded or restricted by non-contractual agreement. For example, the liability of landowners to lawful visitors in respect of dangers on their land can be modified by a non-contractual "notice" the contents of which the visitor knew or ought to have known. Again, liability for negligent misstatement may be modified by a "disclaimer" given to its addressee at or before the time the statement was made. The basis on which such non-contractual exclusions or limitations of tort liability are effective is that if (as is generally the case) the landowner was free not to allow visitors onto the land, or if the person making the statement was free to remain silent, the landowner and the speaker respectively were also free to specify the conditions on which the freedom would be exercised in the plaintiff's favour. Under the Unfair Contract Terms Act non-contractual notices and disclaimers of negligence liability are subject to similar controls as apply to contractual provisions.

What, if anything, can we learn about the nature of tort liability from the fact that it can be excluded or limited in these ways? We learn, I think, that the rules of tort law (amongst others) are designed to provide a set of background principles or "default rules" for the conduct of social life and personal interactions. Some legal rules are considered of such basic importance to human well-being in our society that people are not free to "bargain around" them. People are not allowed to sell themselves into slavery, and consent is not, generally, a defence to a criminal charge (although lack of victim's consent is an element of some crimes, such as rape). Many of the rules of tort law are not considered to be of such fundamental importance that individuals should not be allowed to waive them by agreement: a person can consent to a defamatory publication, for instance; although not, probably, to the deliberate infliction of serious physical injury. The existence of the defence of assumption of risk shows that people are free to take risks if they freely choose to do so. The possibility of excluding or restricting certain tort liabilities by contractual provisions and non-contractual notices and disclaimers similarly reflects the "default" nature of many of the rules of tort law. Conversely, an exclusion of tort liability for serious deliberate injury would probably be given no more effect than consent to such injury. Through tort law, the state offers people protection, but does not always force them to take it. The law thus recognizes that people are often the best judges of their own interests, and that there may be no reason to prevent a person trading off freedom from tortious invasion of their interests for some other benefit perceived to be greater. At the end of the day, however, the state also decides to what extent this freedom to forego its protection should be constrained in the interests of individuals or society. Tort law thus strikes a complex balance between responsibility and freedom and between the interests of plaintiffs and defendants.

CONCLUSION

On the one hand, the idea of "protected interests" is a useful conceptual tool for focusing attention on the plaintiff's side of a tort claim. It has the advantage of uncovering the substance of the plaintiff's complaint in a way that the terminology of individual torts cannot, if only because the names of torts all refer only to what the defendant did ("trespass", "negligence", "defamation", "intimidation", and so on). Much of the distinctiveness of tort law as a protective mechanism is disguised by the traditional organization of the subject around "torts". In particular, focusing on interests yields important insights into the role of tort law in protecting property, and into the relationship between tort and contract, between common law and equity, and between judge-made and statutory rules.

On the other hand, the idea of protected interests, when combined with the concept of correlativity, can be used to throw light on the role of interests of individuals and of society in setting limits on tort liability. Responsibility for conduct must be balanced against freedom of action, and people must be allowed, to some extent at least, to decide when risk-taking is a desirable strategy for them personally. Analysis of tort law in terms of correlativity, protected interests and sanctioned conduct brings out much more clearly than the traditional analysis the fact that tort law is a balancing exercise; and it helps us to appreciate the complex and delicate nature of the balance struck by the law.

4. SANCTIONS

In this chapter we examine the sanctions triggered by the imposition of tort liability. Sanctions are obviously relevant to the analysis of sanctioned conduct. However, they are also an important aspect of the portrait of protected interests. For instance, part of the definition of a property interest consists of the forms of legal protection which are accorded to certain types of interest. In turn, sanctions are an aspect of the forms of legal protection. At one level, sanctions fit easily into the correlative analysis of tort law. There are sanctions for liability-attracting conduct and sanctions for victim's conduct, and the arrangement of this chapter reflects this neat divide. However, in another important respect it is harder to give an account of the place of sanctions in the correlative analysis of tort law than it is to expound and understand the concepts of protected interest and sanctioned conduct within that framework. This is because when discussing the latter concepts, it is possible to look at each of the correlative poles in turn. But sanctions are not bipolar. They are the law's response to the complex balance struck between the two correlative poles. Sanctions, in other words, look two ways at once: they embody the tension in the law between the interests and conduct of the two parties. This can make it very difficult to know how particular sanctions relate to the two poles. An important aim of this chapter is to give an account of sanctions which is sensitive to the correlative structure of tort law and to the ideas of tension and balance between the two poles of that structure. In the process, issues will arise, for instance, about the relationship between tort law and restitution and about the balance between compensation and punishment in tort law.

Although the word "remedy" is normally used to describe the subject-matter of this chapter, "sanction" is more accurate in at least two ways. First, this chapter deals not only with sanctions imposed on tortfeasors in favour of tort victims (to which the word "remedies" aptly applies), but also with the sanctions which tort law attaches to conduct of tort victims for which tort law holds the victim responsible. This latter type of sanction is not, in any normal sense of the word, a "remedy" given to the tortfeasor. Secondly, in a non-legal sense we might speak of the process of making a tort claim against another as a "remedy" for that tort. But in the legal sense, "remedy" refers only to that part of the process of claiming which is concerned specifically with what the defendant must do for the plaintiff on account of being held responsible for a tort. The process of making tort claims is, nevertheless, a very important aspect of the practical operation of tort law, and it is discussed in some detail in Chapter 7. Despite these shortcomings of the word "remedy", I have felt free to use it throughout this chapter except when it would obviously be inappropriate to the context.

SANCTIONS FOR LIABILITY-ATTRACTING CONDUCT

Judicial and Non-Judicial Remedies

By far the most important remedies in tort law are judicial remedies. Some judicial remedies, such as declarations and injunctions, can only be given by a court. However, a payment of money received by a tort plaintiff pursuant to an agreement by the defendant's insurer to settle a claim for personal injuries arising out of a road accident "out of court", and without recourse to litigation, may also be treated as a judicial remedy because monetary payment is a remedy which a court could award in such a case if it went to court.

To be contrasted with judicial remedies are non-judicial (or "self-help") remedies, that is remedies which a tort victim can secure personally without the intervention of a court. Tort law recognizes only a few such remedies. For example, if the branches of a tree planted on D's land overhang P's property without P's consent, D may have committed an actionable tortious invasion of P's property amounting to a "nuisance". If so, P is entitled to "abate the nuisance" by cutting off the branches which overhang the land. Another non-judicial remedy is "recaption of chattels" – in certain circumstances a person may physically reclaim his or her property which has been tortiously taken by another. The reason why such actions are called "self-help remedies" rather than just "self-help" is that they could, in themselves, amount to a legal wrong if there was no legal rule authorizing them. Writing a letter to the neighbour who owned the overhanging tree asking him to come and prune it would be an act of self-help; but it would not be a self-help remedy because it is, in itself, perfectly lawful.

The reason why there are very few self-help remedies is that it would be undesirable to encourage people to do things which would normally be unlawful. It is preferable for such things to be done by state officials. For instance, it would be a recipe for social conflict and disorder if tort victims were allowed to seize tortfeasors' property and sell it to provide themselves with a monetary remedy. One of the main social functions of civil law is to facilitate and encourage the orderly resolution of disputes. Widespread availability of self-help remedies would greatly threaten the performance of this function.

Amongst judicial remedies in tort law a distinction may usefully be drawn between monetary and non-monetary remedies. In practice, judicial monetary remedies are much more common and important than judicial non-monetary remedies, and so I shall first deal quite briefly with the latter.

Non-Monetary Remedies

There are only two types of non-monetary remedies of any significance in tort law: injunctions and orders for the return of property. In an action for the misappropriation of chattels (called "conversion" or "interference with goods")[1] one of the remedies available from a court is an order for the return of the chattels. However, such an order will be awarded only if a monetary remedy would not be "adequate" because the chattel has some non-monetary value for its owner. Money would be an adequate remedy if the plaintiff could go out and buy a replacement for the misappropriated chattel. But this would not be possible if the chattel was unique or very rare, or if (even though it was of a commonly available type) the particular chattel had "sentimental value" for the plaintiff. The availability of an "order for specific return" in a conversion action rests on the basis of the plaintiff's claim in such an action, namely that the misappropriated chattel is the plaintiff's property. This is also the reason why the basic measure of a monetary remedy in such an action is the value of the property. However, "value" in this context means "market value', and if the value of the chattel to the plaintiff exceeds its market value, the court may be prepared to order the defendant to return the chattel rather than to pay money.

The distinction between "market value" and "sentimental (or "non-market") value" is an instance of a distinction of general importance in tort law between "pecuniary loss"[2] and "non-pecuniary loss'. Pecuniary loss is loss of money or "money's worth',

[1] See Torts (Interference with Goods) Act 1977.
[2] I use the word "loss" to include concepts such as "damage", "injury" and "harm" as well.

whereas non-pecuniary loss is loss on which no money value can be put. The mechanism by which we put money values on things is the market. Money (besides being an asset) is a universal medium of exchange, and the money value of a thing is the amount which a "willing buyer" would pay a "willing seller" for the thing. The distinction between pecuniary loss and non-pecuniary loss is related to another distinction between what may be called "economic interests" and "non-economic interests". An economic interest is one for interference with which a finite sum of money would constitute full recompense. A party whose economic interests have been injured should feel no further sense of loss after receiving a sum of money which accurately reflects what has been lost. If the party does feel a sense of unsatisfied loss, then his or her interest is not economic; or, more accurately, the party has some non-economic interest in addition to the economic interest. A person may have both an economic and a non-economic interest in the same thing – for instance, an object of a type commonly available in the market but which has some sentimental value for its owner.

As we will see in detail later in this chapter, tort law provides monetary remedies for interferences with both economic and non-economic interests, for pecuniary and non-pecuniary losses. It is a noteworthy feature of the law governing tort liability for misappropriation of chattels that the way a non-economic interest in a chattel can be protected is by ordering return of the chattel rather than awarding a sum of money representing the plaintiff's non-economic interest. In most situations, as where a personal injury victim suffers non-pecuniary loss, the only way the law can make up for such loss is by a monetary payment because the cause of the loss is an irreparable change in the plaintiff's circumstances.

Non-monetary remedies are more important in relation to misappropriation of real property than of personal property. The remedy is called an "order for possession", and over the past 30 years or so, various statutory changes to the law have been designed to make it increasingly easy for owners to recover land from squatters. This is a reflection of the value which we put on real property in our society. Every piece of land is considered special even if the owner views it purely as a financial investment. A landowner is not expected to accept a money remedy for misappropriation of its land, even if the owner's only interest in the land is economic.

The other important non-monetary remedy available in tort is the injunction. The basic rule is that if it is likely that D will, in the

future, tortiously interfere with some property interest of P, P is entitled to an order requiring D not to interfere. Disobedience of an
injunction (as of any court order, including an order for the payment
of money) is a contempt of court summarily punishable by fine or
imprisonment. Injunctions play an important part in protecting
against trespassory exploitation of real property, infringements of
intellectual property rights and interferences with the use and enjoyment of land (nuisances). Instead of an injunction, a plaintiff may be
required to accept a monetary remedy called "damages *in lieu*" of an
injunction, but only if the damage likely to be inflicted by the defendant's tort is small and easily compensated for in money.

Injunctions may also be available to protect certain non-property
interests. For example, an injunction may be awarded to prevent a
threatened defamation or a likely breach of a statutory duty or prohibition, or "harassment". In these non-property cases, however, an
injunction will be awarded only if a monetary remedy would not be
adequate. Whereas a victim of an interference with property is entitled to an injunction unless, exceptionally, a monetary remedy would
be adequate, a victim of an interference with any other type of interest will be awarded an injunction only if a monetary remedy would
not be adequate; and the fact that the plaintiff may suffer non-
pecuniary loss if an injunction is not awarded would not by itself
make damages an inadequate remedy. While this difference may
seem to be concerned only with who has to establish the (in)ade-
quacy of damages, in practice the way "burdens of proof" are distributed may be of great importance to the outcome of a case. At all
events, it reflects the high value which tort law puts on interests classified as "property" interests. Indeed, as noted in the last chapter, in
the case of interferences with property which are actionable *per se*, an
injunction may be awarded even if the likely interference will inflict
no injury on the plaintiff beyond the interference itself.

The idea underlying the remedy of an injunction is that "prevention is better than cure". It is better to forestall tortious behaviour
than to make good its adverse effects after the event. The availability
of preventive remedies in tort law marks an important point of distinction between this body of law and the criminal law. Because, in
general, criminality carries with it greater social stigma than breach of
the civil law, we normally insist that criminal sanctions should attach
only to conduct which has already taken place. The maxim "innocent until proven guilty", which applies centrally to past conduct,
implies, *a fortiori* that we should assume that when faced with the

choice, people will not commit criminal offences. When it comes to torts, however, we are not so respectful of the individual whose future conduct is in issue. More weight is put on the interest of the plaintiff in being free of tortious interference.

The injunction was a remedy developed by the courts of equity. As a general rule, equity courts did not provide monetary remedies, and it was not until the mid-nineteenth century that statute created the remedy of damages *in lieu* of an injunction. Unlike the injunction, damages *in lieu* are not primarily a preventive remedy. Indeed, the legal effect of an award of such damages is to "license" the defendant to do what the injunction would have ordered D not to do. On the other hand, like an injunction, damages *in lieu* do relate to tortious conduct and damage which have not yet occurred at the date the remedy is awarded; and in a case of nuisance, for instance, damages *in lieu* of an injunction to restrain the nuisance might be designed to enable P to reduce the interference to a reasonable level.

By contrast, the remedies developed by the common law courts (damages and orders for the specific return of property considered above) relate to torts committed and damage inflicted in the past before the granting of the remedy. This does not mean that common law damages cannot be awarded in respect of the future. For instance, as we will see in detail later, in a personal injury action in respect of long-term injuries, the court will compensate the victim not only for effects of the injuries which occur before the award is made, but also for likely future effects. However, common law damages can only be awarded for torts which have already been committed before the remedy is awarded and for injuries which have already been suffered (even if all their effects have not yet materialized). So, for instance, in a case where P acquires a building which, because of D's negligence, has a defect which is likely to cause damage or injury in the future, damages representing the cost of preventing the likely future damage cannot be awarded in a tort action "at common law".[3] Common law damages relate to the past whereas "equitable" damages *in lieu* of an injunction relate to the future. Furthermore, in the defective building case, damages *in lieu* of an injunction could, apparently, not be awarded because an injunction cannot be awarded in a negligence action.[4] This distinction between common law and equitable remedies is an anachronistic hangover of the period when the common law courts and the equity courts were quite separate. Now, in any

[3] *Murphy v. Brentwood DC* [1991] 1 AC 398.
[4] See further p. 131 below.

case where there is a likelihood that in the future D will inflict tortious injury on P, the court should ask itself whether awarding a preventive remedy would be an appropriate course of action. One reason why the courts are wary of awarding "preventive damages" is a fear that this would encourage "speculative" claims in cases where the risk of tortious damage in the future was very slight or, at least, very difficult to estimate. However, this fear has not hampered courts in awarding damages *in lieu* of injunctions, and could easily be met by requiring, as a condition of an award of preventive damages, convincing proof that damage was very likely to occur in the relatively near future.

Finally, we should note that a court may award a declaration in a tort action. In one sense, a declaration is not a "remedy" or a "sanction" because all it does is to state what the legal rights and obligations of the parties are. Thus, failure by the defendant to do something which the court declared D to have an obligation to do would not amount to a contempt of court. On the other hand, a declaration can provide the basis for the award of a coercive remedy (such as an injunction) in case a party fails to act in accordance with the terms of the declaration. An analogous remedy available in tort law which relates to the past is nominal damages (say, 1p). The effect of this remedy is to acknowledge (or declare) that the defendant has committed a tort against the plaintiff. Nominal damages are only awarded where any loss suffered by the plaintiff was non-pecuniary. In a suitable case, the court may brand such damages as "contemptuous" to express its view that the plaintiff, although the victim of a tort and so entitled to a monetary remedy, is unworthy of the court's assistance.[5]

Monetary Remedies

The most important monetary remedy available in tort law is called "damages", and I shall use this term to refer generally to monetary remedies. In discussing damages we need to distinguish between the "measure" of damages and the "quantum" of damages. "Measures" of damages are principles according to which damages are calculated; and the "quantum" of damages is the amount produced by applying a measure to the facts of a particular case. Calculation of the quantum of damages is called "the assessment of damages". We also speak of "heads" of damages. The term "heads" refers to the damage or loss

---

[5] Cf the rule under the Criminal Injuries Compensation Scheme that compensation may be reduced to reflect the applicant's bad character.

in respect of which the damages are being awarded. So, for example, "loss of wages" is a head of damages; and the measure of damages for loss of wages suffered before the date when the damages are assessed is net, take-home pay (that is, gross wages minus tax and national insurance contributions) for the period when the victim was unable to work. The quantum of the damages in a particular case might be, say, £10,000. Tort damages perform three main functions: compensation, disgorgement and punishment.[6]

Compensatory Damages

The Meaning of "Loss"—The prime focus of tort law is on "loss", and the term "compensation" refers to making good a loss that a person has suffered as a result of tortious conduct. It is a general principle of tort law that a plaintiff who suffers actionable loss as a result of a tort is entitled to be compensated for it. This general principle applies to all tort actions, even those relating to conduct which is actionable *per se*.[7] However, the word "loss" is rather vague, and we need to spell out in more detail what it means. For this purpose it will be convenient to refer to tortious conduct which gives rise to a right to compensation as "the tort".

(a) The word "loss" refers most centrally to things which P had before the tort occurred but which P does not now have. As a result of the tort, P might have lost an arm, or a piece of property, or a sum of money, or personal freedom, or a good reputation which P had before the tort occurred. But we also use the term "loss" to refer to a number of other situations:

(b) Where, as a result of the tort, P failed to get something in the past (i.e. before the date of assessment of compensation) which P would have got but for the tort. Thus we refer to loss of wages or profits; for example, a person in work who is injured in a road accident might not be able to go to work and so might be entitled to be compensated for "loss" of the wages which would have been payable if they had been able to go to work.

(c) Where, as a result of the tort, P will not get something in the future (i.e. after the date of assessment of compensation) which P would probably have got but for the tort. Thus, we refer to loss of future wages or profits. For example, a working person may be so badly injured in a road accident that they will never be able to work

---

[6] See also P. Cane, "Exceptional Measures of Damages: A Search for Principles" in P. Birks (ed), *Wrongs and Remedies in the Twenty-First Century* (Oxford, 1996), ch. 13.

[7] See p. 90 above.

again. Such a person could be compensated in tort not only under head (b) for "past loss of wages" but also under head (c) for "future loss of wages" in respect of the period when they would normally have been expected to go on working if they had not been injured. Compensation for future losses of this sort may be called compensation for loss of "expectations". Another example of compensation for loss of an expectation would be a case where P was meant to receive a legacy under a will which, because of the negligence of the testator's solicitor, is ineffective to pass the legacy to the intended beneficiary.

(d) Where, as a result of the tort, P has (before the date of assessment of compensation) incurred expenses which P would not have incurred but for the tort, such as medical or hospital expenses.

(e) Where, as a result of the tort, P will probably in the future (after the date of assessment of compensation) incur expenses, such as medical expenses, which P would not have incurred but for the tort.

(f) Where, as a result of the tort, P suffers some harm, such as distress, anxiety or inconvenience, or some damage, such as a broken arm or a mangled bicycle.

We refer to damages awarded in all these situations (b) to (f) as "compensatory" even though each involves a greater or lesser departure from the central meaning of "loss" in situation (a). Indeed, the words "loss", "injury", "damage" and "harm" tend to be used interchangeably in tort law according to which best fits the circumstances being referred to. What all of the uses of the term compensation have in common is that they refer to situations in which P (judged at the date of assessment of compensation) is, or will probably be, worse off (in some sense) as a result of the tort than P would have been if the tort had not occurred. Compensation is designed to provide P with a money "equivalent" of the actual or hypothetical deterioration in P's position as a result of the tort; to put P in the position, in respect of "loss" suffered, that P would have been in if the tort had not occurred. It is worth emphasizing that because compensation may be payable in respect of the period after the date of assessment as well as the period between that date and the date of the tort, compensatory damages in tort may not only replenish the plaintiff's financial resources as they were at the date of assessment, but also supplement them.

The centrality of compensation in tort law distinguishes it from the criminal law, which focuses more on punishment. Criminal law is more concerned with retributive justice (that wrongs should be punished) than tort law, which chiefly embodies the idea of corrective justice (that wrongs should be righted). So whereas the prime focus of criminal law is on the offender's "wrong", tort law is concerned equally with the defendant's "wrong" and the plaintiff's "right". This is the basis of the correlative structure of tort law. Another important justification for the compensatory response is that compensation minimizes the disruption to people's lives and life-plans caused by torts.[8]

Compensatory damages, then, compensate for "losses" (in the broad sense just described) suffered by P. For the purposes of assessing compensatory damages, a distinction is drawn between compensation for "pecuniary" losses and compensation for "non-pecuniary" losses. As noted earlier, pecuniary losses relate to things on which a money value can be put because they are the subject of market transactions. By contrast, non-pecuniary losses relate to things which are not traded in markets. In a personal injury action, the main heads of pecuniary loss are loss of income; medical, hospital and nursing expenses; loss of ability to perform unpaid domestic services for the members of one's immediate family; and the value of gratuitous care provided by relatives or, perhaps, close friends. The main heads of non-pecuniary loss are "pain and suffering"; loss of "amenities" or of "life's enjoyments"; and "bereavement" (payable to certain relatives of a person who is tortiously killed). However, these heads are only applications of the general principle of compensation that P is entitled to be compensated for all losses which, according to the rules of tort law, are actionable and were caused by the tortious conduct.

In actions relating to damage to tangible property, the distinction between pecuniary and non-pecuniary losses is reflected in the rules which determine when two competing measures of damages, namely reduction (or "diminution") in value and cost of repair,[9] are available. The basic measure of damages for physical damage to tangible property is the difference between the market value of the property before it was damaged and its market value in its damaged state. However, in practice, if the cost of repairing the damage would be less than the reduction in market value, the cost of repair will be the measure of damages because the law requires the plaintiff to "mitigate" the damage by having the property repaired. If the cost of repair would exceed the diminution in value, a plaintiff will not be awarded the former unless it can be shown that the property had some special (non-market) value for P over and above its market value. In that

---

[8] R.E. Goodin, *Utilitarianism as a Public Philosophy* (Cambridge, 1995), ch. 13.

[9] Or replacement in the case of destruction.

case, the difference between the reduction in market value and the cost of repair would represent compensation for non-pecuniary loss.

The law governing assessment of compensatory damages is complicated and technical. It is not necessary or appropriate to examine all the details here. Only a couple of general principles demand discussion.

The Once-For-All Rule—The first is the rule that damages are to be assessed once only in respect of all the loss suffered in the past or likely to be suffered in the future as a result of the tort. Suppose that a young person is tortiously injured in a way which will have permanent detrimental effects on their health, lifestyle and earning capacity. When awarding tort damages the court will have to assess damages as a single "lump sum" designed to compensate the victim for all past and future losses resulting from the tort. It is assumed that the plaintiff will invest this lump sum to produce a continuing income for the rest of his or her life. A court cannot order the defendant to pay damages in the form of "periodical payments" or a "pension". Originally, this rule was probably a product of the fact that the courts had no mechanism for supervising compliance with such an order. The result is that in assessing damages the court must speculate about the future in great detail in an attempt to calculate a lump sum which will, as nearly as possible, compensate the plaintiff in respect of losses yet to accrue. Since the purpose of compensatory damages is to put the plaintiff into the position he or she would have been in if the tort had not occurred, the court must speculate not only about what the plaintiff's position will be over a long period of time as an injured person (including, for instance about whether P's health will deteriorate further in the future as a result of the injuries), but also about the position P would have been in if P had not been injured. Speculation is required not only about P's health and other personal circumstances, but also about matters such as inflation, and tax and interest rates (which affect the amount of income which any lump-sum award will be able to generate).

The once-for-all rule means that the assessment of damages is a hit-and-miss affair. Indeed, in very many cases it authorizes awards of damages which inevitably either overcompensate or undercompensate the plaintiff, if only because the future is impossible to predict with complete accuracy. In some cases, the source of inaccuracy is plain at the time of assessment. For instance, suppose that P receives head injuries in a road accident, and that as a result there is a 40 percent chance that P will develop epilepsy in the five years after the date of assessment of the damages. The once-for-all rule requires damages to be assessed as 40 percent of the amount that would have been awarded if it had been certain that P would develop epilepsy. If P does develop epilepsy, the damages will be undercompensatory, and if P does not develop epilepsy they will overcompensatory. Moreover, plaintiffs who receive large amounts in respect of long-term injuries carry a heavy burden in investing the damages wisely so as to produce a continuing income. There is a statutory exception to the once-for-all rule which allows a court to award "provisional damages" and the plaintiff to come back to court within a specified period and claim more damages if their medical condition deteriorates. But the specified period can be no more than three years, and it has been held that the deterioration in medical condition has to be sudden rather than gradual. Moreover, the plaintiff can only come back to court once. The once-for-all rule can also be evaded in some cases by the use of what is known as a "structured settlement". Under this sort of arrangement, the defendant purchases an annuity policy from a life insurer to provide the plaintiff with specified income (and, perhaps, capital) payments over a period of time. However, the amount available to purchase the annuity is calculated according to the same rules as apply to the calculation of lump sums, and once the annuity has been purchased, it is difficult to alter the schedule of payments to accommodate changed circumstances. Moreover, while a court has power to approve a structured settlement to which both of the parties agree, there is no power to force a structured award on an unwilling party.

Research over the years has tended to show that when asked, some people prefer the idea of receiving a lump-sum award and others would prefer a periodical award. The choice between these two positions does not seem to be a matter of ethics. There are pragmatic arguments for and against both lump sums and periodical payments; and both are arguably plausible interpretations of the idea of compensation for tortiously-caused losses. Ethical principles go little further than supporting compensation in a general sense, and tell us little about how this goal should be pursued in detail. There is, perhaps, an argument for giving plaintiffs the freedom to choose between the two forms of compensation.

Full Compensation—The second general point to make about compensation is that tort law interprets this to mean "full compensation'.

The concept of full compensation encompasses two principles, the "100 percent principle" and the "standard-of-living principle". The former says that the victim of a tort must be compensated for all the actionable losses flowing from the tort. This principle is most easily applied to past pecuniary losses – they have already occurred, and they can be assessed reasonably accurately by taking evidence of market values of goods and services. The full compensation principle is less easily applied to future pecuniary losses because of the uncertainties inherent in predicting the future; but the difficulties are practical rather than conceptual. The principle is least easily applied in relation to non-pecuniary losses (whether past or future). Such losses relate to things which, by definition, have no market value; and in this context, full compensation is usually interpreted to mean "fair" compensation – that is, an amount which seems large enough to recognize the seriousness of what P has suffered but not so large that it seems "unfair" to D. In practice, in personal injury cases, damages for non-pecuniary loss are calculated according to a quite detailed set of guidelines published by the Judicial Studies Board (the body responsible for the continuing education of judges). It should be noted, however, that these guidelines relate solely to the nature and extent of the injuries suffered by the plaintiff and in no way to the nature or seriousness of the defendant's conduct. Indeed, one aspect of the full compensation principle is that whereas the nature and seriousness of the defendant's conduct is relevant to the issue of liability, it is not relevant to the assessment of damages. I shall return to this point a little later in this chapter.

Such guidelines can work in this area because in cases which go before a court, damages for personal injury are assessed by judges, not by a jury. By contrast, damages for injury to reputation in defamation cases are nearly always assessed by a jury. Injury to reputation is a non-pecuniary loss, and until recently, there was no effective way in which decisions of juries about assessment of damages could be guided or controlled by the judge in charge of the trial or by an appeal court. As a result, damages awards for injury to reputation in a number of high-profile cases were much higher than the total which would be awarded for non-pecuniary loss in even the most serious cases of personal injury. This caused a great deal of controversy, and now a mechanism exists for interfering with damages awards by juries in defamation cases which will allow the generation of guidelines about levels of awards for damage to reputation. As in the case of personal injuries, such guidelines perform two functions:

they can facilitate the like treatment of like cases (larger awards for more "serious" cases and smaller awards for less "serious" ones), and they can secure that the amounts actually awarded are considered "fair". Since, by definition, non-pecuniary loss has no market "value", "fair" in this context means something like "generally acceptable in society". The personal injury guidelines mentioned above set an upper limit of about £130,000 for the most serious cases. Although some consider this figure too low, its rationale is, perhaps, that for most people, such a sum is a lot of money, and large enough to acknowledge the wrong done and the injury suffered.[10]

The second principle encompassed by the concept of full compensation is the standard-of-living principle. It dictates that compensation for pecuniary loss should reflect the plaintiff's pre-tort position. The tort system does not seek to redress inequalities in the distribution of income and resources in society. Rather, by awarding to plaintiffs compensation related to pre-tort standard of living, its aim is to minimize disruption to their lives and life-plans. The basic principle of compensation in tort law is restorative or corrective, not redistributional. The standard-of-living principle implies not only that compensation for loss of income should be "earnings-related" but also that someone who, as a result of a tort, is unable to continue to do productive but unpaid work consisting of familial caring (such as cooking and cleaning a house) should be compensated for the value of that work. Compensation can also be awarded to an injured plaintiff representing the value of nursing and other domestic services made necessary by the tort and provided gratuitously to P by a family member or friend, whether or not the carer gave up paid work in order to be able to provide the care. Such damages are held on trust for the carer and so are, in effect, compensation for the carer's expenditure of time and effort. The basic measure of damages for unpaid services is the market value of the services.

On the other hand, if a tort plaintiff was, as a result of the tort, no longer able to do voluntary work for a charity, tort damages would not provide compensation for the value of the work previously done by P for the charity which P could give to the charity. Tort law is only prepared to compensate for loss of ability to do unpaid work if the beneficiaries of that work are intimates of the plaintiff. This limitation is, perhaps, not an unreasonable position for the law to adopt.

[10] The Court of Appeal has recently issued guidelines for the assessment of damages for non-pecuniary losses by juries in cases of wrongful imprisonment and malicious prosecution by police authorities: *Commissioner of Police for the Metropolis* v. *Thompson* [1997] *New LJ* 341.

Still, some might want to argue that in this respect, the law systematically discriminates against women who do much more unpaid work outside the family circle than do men; and that it is based on a distinction between the private world of the home and the public world of social charity which reflects male attitudes to life, not female ones. This debate is an illustration of a wider phenomenon: charges of discrimination have frequently been levelled at the law relating to assessment of damages because implicit in it are judgements about the relative worth of various human activities.

Criticisms of the Full Compensation Principle—The full compensation principle is sometimes criticized for taking no account of the degree of culpability of the tortfeasor's conduct relative to the objective standard of conduct against which the defendant is judged. This criticism is usually made specifically in relation to liability for negligence by pointing out that the tortfeasor is required to compensate the victim fully whether the tortfeasor's conduct was a slight inadvertent lapse from the standard of reasonable care or a gross and deliberate departure from it. But the criticism could be forcefully extended because the full compensation principle applies across the whole range of tort law whether the tortious conduct which inflicted the losses was inadvertent and completely innocent or intentional and malicious. In tort law, any tortious conduct attracts the obligation to compensate in full, however slight or great its culpability. There are only two grounds on which, in tort law, a tortfeasor's obligation can be reduced. First, if the victim has been contributorily negligent, the amount payable by the tortfeasor may be reduced to reflect the plaintiff's responsibility for the loss suffered.[11] Secondly, where two or more tortfeasors are held liable in respect of the same loss, although each is liable to compensate the victim in full, as between themselves they may each be required to "contribute" a proportion of the damages reflecting the responsibility of each for the victim's loss. But neither rule represents a true exception to the full compensation principle. In the latter case, the victim can recover full compensation from any of the tortfeasors,[12] and in the former the plaintiff receives

[11] See p. 120 below.
[12] This rule, referred to by the term "solidary liability" is very controversial. It is designed primarily to protect victims, but it can operate harshly in cases where one tortfeasor is very much more responsible than the other and the one less responsible is alone sued and held liable while the other has no funds to contribute to the damages. The alternative of "proportionate liability" is currently being considered for certain types of case by the Department of Trade and Industry.

full compensation for so much of the loss as is the legal responsibility of the defendant.

What is the ethical basis of the full compensation principle? The answer would appear to be that however slight the culpability of the tortfeasor, if the victim is not culpable at all, there is no reason why the defendant should not be required to pay full compensation. The relevant point is not whether the tortfeasor is slightly or grossly culpable but that the victim is not culpable at all. On the other hand, it might be argued that just as in criminal law, fairness ("retributive justice") is thought to require "that the punishment fit the crime", so in tort law fairness requires that the sanction should fit the tort. Indeed, it might be argued that it is only the existence of liability insurance which overcomes the potential for unfairness in the operation of the full compensation principle.[13] However, the difference between crime and tort would appear to lie in the fact that protecting the interests of the victim is just as important to tort law as sanctioning the tortfeasor. This is the force of the correlativity of tort law. By contrast, criminal law focuses on the impact of the criminal's conduct on the interests of society, not of individual victims.

Another criticism of the full compensation principle is that it takes no account of the wealth of the tortfeasor or the victim: a poor tortfeasor may be under an obligation to pay a very large amount of damages to a rich victim. In practice, this is unlikely to happen because it is not worthwhile making a tort claim against a tortfeasor who is not either insured against liability or wealthy enough to pay any damages awarded. However, within the ethical framework of tort law, the wealth of the tortfeasor and of the victim is simply irrelevant to their personal responsibility for the victim's losses (except to the extent that wealth might be thought relevant to judging reasonable care).[14] Of course, it is possible to reject the ethical principle of personal responsibility on which the tort system is based; but if this is done in order to undermine the full compensation principle, it is bound to result in the demolition of the whole edifice of tort law. Even replacement of the full compensation principle with one of compensation proportional to culpability would alter the anatomy of tort in a significant way. But replacement of full compensation by a principle of liability

---

[13] T. Honoré, "The Morality of Tort Law" in D.G. Owen (ed), *Philosophical Foundations of Tort Law*, (Oxford, 1995), 86–90 (but note that Honoré is talking about the potential unfairness of strict liability, not of the full compensation principle).

[14] See p. 43 above.

based on ability to pay would be the death of tort law. We will discuss this important issue further in Chapter 7.

Losses, not Needs—The third general point to be made about compensation is that its subject is "losses", not "needs". This explains a number of aspects of the law. For example, a person is entitled to full compensation for loss of income even if they are so wealthy that they do not in any sense "need" the compensation to maintain their pre-tort standard of living or to ensure that they have as good a life as is possible. Again, a person is entitled to full compensation for loss of income in addition to full compensation for medical care even if the person is single and without dependants and is likely to be unable to use such damages because he or she is in a comatose or near-comatose state. Indeed, a permanently unconscious victim is also entitled to (non-pecuniary) damages for loss of enjoyment of life, even if they can have no use for the damages. The fundamental ethical principle underlying the assessment of compensatory damages in tort is that the victim of a tort is entitled, as far as money can do, to be put in the position they would have been in if the tort had not been committed. It may be argued, however, that this principle should not be applied in cases where the plaintiff is unable to use the damages in any way at all.

Disgorgement Damages

Whereas compensatory damages focus on the position of the victim of a tort by making good actionable losses flowing from the tort, disgorgement damages focus on the position of the tortfeasor by requiring the defendant to give up (or "disgorge") certain gains generated by the tortious conduct. The purpose of compensatory damages is to put the victim in the position he or she would have been in if the tort had not been committed so far as losses are concerned; while the aim of disgorgement damages is to put the defendant in the position he or she would have been in if the tort had not been committed so far as gains are concerned. To the extent that any actionable loss suffered by the victim as a result of the tort corresponds to a gain received by the tortfeasor as a result of the tort, the purposes of compensatory damages and disgorgement damages coincide. For instance, if D converts P's chattel, and P is awarded damages representing the value of the chattel, the damages may be viewed either as achieving compensation or disgorgement or both. But it is only compensation which is concerned with losses of the victim which do not correspond to gains received by the tortfeasor (such as loss of an eye in an accident), and only disgorgement which is concerned with gains received by the tortfeasor which do not correspond to losses suffered by the victim (such as expense saved by using another's property without their consent in circumstances where the owner could not and would not have used it).[15] The following discussion is concerned only with disgorgement of gains which do not correspond to losses.

Because of the strength of the "harm principle" ("avoid harming others"),[16] the ethical case for compensating for losses, whether or not they correspond to gains made by the tortfeasor, is generally thought to be stronger than that for requiring the disgorgement of gains which do not correspond to losses. This opinion explains why the principle of compensation applies generally throughout tort law while the principle of disgorgement has a narrower field of operation. It may also explain why tort law adopts the principle of full compensation but does not adopt a principle of full disgorgement.[17] In fact, there are two measures of disgorgement: profit made and expense saved. For example, suppose D uses P's property without P's consent for some profitable enterprise. In doing so D will have both saved the expense of paying for the use of the property (in the form of rent, or a licence fee, or a royalty) and earned an income. In this context, "profit" means "income *plus* expense saved". The remedy available in tort law to secure disgorgement of profits received is called "account of profits". It seems that the main type of tort cases in which courts are willing to award an account of profits are ones in which D has infringed P's statutory intellectual property rights. Analogously, an account of profits may be awarded in an action for breach of confidence or for passing off. In tort cases of other types in which disgorgement has been ordered, the measure has been expense saved.

[15] Disgorgement damages are one of two types of "restitutionary" damages. The other type I call "restorative" damages. An obligation to pay restorative damages is an obligation to pay back to P gains which represent a loss to P. See further p. 194 below. Another way of viewing liability to pay damages representing expense saved by unauthorized use of another's property is as compensation for (non-pecuniary) loss suffered as a result of interference with the right to control the use of one's property: P. Cane, *Tort Law and Economic Interests*, 2nd edn (Oxford, 1996), 44.

[16] The most famous discussion of this principle is J.S. Mill's *On Liberty*.

[17] Although tort law compensates for certain non-pecuniary losses, it never requires the disgorgement of non-pecuniary gains. The strength of the compensation principle is also reflected in the fact (which is discussed in Chapter 6) that although there are some cases (in the law of restitution) in which the obligation to disgorge is limited to such gains received by the defendant as correspond to loss suffered by the plaintiff, there are no cases in which the obligation to compensate is limited to such losses suffered by the plaintiff as correspond to gains received by the defendant.

But even in intellectual property cases, the culpability of the defendant's conduct may be relevant to the measure of disgorgement. For instance, if D wrongly thought that the property being used belonged to D, or if the profits were significantly the result of the lawful exertions of D, a court would be unwilling to award P an account of profits and might only award a licence fee or a royalty. Thus liability to disgorge seems related to the culpability of the defendant's conduct in a way in which liability to compensate is not.

There are certain cases in which disgorgement damages may be awarded under the head of "punitive" or "exemplary" damages. As we will see below, the purpose of punitive damages, as the name implies, is to punish the tortfeasor. To this end, if a tort is committed deliberately, then in order to make the point that "tort does not pay", the tortfeasor may be stripped of any gain arising from the tortious conduct. Disgorgement by this indirect route is available only in relation to heads of tort liability to which punitive damages also attach; and as we will see below, the law currently contains no rational principle governing the availability of punitive damages. Nevertheless, the availability of disgorgement *via* the punitive damages route does reinforce the point that tort liability to disgorge is related to the culpability of the defendant's conduct in a way in which tort liability to compensate is not.

It is worth noting at this point that in the property context, disgorgement damages may be awarded even in respect of innocent exploitation of another's property, while in other contexts, such damages are a response to deliberate gain-seeking. The significance of this surprising contrast will be considered below.

Punitive Damages

As just noted, the purpose of punitive (or "exemplary") damages in tort law is to punish the tortfeasor. For this reason, punitive damages may be seen as "civil (as opposed to criminal) fines". Punitive damages are sometimes distinguished from "aggravated damages" which are said to be designed not to punish the defendant but to compensate the plaintiff for non-pecuniary loss arising from the commission of a tort in a way which demonstrates extraordinary disrespect for the plaintiff. However, aggravated damages are effectively indistinguishable from punitive damages, and in my view, they should be abolished.[18]

---

[18] But the Court of Appeal has recently laid down guidelines for the calculation of aggravated damages by juries in cases of wrongful imprisonment and malicious prosecution by the police: *Commissioner of Police for the Metropolis* v. *Thompson* [1997] New LJ 341.

Punitive damages are available in tort in three situations:[19] where such damages are provided for by statute; where a person exercising governmental (or "public") powers has been guilty of "oppressive, arbitrary or unconstitutional action"; and in some cases where D has acted in "cynical disregard for a plaintiff's rights" with a view to making a profit. Under the second of these heads, punitive damages are often awarded against the police in actions for wrongful imprisonment or malicious prosecution.

The intended message of punitive damages under the third head is to show that the law "cannot be broken with impunity". Although, as noted above, damages under this head provide a means by which a person who has made gains at the expense of another may be required to disgorge those gains, the prime purpose of such damages is to punish, not to secure disgorgement; and so they are available only in cases where D has been guilty of deliberate conduct designed to acquire some benefit at another's expense. By contrast, disgorgement damages may be available, for instance, against innocent exploiters of another's property. Furthermore, damages under this head are not limited to the amount of any gain made by D but may be awarded even if D made no gain by the tort. Conversely, a plaintiff may be awarded such damages even if it cannot be proved that D's gain was a result of the tort rather than D's own lawful exertions. In short, punitive damages are a very blunt instrument of disgorgement.

Punitive damages under the third head are most commonly awarded in tort actions for defamation and trespass to land; and they may only be awarded in relation to heads of tort liability for which, prior to the House of Lords' decision in *Rookes* v. *Barnard* in 1964, it had been held that punitive damages could be awarded.[20] This extraordinary restriction is a product of a simple refusal on the part of the courts to extend the grounds on which punitive damages may be awarded, not of any rational argument.

The Ethical Underpinnings of the Law of Tort Damages

There are, then, three types of tort damages: compensatory damages, disgorgement damages and punitive damages. Of these three, compensatory damages are, as noted above, generally thought to be the easiest to justify. After all, they give effect to the uncontroversial idea that we should avoid harming others. To the extent that

[19] *Rookes* v. *Barnard* [1964] AC 1129.
[20] *AB* v. *South West Water Services Ltd* [1993] QB 507.

disgorgement damages may require a tortfeasor to give up gains resulting from the tort which do not correspond to any loss suffered by the victim, many people would find them harder to justify: if P lost nothing by D's gain, then even if D made the gain by acting tortiously towards P, would P not be receiving an undeserved and unfair windfall if D was required to hand over the gain to P? Pursuing such reasoning further, many find punitive damages ("civil fines"), which represent neither losses suffered by the plaintiff nor gains made by the defendant, simply inconsistent with the correlative nature of tort law because they bear no relationship at all to the plaintiff's interests. In my view, this line of argument rests on two mistakes. The first is an assumption that compensation for loss is the only function of tort law; and the second is that each of the types of damages should be viewed in isolation from the others. As for the first mistake, the analysis of tort law so far in this book has shown that tort law is not just about making good losses, but is also concerned to protect certain rights irrespective of whether interference with the right causes damage. The analysis has also shown that tort law is concerned to sanction conduct as well as to protect interests. As for the second mistake, it is important to understand that the three types of damages are not mutually exclusive: in a suitable case, all three might be awarded. For this reason, we need to consider them not just individually, but also as a set.

First, let us consider the three types of damages individually. From the fact that compensatory damages are available under heads of tort liability which are not based on fault as well as under those which are, and that the full compensation principle takes no account of the culpability of the defendant, it is apparent that the prime focus of compensatory damages is on the plight of the plaintiff rather than the conduct of the defendant. It does not follow, however, that compensatory damages may not also be seen as a sanction. Indeed, the "economic interpretation" of tort law views all tort remedies as designed primarily to provide incentives for the avoidance of tortious conduct. We need not go this far in order to recognize that even compensatory damages may have, as one of their rationales, expressing disapproval of and discouraging certain kinds of conduct.

Turning to disgorgement damages, we noted above that these are available in two main types of case: where D exploits P's property and where D commits a tort deliberately with a view to making a gain. In the former type of case, the emphasis is on protection of an interest while in the latter case it is on sanctioning conduct. So far as conduct is concerned, the justification for requiring D to give up gains even though they do not correspond to any loss suffered by P is that deliberate gain-seeking by tortious conduct is particularly reprehensible. Liability to disgorge expresses stronger disapproval of such conduct than liability to compensate would by itself. So far as interests are concerned, the justification for the obligation to disgorge is that the interest of P which D has interfered with is of great value not only to P but also to society more widely. Liability to disgorge gains made by unauthorized exploitation of another's property signals the high social value attached to property rights, and the importance to the stability of the market that property rights be jealously guarded. What makes the tortfeasor's conduct especially worthy of sanction is not its impact on the interests of the plaintiff as a property owner but its impact on property as a social institution.

Because the disgorgement principle is, in the way just explained, not primarily concerned with the plaintiff's interest as such, the "windfall" objection to disgorgement damages, mentioned above, seems less compelling. The fairness of disgorgement damages should not be judged primarily from the victim's point of view but from the tortfeasor's. The important ethical issue does not concern the destination of the gain. If disgorgement damages are to be pronounced unfair, it must be on the ground that they are an unfair reaction to the tortfeasor's conduct: is it an over-reaction to the sort of tortious conduct which the defendant committed to strip D of gains which do not correspond to losses suffered by the victim? This is not to say, however, that the victim might not have a stronger claim to receive the gain in some cases than in others. For instance, in cases where the tortfeasor has made a gain by interfering with some property right of the victim or by damaging the victim's reputation, we might feel that the victim has a reasonably strong claim to the gain. By contrast, consider a case where a transport company deliberately adopts a policy of cutting corners on safety to maximize profits; as a result, numerous passengers in one of the company's vehicles are killed and injured in an accident involving the vehicle. Many would argue that an obligation to disgorge would be an appropriate response to such conduct even though the present law seems not to impose such an obligation. In such a case, however, it might be thought that it would be more appropriate that the gain be paid into some fund which could be used to improve enforcement of safety regulations against transport companies than that it should be paid to the victims and their relatives.

The "windfall" objection can also be made against punitive damages. Punitive damages are concerned solely with the defendant's conduct, with expressing disapproval of it and with discouraging like conduct. Leaving aside the indirect disgorgement aspect of such damages, punitive damages are fines in the sense that they relate neither to any loss suffered by the victim of a tort nor to any gain made by a tortfeasor out of the tort. It is often said that fines have no place in the law of tort (or, indeed, in any area of the law except the criminal law). The objections to punitive tort damages fall into two groups: pragmatic objections and objections of principle. By pragmatic objections, I mean objections which do not attack the idea of civil fines as such but only some aspect of the way they operate in practice. The windfall objection is pragmatic in this sense: it could be met by providing that punitive damages should go to the State, not to tort victims. Another pragmatic objection is that whereas in criminal law, fines are only imposed if it can be proved "beyond reasonable doubt" that D committed a crime, in tort a fine can be imposed provided only that it can be proved "on the balance of probabilities" that D committed a tort. This objection could be met by requiring a higher than normal standard of proof in tort cases before punitive damages could be awarded. A third pragmatic objection is based on the idea of "double jeopardy": in a case where D's conduct constituted both a tort and a crime, it would be unfair if D could be fined twice, once for the crime and a second time for the tort. This objection could be met by a carefully drafted rule against such double fining.

There are two main objections of principle to punitive damages. The first is that to allow courts to impose fines in tort cases is to give them the power, in effect, to criminalize conduct. Because of the peculiar social stigma attaching to criminal sanctions (so the argument would go), conduct should only be criminalized by the legislature. Even if we accept this argument, there would be no objection to the imposition by a court of a fine in a tort case provided the tortious conduct in question also constituted a crime or there was a statutory provision conferring the power to award punitive damages in respect of tortious conduct of the type in question. The second objection of principle is that whereas criminal proceedings are normally instituted by, or at least under the ultimate control of, state authorities, tort actions are normally brought by citizens. Because of the peculiar social stigma which attaches to criminal sanctions (so the argument goes) individuals should not have an unfettered power to institute proceedings which may culminate in the imposition of a fine.

However, although there are some crimes which can only be prosecuted by or with the consent of state officials, many crimes can be and are prosecuted by individual citizens. If it were thought desirable to have some state control over applications for punitive damages, it would not be impossible to require the consent of a state official to applications for punitive damages in tort cases.

It is often said that punitive damages ought not to be available in tort cases because tort law is part of civil law, and that it is the purpose of the criminal law, not the civil law, to punish. However, punishment can be seen as a particularly emphatic way of expressing disapproval of and discouraging (or "deterring") certain types of conduct. Few would deny that expressing disapproval of and discouraging certain types of conduct is also a legitimate function of the civil law, including the law of tort. Indeed, I have argued that even compensatory damages in tort can be seen as expressing disapproval of and as discouraging certain kinds of tortious conduct. Disgorgement damages can also be seen as performing such a function. Once we accept that civil law sanctions may legitimately be seen as expressing disapproval and discouragement of conduct, there is no conclusive reason of principle why punitive damages should not be available to sanction tortious conduct of a particularly reprehensible kind.[21]

I said earlier that we should not fall into the trap of considering the three types of damages in complete isolation from one another, but that they should be viewed as a set. There are two reasons why. First, as I explained at the beginning of this chapter, remedies embody the tension and give expression to the balance inherent in the correlative structure of causes of action in tort. Secondly, the measures of damages may be awarded cumulatively in appropriate cases. These two reasons taken together suggest that the three ideas of compensation, disgorgement and punishment not only individually give expression to aspects of the balance struck in tort law between the positions of the two parties in terms of protected interests and sanctioned conduct, but also together give fuller expression to the complexity of that balance. In the correlative analysis of tort law, one would expect tort remedies to be concerned with sanctioning conduct as well as with protecting interests.

---

[21] Whether this argument is acceptable or not, the present state of English law in which punitive damages are available, but only available, in relation to torts in respect of which it was held before 1964 that they were available, is nonsensical.

SANCTIONS FOR VICTIM'S CONDUCT

As noted several times before in this book, tort law is concerned not only with the responsibility of tortfeasors for torts, but also with the responsibility of tort victims for what has happened to them. Sometimes, tort law gives effect to judgements about the responsibility of the victim by denying tort liability. For instance, if a person unreasonably (that is, negligently) relies on a statement made by another or unreasonably fails to check its accuracy, and suffers economic loss as a result, the maker of the statement may not be liable to that person at all. Here, we are not concerned with this type of case, but rather with situations where the law imposes tort liability in respect of someone's conduct but modifies the sanction attaching to the conduct to take account of the victim's responsibility.

There are two types of sanction imposed on victims: either a partial reduction of damages or a total denial of damages. In a sense, of course, a total denial of damages is equivalent, from the victim's point of view, to a denial of liability. Indeed, as we saw in Chapter 2,[22] in certain types of case failure by the victim to take reasonable care for his or her own interests provides the basis for a denial of liability. Perhaps the most that can be said in general terms is that the choice between a denial of liability, a total denial of damages and a partial reduction of damages is influenced by ethical judgements about the proper allocation of responsibility for injuries and losses in various types of situations and in particular cases.

Total denial of damages is the sanction attaching to illegal conduct by the victim giving rise to a defence of illegality, and also to effective consent and assumption of risk. Partial reduction (or "apportionment") of damages is the sanction attaching to contributory negligence. The difference between these two outcomes has had an important influence on the way the various defences are used and perceived. Damages are apportioned in cases of contributory negligence as a recognition that the tortfeasor and the victim were both responsible in some way for the impact of the tort on the victim. Apportionment was introduced by statute to obviate the perceived unfairness of the pre-existing law under which a finding of contributory negligence led to a complete refusal of damages. Over the years, the definition of contributory negligence had been increasingly narrowed to reduce the unfairness, but in the end[23] apportionment

---

[22] See p. 60 above.
[23] Law Reform (Contributory Negligence) Act 1945.

was seen as the only fair rule. The term "apportionment" is slightly misleading because whereas its effect on the tortfeasor is to reduce the liability to pay damages, the effect on the victim is that he or she must absorb a proportion of the losses flowing from the tort. It is more accurate to say that the effect of a successful defence of contributory negligence is to reduce the amount of damages which the tortfeasor is obliged to pay to the victim.

The amount of that reduction (which will be expressed as a percentage) is entirely in the discretion of the court guided only by two extremely vague concepts, namely the relative culpability and the relative causal "potency" of the conduct of the tortfeasor and the victim respectively. Relativity is a crucial idea: the question is not how far the victim's conduct departed from the standard of the reasonable person in the victim's position but rather how responsible the victim was relative to the tortfeasor. Despite the inherent vagueness of the concepts central to apportionment for contributory negligence, in juristic terms the apportionment legislation has been a great success. It seems impossible to attack apportionment given the ethical structure of tort law. As against a tortfeasor, it is fair that a wholly innocent victim should recover compensation for all their losses regardless of how culpable the defendant's conduct was relative to some objective standard; but not if the victim was less than wholly innocent. However, it is probably true to say that in practice, apportionment has a more negative impact on the position of victims than in theory it should have. This is because in the case of very many tort claims, it can be plausibly argued that the victim was to some extent contributorily negligent. This gives the tortfeasor a very useful bargaining chip in the settlement process[24] which may result in delay and enable the tortfeasor to secure a disproportionately favourable settlement.

Nevertheless, part of the cake is clearly better than none, and once apportionment for contributory negligence was introduced, the position of assumption of risk and illegality as defences became suspect, because to each attached the draconian sanction of a complete denial of damages to the victim. This probably provides part of the explanation of why these defences play a very small role in tort law today. Without too much difficulty, most cases of causally-relevant illegal conduct or assumption of risk by the victim can be interpreted as cases of contributory negligence, and thus as grounds for

---

[24] Almost all tort claims are settled out of court.

apportionment. Only two things have stood in the way of the complete demise of these defences. One is a decision that the legislation which authorizes apportionment does not allow a court to reduce the damages payable to a contributorily negligent victim by 100 percent (that is, to refuse the victim any damages at all).[25] The other is a statutory rule that the defence of assumption of risk cannot be pleaded in the typical road accident case.[26] Because of the first, the defence of assumption of risk has been revived to deal with cases in which, despite the defendant's tortious contribution to the plaintiff's loss, the plaintiff "only had herself to blame for what happened"; as in a case where P willingly flew as a passenger in a small plane being piloted by a companion who had, to the plaintiff's knowledge, been drinking alcohol for most of the day.[27] The second factor has provided a role for the defence of illegality in road accident cases where the plaintiff's conduct was both illegal and very foolish. Typically, in both types of case, the conduct of the plaintiff is considered so outrageous that P should receive nothing even though the defendant was significantly to blame for what happened.

CONCLUSION

In this chapter I have attempted to show how sanctions fit into and express the correlative structure of tort law. The crucial point to emphasize is that remedies should be seen as embodying the tension and giving effect to the complex balance the law strikes between the positions of the two parties in terms of protected interests and sanctioned conduct. It is a mistake to view sanctions, either individually or as a set, exclusively from one angle or the other.

[25] *Pitts* v. *Hunt* [1991] 1 QB 24.
[26] Road Traffic Act 1988, s. 149(3).
[27] *Morris* v. *Murray* [1991] 2 QB 6.

5. RECONSTRUCTING TORT LAW

Now we have examined the three main components of tort law, namely protected interests, sanctioned conduct and sanctions. In this chapter we will see how these components fit together to form the structure of tort law. This is a complex task, and to do it in full detail would require a much longer treatment. My aim here will be to produce a line-drawing rather than a fully worked-up portrait. Because there are three variables to fit into the picture – protected interests, sanctioned conduct and sanctions – the first question to be resolved is how to organize the discussion. I have decided to do this in terms of protected interests in the sense of "assets" or "resources". There are two related reasons for this. The first is that tort claims are, of course, always initiated by plaintiffs. In *practical* terms, tort law is first and foremost a resource which people can utilize to protect and further their interests, to resolve disputes and to seek redress for wrongs done and injuries inflicted. The second reason is that (as I argued in Chapter 2) when it comes to applying the correlative analysis of tort law to concrete situations, it is better to start with protected interests (in the sense of assets or resources) than with sanctioned conduct. The discussion in Chapter 6 will make this clearer.

Before we start the process of reconstruction, it is important to understand how this operation relates to the correlative analysis adopted so far. Causes of action in tort are two-sided, looking to the plaintiff on one side and the defendant on the other; and on each side there are elements relating to protected interests and sanctioned conduct. Each cause of action holds the positions of the two parties in a sort of tension, and the sanctions available under each head of liability express and give effect to the balance which the law strikes between those two positions as described in terms of protected interests and sanctioned conduct. The liability and its limits under each head take into account the interests and the conduct of both parties, and the available sanctions (as it were) reflect the balance of the account between them.

As will become clear in the course of this chapter, reconstructing tort law in the way just outlined brings to light many neglected or unnoticed features of and anomalies in the law. It also lays the groundwork for the exploration in Chapter 6 of the distinctiveness of tort law and of its relationship to other areas of the law.

INTERESTS IN ONE'S PERSON

Physical Interests

Sanctioned Conduct

Personal health and safety lie at the core of tort law. The only other area of civil law which protects this interest is contract; but "personal injury claims" based on contract are, both in theory and in practice, of marginal importance in the total picture of contract law. Criminal law is also much concerned with personal health and safety; and in practice, the conduct which forms the basis of very many tort claims for personal injuries (in respect of accidents on the road and at work) is also criminal. On the other hand, much criminal behaviour which results in personal injuries never becomes the subject of tort claims. Other sources of compensation are important here, notably "compensation orders" made by criminal courts and awards made under the Criminal Injuries Compensation Scheme (CICS). Compensation orders follow conviction just as tort damages follow a finding of tortious conduct. By contrast, an award may be made under the CICS despite the fact that the perpetrator of the crime has not been convicted or even identified. Moreover, the CICS is funded by general taxation, not by criminals. Thus while the CICS is based on concepts of personal responsibility, in important respects it is more like a social security scheme based on ideas of social responsibility for those in need than like the tort system.

Fault-Based Liability—In tort law there is an important difference between bodily ("physical") injuries to the person and mental (or "psychiatric") injuries. Dealing first with physical injury, there can be tort liability for such injury if it is inflicted intentionally, recklessly or negligently. In relation to such injury, the distinction between acts and omissions is relatively unimportant. Although cases can be imagined in which tort law would not hold a person liable for failing to take difficult, costly or risky steps to prevent a complete stranger suffering personal injury, in practice there are many types of case in which tort law imposes liability for failures of physical protection. In the "tort of negligence" the device used to do this is the "duty of care". This device deserves an explanatory digression because most personal injury tort claims are based on the tort of negligence. This tort has three elements: duty of care, breach of duty, and damage, not too remote in law, caused by the breach of duty. There can be no liability "in the tort of negligence" unless D was under a duty of care to P and committed a breach of that duty which caused actionable damage to P. The third element is discussed later in this chapter under the heading of causation. The discussion of negligent conduct in Chapter 2 above was largely a discussion of the second element. The first element deserves a little explanation here.

In terms of the framework suggested in this book, the duty of care element of the tort of negligence is used to refine and give more detailed content to the concepts of protected interests and sanctioned conduct. Important rules about the scope of liability for negligent conduct are framed in terms of whether the defendant "owed a duty of care" to the plaintiff. The classic general statement about when a duty of care is owed is the "neighbour principle" enunciated by Lord Atkin in 1932 in *Donoghue* v. *Stevenson*.[1] Everyone owes a duty of care to their neighbours. A neighbour is someone you ought to foresee as likely to suffer injury as a result of negligence on your part. The neighbour principle has since been fleshed out by a three-stage test under which a duty of care will be owed by D to P if D ought to have foreseen injury to P, there was a sufficient relationship of proximity between D and P, and it would be "just and reasonable" to impose a duty of care.[2] The first element (foreseeability) is more or less redundant because foreseeability of risk is central to the concept of negligent conduct. The other two elements (proximity, and justice and reasonableness) are no more than labels which can be attached to the various grounds on which the courts think it right to restrict the scope of liability for negligently-caused injury. The duty of care concept operates negatively to impose limits on the potentially enormous breadth of the principle that people ought to be legally liable for negligently-caused injury. It is a repository of principles relevant to the concepts of protected interests and sanctioned conduct which, for purely organizational reasons, it is convenient to separate out from those concepts and which lend themselves to being explained in terms of the concept of "duty".

To return to the distinction between acts and omissions which prompted this digression, tort law reflects non-legal ethics in

[1] [1932] AC 562.
[2] *Caparo Industries Plc* v. *Dickman* [1990] 2 AC 605.

drawing a distinction between the two and in attaching fewer sanctions (other things being equal) to the latter than the former. A person who causes physical injury to another person by a negligent act will, as a general rule, be held to owe a duty of care to that person unless some countervailing reason not to recognize a duty can be found. In relation to negligent omissions, the law starts from the other end and looks for some justification for imposing a duty of care or, as it is often put, a "duty of positive action". There are many of these recognized in tort law. For example, employers owe duties of positive action to protect the health and safety of their workers; and occupiers of land owe such duties of positive action to visitors coming onto the land. There may be no duty to protect or rescue a complete stranger from danger, particularly if doing so would be costly or dangerous, but doctors have "duties of physical protection" towards their patients, as do parents towards their children, school authorities towards their pupils and prison authorities towards prisoners. A surveyor or architect employed to certify the safety of a building would also owe a duty of positive action to someone injured by the building, whether the employer or not. A person who creates a dangerous situation may be under a duty to protect or rescue a person who falls into the danger, even if that person is a stranger.

One question to which the law currently gives no clear answer is whether a public regulatory body charged with the function of monitoring and enforcing compliance with health and safety regulations and standards by citizens, would owe a duty of care to a person for whose benefit the regulations and standards existed and who was injured as a result of non-compliance with them, such that the body could be held liable for negligent failure to monitor and enforce compliance. The ethical question here is whether the regulatory body's responsibility should be treated as outweighed by the responsibility of the law breaker. It is the latter, we might say, who was "primarily responsible" for the injuries; the former was only "secondarily responsible".[3] From an ethical point of view, it is not obvious, given the monitoring and enforcement functions of the regulator, that the regulator should be totally relieved of liability simply on the ground of being only secondarily responsible; especially since the law breaker

[3] In this context, "primarily responsible" and "secondarily responsible" are not synonyms of "primary liability" and "secondary liability". For a definition of secondary liability see p. 32 above. Here "primarily" means "more" and "secondarily" means less, whereas the basis of secondary liability for a tort is that a person who induces or assists the commission of a tort is as culpable as the person who perpetrates it.

could also be held liable and since, as between the two tortfeasors, the lawbreaker would be held liable to pay more of the damages than the regulator.[4] In practice, however, if regulators owed duties of care to individual beneficiaries of regulatory schemes, they would present very attractive targets for tort actions because their liabilities are ultimately underwritten by public funds (tax revenue). It might also prove very difficult for a regulatory body held liable in tort successfully to offload part of the burden of liability on to the law breaker even though the law breaker may well have been, from an ethical point of view, much more responsible for what happened than the regulator.

This dilemma about the imposition of duties of positive action on regulators uncovers two points of fundamental importance to our understanding of tort law as a system of ethical principles. The first is this: what is the significance of the fact that any damages paid by D to P will not come out of D's pocket? Should a person's tort liability be affected by the source of the funds which will be used to meet that liability? Would it be right to allow a judgement about a person's responsibility for injury to be influenced by the facts about how that responsibility will be financially discharged? This question arises very commonly in relation to tort law because most tort damages are paid by liability insurers. The general relationship between tort liability and liability insurance is considered in Chapter 7. In the present context, the more specific issue concerns the significance of the fact that any damages paid by the regulator will come out of "public funds", that is, tax revenues. The second of the two points mentioned above is this: what is the significance of the fact that in reality a person may not end up paying the damages which, according to the principles of tort law, they should pay? In the present context, should our judgement about the responsibility of the regulator be affected by the fact that if the regulator can successfully be sued in tort, in practice it alone may be sued and it alone may, in the end, bear the whole burden of the damages awarded to the injured person while the law breaker escapes being sued and pays no damages?[5]

Concerning the first point, some would argue that regulators and other public bodies have responsibilities to the public as well as to individual citizens; and their responsibilities to the public should be taken into account in determining if and when they should be subject to tort liability. To impose tort liability on a public body in favour

[4] See the discussion of contribution at p. 129 below.
[5] The injured person is free to choose whom to sue.

of individuals (so the argument goes), at least in relation to "policy decisions", would hamper the freedom of the body to use its resources in the way best calculated, in its view, to balance its responsibilities to the public on the one hand and to individuals on the other. This sort of argument rests on the idea that individual responsibility in tort law must be understood in a social context.[6]

So far as the second point is concerned, some people would argue that despite their being in a real sense partly responsible for injuries resulting from negligent failure to perform their monitoring and enforcement functions, regulators should owe no duty of care in tort to individual beneficiaries of regulation in relation to personal injuries because, in reality, if regulators were held to owe a duty of care to injured persons in the sort of situation we are considering, regulators would likely be the sole targets of tort litigation, letting law breakers entirely off the hook because it would, in practice, be difficult or impossible for the regulator to recover from the law breaker in contribution proceedings. This argument rests on a distinction between principles of personal responsibility and the practical impact of applying those principles in the law. What I have argued so far in this book is that the best way to understand the structure of tort law is to treat it as a system of ethical rules and principles of personal responsibility for conduct. We could go further and say that the practical effects of imposing tort liability on matters such as who pays tort damages should simply be irrelevant to deciding the ethical issues which underpin tort law. If we took that view, we would reject the argument at the beginning of this paragraph and impose a duty of care on regulators in the sort of situation we are considering. By contrast, we could say that giving effect to ethical principles of personal responsibility is only one of the social functions of tort law, and that achieving a socially fair distribution of the burdens of meeting tort liabilities is another. This approach would involve an admission that tort law legitimately serves a number of different social goals which may conflict with one another. Taking this view, we might accept the argument at the beginning of this paragraph if we thought that a rule of no-liability in relation to regulators represented a reasonable compromise between the conflicting goals of enforcing principles of personal responsibility and ensuring a fair distribution of the costs of negligence. We will return in Chapter 7 to the whole question of the relationship between the ethical structure of tort law on the one

[6] See pp. 38, 92 above.

hand, and the goals of tort law and the effects of the imposition of tort liability on the other.

A third possible approach to the dilemma we are considering might be to say that the problem actually lies in the rules of tort law. Under present law, where more than one tortfeasor is responsible for one and the same loss, the victim may sue one or other or all of the tortfeasors and may be awarded a judgment for full compensation against any or all of them (although, of course, P may not actually recover in total an amount greater than "full compensation"). Each of the tortfeasors may then sue the other(s) for "contribution" which is determined according to the relative causal relevance and the relative culpability of each of the tortfeasors. But each tortfeasor is liable to pay full compensation for the whole of P's loss, and must do so unless successful contribution proceedings are brought against the other tortfeasor(s). Some would argue that these rules are ethically suspect on the basis that liability should be proportional to culpability. On this basis, if one tortfeasor was only 30 percent responsible for P's injuries, that tortfeasor should only ever have to pay 30 percent of the damages. The ethical argument against this is that if P was in no way responsible for the injuries, P should not have to sue more than one person in order to recover full compensation. Those who support proportional liability typically (and perhaps inconsistently) do not argue that it should be a general rule in tort law, but they do advocate it as between multiple tortfeasors. However, it should be noted that if applied to the situation we are considering, the argument for proportional liability would not justify a rule that regulators owe no duty to individual plaintiffs but only that they should not be held liable in tort for more than their "fair share" of the damages awarded to such plaintiffs.

The duty of care concept is also used to regulate the scope of liability for negligently-caused psychiatric injuries ("nervous shock"). The relevant rules were discussed in Chapter 3,[7] and there is no need to repeat the discussion here. So far as concerns psychiatric injury, such as grief or anxiety, which does not amount to nervous shock (that is, a recognized psychiatric illness or condition), compensation for such injury can, it seems, be awarded in a negligence action only if it is an accompaniment of some other actionable injury, such as physical injury. The only exception is that damages for "bereavement" may be awarded in a claim under the Fatal Accidents Act 1976

[7] See p. 68 above.

to a limited class of relatives of a person who has been tortiously killed, even if this is the only actionable injury which has been suffered by the relative. There is some authority for the proposition that it is tortious intentionally to inflict mental injury even if it does not constitute a recognized psychiatric illness. It is to such conduct that the developing "tort of harassment" seems directed.

Strict Liability—Strict liability for personal physical injury is the exception in tort law. In practice, the most important head of strict liability in this context is vicarious liability, which is a form of secondary liability.[8] The liability of importers and distributors for injuries caused by defective products under the Consumer Protection Act 1987 (Part I) may perhaps be seen as a form of vicarious liability. Primary liability which is negligence-based in theory may be strict in practice if the defendant bears the burden (which is typically very difficult to discharge) of disproving negligence under the so-called doctrine of *res ipsa loquitur*. The combination of vicarious liability and reversal of the burden of proving negligence can produce a particularly powerful form of strict liability. For instance, if a patient undergoes surgery to restore movement to a stiff finger and ends up with two stiff fingers, the hospital may be liable even if it cannot be proved that any member of the theatre staff was negligent, simply on the basis that this sort of thing does not normally happen without negligence, and the hospital cannot prove that none of the staff was negligent.

Most supposed instances of strict primary liability for personal injuries are not such on closer inspection. Even if liability does not depend on proof by the plaintiff that the defendant caused the injuries intentionally, recklessly or negligently in the senses of these words explained in Chapter 2, in most cases the plaintiff must prove that the defendant was at fault in some sense (such as that D ought to have foreseen P's injuries), or it is open to D to plead lack of fault as a defence (as where D can plead that the injury was the result of an unforeseeable act of a third party). Why is "fault" (in the sense of intention, recklessness or negligence) such a pervasive feature of primary tort liability for personal injuries? In general terms, this question is extremely difficult to answer. It is sometimes argued that fault-based liability is and that strict liability is not "fair". On this basis, however, large parts of the civil law of obligations would have to be condemned as unfair when they are clearly not thought to be so by

[8] See p. 46 above.

many people. As we saw in Chapter 2,[9] an ethical case can certainly be made in favour of strict liability in tort law. In fact, at a general level, there seems to be no convincing ethical reason to prefer fault liability to strict liability. Ethically-based criticisms of particular instances of strict liability are more often based on perceived anomalies generated by applying different standards of liability to essentially similar types of case, or vice versa, than on objections to strict liability as such. Why, for instance, are people prepared to contemplate strict liability for injuries caused by defective products but not for injuries caused by defective services?[10]

If we take the view that interests protected by strict liability are more highly valued by tort law than interests protected by fault-based liability, a very significant fact emerges, namely that tort law values property interests more highly than a person's interest in health and safety. As we will see, strict liability for interferences with property interests is much more common than strict liability for personal injuries. However, a better explanation for this initially puzzling feature of tort law lies in the function of the concept of common law property rights, which is to mark the distinction between "what is mine and what is yours". This distinction is fundamental to the operation of a market economy, and strict liability for misappropriation or unauthorized exploitation of another's property is an important mechanism for vindicating property rights.

Victim's Conduct—The fact that tort liability for personal injuries is typically fault-based means that contributory negligence is a very important defence in personal injury cases. But even in cases where liability for personal injuries is, in some sense, strict (as in relation to defective products under the Consumer Protection Act 1987), contributory negligence is usually available as a defence. The defence of assumption of risk also finds its most important (though small) area of operation in personal injury claims.

Sanctions

To all intents and purposes, the only remedy for personal injuries is compensatory damages. Injunctions are assumed not to be available to restrain negligence, which forms the basis of the typical personal injuries tort action. The unavailability of injunctions to restrain negligence may be the result of a false equation of negligence with

[9] See p. 49 above.
[10] J. Stapleton, *Product Liability* (London, 1994), 323 ff.

inadvertence. It would be illogical to order someone not to act inadvertently. However, as we saw in Chapter 2,[11] negligence is not a
state of mind but a failure to comply with a standard of conduct.
Deliberate and even intentional conduct can meet the definition of
negligence. Much unsafe practice in industry, for instance, probably
results from conscious decisions deliberately to "cut corners on
safety". There is no obvious reason why an injunction should not be
available in suitable circumstances to order a person to refrain from
specified conduct or to perform specified acts with a view to remov-
ing foreseeable risks of injury to a plaintiff. This is particularly so
given that much risky conduct is not only negligent but also in breach
of statutory regulations; and injunctions are available (in addition to
damages) to enforce statutory duties or prohibitions which are
actionable by individuals. At all events, the unavailability of preventive remedies in negligence actions has had the result that, in this
respect, the interest in bodily and mental health and safety is less well
protected by tort law than property interests are – which, to modern
eyes, may seem to involve a strange inversion of moral values.

As for monetary remedies, disgorgement damages are not, it seems,
available in a negligence action. It is, nevertheless, surely true that
many unsafe practices are the result of conscious decisions to save
money. In other words, financial gains are often made at the expense
of personal injury victims. It would, no doubt, often be very difficult
in practice to prove that a gain was made at the expense of any particular personal injury plaintiff and to quantify such gain. In theory,
however, is there any reason why, if this difficulty could be overcome, disgorgement damages should not be available in personal
injury cases? As we saw in Chapter 4,[12] under the present law, the
grounds on which such damages can be awarded are that D has
exploited P's property without consent or authority, and that D has
committed a tort with the conscious aim of making a gain at P's
expense. Although instances of negligently creating risks of personal
injuries with the conscious aim of making a gain at the injured person's expense may not be common, it is certainly not unknown for
commercial enterprises to be accused of such conduct. Once we
reject the mistaken equation of negligence with inadvertence, it is
possible to conceive of negligent conduct which could attract an
obligation to disgorge, even if we accept the basis for the current limits on the incidence of such obligations.

[11] See p. 36 above.
[12] See p. 112 above.

Whatever the position may be in regard to disgorgement, it is perfectly clear in English law that punitive damages are not available in a negligence action for personal injuries. Once again, however, since deliberate, gain-seeking conduct may satisfy the definition of negligence, unless punitive tort damages are abolished entirely, there is no logical reason why there should be a blanket ban on the award of punitive damages in respect of deliberate gain-seeking conduct which causes personal injury. If deliberate, gain-seeking conduct is thought to be a proper trigger of punitive (or disgorgement) damages, it should make no difference under what head of tort liability the plaintiff seeks a remedy for such conduct.

In a personal injury action brought by the victim during his or her lifetime, the aim of compensatory damages is to put P in the position he or she would have been in if the injuries had not been suffered, so far as money can do this and within the considerable constraints imposed by the lump-sum system of tort compensation. Thus the plaintiff is compensated in full for any reduction of income or earning capacity as a result of the injuries; and if the victim's life expectancy was reduced as a result of being injured, compensation is given for income which would have been earned during the period when, but for the injuries, P would have been alive and earning (the "lost years"). The victim is also compensated in full for any additional expenses incurred as a result of the injury; and "fairly" for "nonpecuniary" loss resulting from the injuries – pain, suffering, anxiety, distress, unhappiness, inability to enjoy a full life. In theory, the victim is entitled to be compensated in full at the date of the injuries. In practice, compensation is not received until some time later. So the victim is entitled to be paid interest on the full amount of the damages received for the period between the date of the injuries and the date of assessment of the damages. In cases where the damages compensate partly for loss which has not yet been suffered at the date of assessment, in assessing the damages a "discount" is applied to take account of the fact that P will be able to invest the damages until they are needed to meet future losses. The likely effects of future inflation are ignored on the basis that inflation can be neutralized by sound investment; but in theory, at least, the courts make allowance for tax payable on the income generated by investment of the damages. I have rehearsed these details about the assessment of damages to show the lengths to which tort law goes to give effect to the "full compensation" principle.

Where an injured person dies before commencing an action, the person's estate may sue and recover full compensation in respect of the period between the tort and the death in a so-called "survival action". The original common law rules were that the death extinguished an existing tort claim and could not form the basis of a tort action. In relation to personal injury claims, the second of these rules was reversed by the Fatal Accidents Act 1846, which is discussed further below in the section headed "Non-Contractual Expectancies". The first rule was not abrogated until the introduction of "survival actions" by statute in 1934.

Dignitary Interests

Sanctioned Conduct and Sanctions

The dignitary interest which receives the most protection from tort law is reputation. Reputation is seen as analogous to property, and as a result, liability for damage to reputation is very strict. The only thing a plaintiff in a defamation action has to establish to get the action off the ground is that a statement[13] defamatory of P was communicated to someone other than P (or, in other words, "published"). P does not have to prove damage to reputation as a result of the publication. The publication might be by the maker of the statement or by another. Any and every person who publishes a defamatory statement is *prima facie* liable. In the typical case, publication will be deliberate; but liability may arise for inadvertent publication. The maker of a defamatory statement may be liable for publication by another if the maker is vicariously liable for the torts of the other, or authorized the publication by the other, or intended or ought to have foreseen that publication.

Prima facie liability for defamation represents a very significant intrusion on individual freedom of speech. In modern society, freedom of speech is considered a "fundamental human right" which significantly curtails a person's responsibility for what they say in social contexts. The individual's freedom of speech partly serves and is bolstered by society's interest in the free flow of information about matters of legitimate social concern. However, in traditional English tort law, reputation is more highly prized than (the countervailing interest in) freedom of speech and information, and such protections for the latter as are recognized are embodied in defences to a claim for defamation rather than in the definition of the wrong of defamation.

---

[13] This word refers to material (whether verbal or not) which expresses or implies something defamatory.

INTERESTS IN ONE'S PERSON

It is a defence (called "justification") to prove that the defamatory statement was a reasonable inference from substantially true facts. A person cannot complain if the truth causes them harm. The defendant has a defence (of "fair comment") if it can be proved that the statement was an expression of opinion, that it was an honestly believed (even if unreasonable) inference from substantially true facts, and that it concerned a "matter of public interest". This defence will not succeed if D acted out of what the law regards as an improper motive (with "malice", for some reason other than contributing to public debate); but it is the plaintiff who must prove such an improper motive. "Absolute privilege" protects statements made in the course of parliamentary and judicial proceedings; and qualified privilege protects statements made in situations where the maker and the recipient have what the law considers to be legitimate interests in the making and receiving of the statement. Qualified privilege can, but absolute privilege cannot, be "defeated" by proof by P of malice (lack of honest belief in the truth of the statement, or making the statement for a purpose other than that which the privilege protects) on the part of D.

The defence of justification rests on the simple ethical principle that no-one deserves to have or to retain a good reputation which is based on falsehood. The other defences are designed to protect the interest of citizens in knowing things which are of legitimate interest to them as members of society. As a general rule, it is no defence to a claim in defamation that D took reasonable care not to injure P's reputation. There are two major qualifications to the general rule. One is that if D did not make the statement but only published it (in the strict legal sense of dissemination), there will be no liability if D did not know that the statement was defamatory and took reasonable care not to publish a defamatory statement.[14] Secondly, if the defendant took reasonable care not a defame the plaintiff, and if D makes an "offer of amends" which P refuses to accept, D can plead the making of the offer as a defence to P's claim.[15] However, the effect of this second qualification to strict liability is simply to make it easier for an "innocent defendant" to settle P's claim out of court. The section assumes that the "innocent" defendant has committed tortious defamation.

The strictness of liability for defamation is controversial. The main thrust of criticism is that it unduly protects public figures such as

[14] Defamation Act 1996, s.1.
[15] Ibid, ss. 2–4.

politicians from proper scrutiny by the press who, in an open society, perform a pivotal "quasi-constitutional" role in maintaining the free flow of socially important information and views. In some jurisdictions (in the US, for instance) the standard of liability in defamation actions brought by public figures is much less strict than in England. By contrast, some would argue that strict defamation laws are needed to protect people who have not chosen to put themselves into the limelight from the attentions of less scrupulous sections of the press. Those who argue along such lines are also usually concerned that the law gives insufficient protection to people's privacy. Such arguments about the standard of liability for defamation may be branded as "policy arguments", but they are clearly relevant to ethical judgements about the personal and social responsibility of newspapers. If newspapers have responsibilities towards society, this will inevitably affect their responsibilities towards people whose lives are discussed in their pages.

Injunctions can be awarded to restrain anticipated defamatory publications. In this context, freedom of speech receives some explicit protection in that an injunction will not normally be granted if D claims that the defamatory material is true. A successful defamation plaintiff is entitled to damages for actual financial loss flowing from the publication. However, the main head of compensatory damages available in a defamation action is damages for (non-pecuniary) injury to reputation. Levels of awards for injury to reputation have generated much controversy in recent years. In a number of notorious cases, plaintiffs were awarded (or settled out of court for) amounts much greater than the largest awards for non-pecuniary loss available in personal injury actions (currently around £130,000). Many found it repugnant that anyone's reputation could be "worth more" than the suffering of a person rendered quadriplegic in a road accident, for instance. Appeal courts are beginning to develop ways of controlling defamation awards with a view to reducing the level of the largest awards. However, the controversy raises two important issues relevant to themes of this book.

First, the controversy shows that institutional factors can play an important part in tort law. Damages awards in defamation actions are typically made by juries whereas in personal injury actions they are made by judges (and have been for over 60 years). Appeal courts are much less willing to control juries than to control judges. Moreover, there is a rule that the jury must not be told of damages awards made in other comparable defamation cases. By contrast, judges have always been free to take account of awards of non-pecuniary damages made by other judges in comparable personal injury cases, and there is now a semi-official publication which provides judges with much detailed guidance about conventional awards in various types of case. Consistency is at least as important a feature of awards for non-pecuniary loss as the actual amount awarded because there is no objective way of putting a monetary figure on non-pecuniary loss. If the process of assessing damages for non-pecuniary loss is felt to produce unpredictable and inconsistent results, it will lose much of its legitimacy, whatever the amounts awarded.

In Chapter 1[16] I said that this book was primarily concerned with the substance of tort law and not with the procedures by which tort claims are made. I also pointed out, however, that substance and procedure are not entirely unrelated. Here, I think, we have an example of the interaction of substance and procedure. Because predictability and consistency are important sources of legitimacy of awards for non-pecuniary loss, the nature of the institutional arrangements for making such awards may affect the legitimacy of the awards themselves.

The second important issue raised by the controversy over defamation damages is this. Besides compensatory damages, it is clear that punitive damages may, in theory at least, be awarded in a defamation action if D deliberately set out to make a gain at P's expense. Such damages may, as we saw in Chapter 4, include a component representing gains made by D (that is, a disgorgement component) and a component of pure fine not representing any loss suffered by P or any gain made by D. A jury would not be entitled to award punitive (or disgorgement) damages in a defamation action unless the judge gave a direction to that effect. But because juries give no reasons, it would be impossible to know, in any particular case, whether the jury had or had not been moved by a desire to punish the defendant or to strip it of some of its profits. My suggestion is that some especially high awards by juries in defamation cases might have been so high because, in effect, they were designed not only to compensate P but also to punish D and to strip D of gains. Some awards may also have expressed the jury's "sympathy" for the plaintiff. Although the tort of defamation does not, in theory, protect against hurt feelings, in practice the fact that injury to reputation need not be proved may make it difficult for the lay juror to distinguish rigorously between hurt

[16] See p. 5 above.

feelings and hurt reputation. Popular morality would, no doubt, support the idea that hurting a person's feelings is wrong; but the issue for tort law is whether this moral intuition should be translated into a legal rule. To some extent, this question is fudged by using juries to assess damages – one of the classic justifications for the jury is exactly that it can reflect popular morality in its deliberations regardless of the legal rules which are supposed to guide them.

Tort law can also protect a person against attacks on their dignity by unwanted physical contact, for instance. Such contact would only be tortious if it went beyond what must be accepted as an ordinary part of living in a community. Such contact is likely to be deliberate; but it might be actionable even if it was unintentional and non-malicious. Damages for injury to feelings could be recovered. Damages for injury to feelings can also be recovered in cases brought under the Sex Discrimination Act and the Race Relations Act. Liability for discrimination is strict – the wrong is discriminating on grounds of sex or race, and it makes no difference that the discrimination was unintentional or even non-deliberate. Nor will it help the discriminator that all reasonable care was taken not to discriminate. The sort of conduct at which the developing tort of harassment is directed is, it seems, deliberate, although not necessarily done with the intention of causing offence or hurting feelings. What is not yet clear is whether harassment (that is, behaving towards someone in a way likely to cause them to be hurt or upset) is actionable in the absence of any physical or recognized psychiatric injury.

Civil and Political Interests

The only such interest to which tort law gives direct and significant protection (through the tort of wrongful or false imprisonment) is personal liberty. Deprivation of liberty against a person's will is typically the result of deliberate restriction of movement, but inadvertent restriction might also attract liability. In practice, the most important defence to a claim for deprivation of liberty is legal authority. Such authority may derive from contract.[17] The common law authorizes detention in the name of preserving the peace, and an important ground of statutory authority is law enforcement. There are also some statutory powers to detain people on medical grounds. In the public order and law enforcement contexts, apart from court orders (in the form of warrants for arrest or orders for imprisonment), the

---

[17] J.G. Fleming, *The Law of Torts*, 8th edn (Sydney, 1992), 29–30.

main basis of authorization is reasonable suspicion that a ground for detention exists. The effect of the reasonable suspicion test is to inject an element of fault into a head of liability to which fault is essentially irrelevant: the detainer must take reasonable steps to ensure that the suspicion that a ground of detention exists is well-founded. In relation to the police, suspicion will only be unreasonable if no reasonable police officer would have had a suspicion in the circumstances.[18] The commonest remedy for deprivation of liberty is compensatory damages covering both pecuniary and non-pecuniary loss. Against the police, punitive damages for wrongful arrest and imprisonment are also available.[19] In theory, an injunction might also issue to restrain anticipated wrongful detention.

PROPERTY INTERESTS[20]

Real Property

Liability for misappropriation of real property at common law is strict: there can be liability even if D acted[21] inadvertently and neither knew nor ought reasonably to have known that the property was P's. It is no defence that P failed to take reasonable care to protect the property from the intruders. Moreover, misappropriation of real property is actionable *per se*, without proof of financial or physical damage. The rationale for these rules is that in English law, tort performs in relation to property what might be called a "vindicatory" function or, in other words, the function of marking the boundary between "what is mine and what is yours". What is mine is no less mine because I do not take care of it or because you had no reason to know it was mine. In this respect, tort law is much more concerned with the nature of the plaintiff's interest (which it vindicates) than with the nature of the defendant's conduct (which it sanctions). Every tort claim is a bilateral affair, but the balance between the two poles varies from one type of claim to another. In this context, the rights and freedoms of plaintiffs are given much more weight than those of defendants.

---

[18] *Holgate-Mohammed* v. *Duke* [1984] AC 437.

[19] The Court of Appeal has recently issued guidelines for the assessment of punitive damages in such cases, and has suggested a range of between £5,000 and £50,000: *Commissioner of Police for the Metropolis* v. *Thompson* [1997] *New LJ* 341.

[20] For detailed discussion see P. Cane, *Tort Law and Economic Interests*, 2nd edn (Oxford, 1996), ch. 2.

[21] But mere omission will not amount to misappropriation.

As we saw in Chapter 3, more than one person may have property rights in one and the same piece of property at the same time. Thus, statute and the common law of tort provide remedies not only to dispossessed owners but also to dispossessed tenants. The owner is protected not only against "squatters" but also against "overstaying" tenants. Tenants are protected not only against dispossession by third parties but also against dispossession and "harassment"[22] by the owner during the period of the tenancy. The common law drew a sharp distinction between the rights of tenants (who have a property interest in the demised premises) and "licensees" (who have only a contractual interest in the premises). On the whole, the common law of tort gives no protection to merely contractual interests in real property. However, residential licensees now enjoy, by statute, many of the protections accorded to tenants against the owner; but their position vis-a-vis third parties is still precarious.

Injunctions are available to restrain anticipated misappropriation of real property, but are not commonly sought. For landlords, there are speedy procedures to enable them to obtain "orders for possession" against unauthorized occupants. Landlords may also obtain compensatory damages and, in the form of a claim for "mesne profits", an amount representing the market rental value of the property. Damages of this latter type achieve a measure of disgorgement and are available whether or not the owner suffered any actual loss of rent as a result of the occupation. The main remedy for tenants and licensees is damages; the plaintiff can be compensated for physical injury and damage, pecuniary and non-pecuniary loss. Punitive damages can also be awarded at common law; and under statute an owner can be ordered to pay damages for the gain realized by dispossessing a tenant. In short, for the protection of rights in real property, the law provides a full panoply of remedies: injunctions, and compensatory, disgorgement and punitive damages.

The ideological underpinning for such ample protection of interests in real property against misappropriation is clear enough: private property forms the bedrock of our economic and social life, and real property is one of the most important forms of private property. There is a strong ethical imperative to respect the property of others. In favour of protecting tenants and licensees against owners, there is also a concern to prevent the abuse of economic and physical power.

---

[22] That is, behaviour which causes the tenant to give up the premises. Liability arises under ss. 27 and 28 of the Housing Act 1988, but it is not quite as strict as common law liability for trespass.

However, this ideology has not always gone unchallenged. The late 1960s saw the advent of organized squatting in derelict city buildings and campaigns against both public and private landowners to enforce "social responsibility" in the use of unoccupied property. Proposals have sometimes been made for legislation which would allow community groups to take over empty property which its owner did not intend to use. However, the trend of legislation has been in the opposite direction, making it easier for owners to regain possession from unauthorized occupants. Tort law, both judge-made and statutory, remains a champion of private property rights.

This is true not only in respect of misappropriation of real property but also in relation to its unauthorized exploitation. Here, the concern of the common law to preserve the rights of owners to the full is reflected in the rule that the owner is entitled to an injunction to restrain unauthorized use of the property, and can be required to accept damages *in lieu* only in a very narrow range of circumstances. Thus, at common law a landowner is entitled to refuse a neighbour permission to erect scaffolding on the former's land in order to facilitate work on the neighbour's building, and may obtain an order that the scaffolding not be erected, or even that it be removed, even if the neighbour has offered to pay the landowner for the privilege of erecting the scaffolding and even if the landowner suffers no physical or financial loss as a result of the intrusion.[23] Now, under the Access to Neighbouring Land Act 1992, a court can order a landowner to allow access to facilitate works of "preservation" on condition that the "intruder" pay a reasonable fee and compensate the landowner for any damage. But the Act is quite narrow in scope and would not cover, for instance, the common situation in which the jibs of cranes on building sites intrude into the airspace of neighbouring property. Here, once again, the neighbouring landowner is *prima facie* entitled to an injunction, however costly this might be for the building owner and however little inconvenience the crane might be causing the neighbour. In practice, no doubt, builders usually offer, and landowners usually accept, a licence fee and an undertaking to compensate for any loss caused in return for permission to intrude. The point is, however, that the common law of tort protects landowners not just from unreasonable exploitation of their land but from any significant exploitation, however innocent and however little harm it might cause the landowner; and by doing this it puts them in a

[23] *John Trenberth Ltd* v. *National Westminster Bank Ltd* (1980) 39 P & CR 104.

position to secure payment by waiving their rights. Of course landowners should be protected from damage and should be allowed to exploit their land for their own financial benefit by extracting licence fees from those who wish to use it for *their* own financial benefit. The ideological question is whether landowners should be allowed to deny others the use of their land "just for the heck of it". Provided those seeking to use another's land do not also seek thereby to assert rights of ownership over it, the law should be willing to take account of the reasonableness of the use as against the owner's desire to prevent it.[24]

When we come to liability for interference with the use and enjoyment of land, the legal picture is rather different. Two heads of tort liability are important here – trespass and nuisance. In this context, trespass is used primarily to deal with unwanted entrants. Not all unwanted intrusions are necessarily tortious – for instance, the owner is assumed (in the absence of contrary indication) to be willing to allow people, under normal circumstances, to enter the land to get to the front door of a dwelling; and it is not an actionable trespass to fly in an aircraft over someone's land at a normal height even though ownership of land carries with it ownership of the airspace above it. Both in the law and outside it, people's rights and obligations *inter se* must take account of the accepted necessities of social life. That said, however, liability for unauthorized entry is strict and actionable *per se*: the law gives strong protection to the owner's right to control entry.

Whereas trespass as a head of tort liability deals with interference with the use and enjoyment of land by entry, nuisance deals with interference by things done off the land. In relation to nuisance, although a landowner is *prima facie* entitled to an injunction, interference with use and enjoyment is actionable only if it is "unreasonable" and only if it has caused the landowner some damage (pecuniary or non-pecuniary) or is likely to do so in the near future. Interference with use and enjoyment does not typically challenge the owner's title to the land, and so the law need not take a strict vindicatory attitude to it. The requirement of unreasonableness is practically equivalent to a requirement of negligence: the interference with use and enjoyment must have been foreseeable, and it must be greater than it is reasonable to expect P to put up with. The philosophy of the law of nuisance is mutual tolerance: "live and let live". As in a negligence

---

[24] See further P. Cane, *Tort Law and Economic Interests* (above n.20), 49–56.

action, the likely cost to D of preventing the interference and the social value of D's activity are relevant to judging reasonableness.

Although the basic remedy for likely future interferences with the use and enjoyment of land is an injunction, damages may be awarded *in lieu* of an injunction if the injury likely to be inflicted by the interference is small and easily compensated for in money. Such damages may represent diminution in the value of P's property as a result of the interference, or the cost of "abating" (that is, taking steps to reduce the effect of) the nuisance. They may also include an amount representing gains which D is likely to make as a result of the nuisance. In addition, damages may be recovered for damage suffered in the past, both pecuniary and non-pecuniary; and, it seems, to secure disgorgement of past gains. However, purely punitive awards are, apparently, not available in this context even though spiteful nuisances are certainly not unknown, especially in domestic situations.

In the nineteenth century, the law of nuisance played an important role in resolving conflicts between competing uses of land, particularly industrial and non-industrial. In the twentieth century this function has been largely taken over by the statutory land-use planning system which aims in part to prevent incompatible contiguous uses of land. However, the law of nuisance still operates at the margins of the planning system to deal particularly with problems generated by the day-to-day use of land with which the planning system is not directly concerned. In one case, for instance, houses for which planning permission had been obtained were located so close to a playing field that they became targets for stray cricket balls. In another, a shipping terminal for which planning permission had been obtained generated far more noise and traffic than local residents had anticipated. The law says that if a use of land has been authorized by statute, this provides an answer to a tort claim even if the use causes a nuisance. However, the mere fact that planning permission has been obtained for a particular use does not prevent that use being an actionable nuisance. These rules illustrate two important points: first, that tort law is a complex amalgam of judge-made and statutory rules; and secondly, that although tort law is concerned with the rights and obligations *inter se* of individuals, these rights and obligations are inevitably affected by the social context in which these interactions take place.

Finally, we must consider tort liability for physical damage to or the destruction or loss of real property. The basic standard of liability here is fault – intention or, more commonly, negligence. The few

instances of strict liability are statutory.[25] The most common measure of damages is the cost of repairing the damage or, in the case of
loss or destruction, the cost of replacing the property. However, if the
cost of repairing the property would be greater than any reduction in
its market value caused by the damage, or if the cost of replacing the
property would be greater than its value before the damage, the damages would be limited to the reduction in value or the pre-tort market value (respectively) unless the plaintiff could convince the court
that the property had some special (non-pecuniary) value which
would justify incurring the expense of repair or replacement. The
owner is also entitled to compensatory damages for losses consequential upon the damage, such as the cost of hiring a replacement
while repairs are done. Damages might also be awarded to compensate an individual for psychological injury resulting from the damage
(as in a case where a person had to stand by as their house burnt
down). In the typical case where the action for physical damage to
property is based on an allegation of negligence, neither disgorgement nor punitive damages would be available; nor would an injunction to prevent likely future damage.

It can be seen, then, that whereas liability for misappropriation
and unauthorized exploitation of real property is basically strict,
liability for interference with the use and enjoyment of real property and for physically damaging it is typically based on fault. The
most satisfactory explanation for this difference is that remedies for
the first two forms of interference are designed to protect (or "to
vindicate") the owner's right to control how and by whom the
property is used – which we might call "positive" rights over property, whereas remedies for the latter two forms of interference are
designed to protect the "negative" right that property not be damaged and that use of property not be adversely affected by damage.
The economic and social functions of property are more fundamentally threatened by interferences of the first two types than of
the latter two types because interferences of the former type, if left
unremedied, would be more likely to undermine the distinction
between "what is yours and what is mine" than interferences of the
latter two types, which rarely involve or imply assertions of rights
over the property of another.

---

[25] Liability under the "rule in *Rylands* v. *Fletcher*" is based on fault – liability can arise only
out of an unreasonable use of land and extends only to foreseeable damage. P need not prove
that the escape was the fault of D, but the defences of "act of God" and "act of stranger" are
defences of "no-negligence".

Chattels

The basic pattern of liability rules in this context is the same as that which applies to real property: strict liability for misappropriation and unauthorized exploitation, and fault-based liability for interference with use and enjoyment and for physical damage. In most respects, the pattern of remedies is also similar to that which applies to interferences with real property. However, the scheme of remedies for misappropriation of chattels ("conversion") deserves some discussion. The basic remedy for misappropriation of real property is an order for possession (that is, for the restoration of possession to the dispossessed person). In the case of chattels, an order that D return the misappropriated chattel(s) to P can be made (assuming the chattel(s) are still in D's possession), but this happens only rarely. The normal remedy is an award of damages. This difference reflects the fact that chattels are typically not unique or of special value to their owner. Just as the diminution in value measure sets a ceiling on liability for physical damage to property unless there is some special reason to award the cost of repair or replacement above this ceiling, so an order for return of a chattel will normally be made only if the chattel has some special value to its owner.

A second noteworthy feature of the scheme of remedies for misappropriation of chattels concerns the measure of damages which was, traditionally, the value of the chattel(s). This measure generated a number of rules, the effect of which was that under certain circumstances, a plaintiff in a conversion action could recover by way of compensatory damages more than the financial loss suffered as a result of the misappropriation. Under the Torts (Interference with Goods) Act 1977, a new scheme was introduced, the general aim and effect of which was to prevent a plaintiff in a conversion action recovering more by way of compensation than the financial loss flowing from the misappropriation. On the other hand, it is now accepted that if D saves expense as a result of taking (and using) another's chattel, the owner may recover, in addition to compensation for losses, disgorgement damages representing the reasonable hire value of the chattel.

Intangible Property

This is not the place to examine in detail the statutory rules about liability and remedies for infringement of the various intellectual property rights. A few general points will suffice. The first is that except in a few cases where action cannot amount to an infringement of an intellectual property right unless D knew or ought to have known of P's rights, liability for infringement of such rights is strict. Moreover, various non-monetary remedies (such as injunctions) are available without proof of actual or anticipated financial loss. By contrast, in some cases, monetary remedies are available only if D knew or ought reasonably to have known of P's rights. Secondly, there are some non-monetary remedies which are peculiar to this area of the law, such as orders for delivery-up, forfeiture and destruction of items which infringe intellectual property rights.

Thirdly, by the remedy of account of profits a plaintiff can recover income made by an infringement of an intellectual property right. In assessing the quantum of this remedy in individual cases, account has to be taken of the extent to which any income was the result of D's own legitimate exertions rather than the infringement of P's rights. In the typical case, income will result from a combination of legitimate and infringing activity, and the courts will have to make some apportionment as between the two sources. Account of profits is, in effect, a form of disgorgement damages. It is noteworthy that in cases of unauthorized exploitation of tangible property, the measure of disgorgement damages seems limited to the value of the use of the property in the form of a licence fee or royalty. In that context, income made by the exploitation cannot be claimed by way of damages. By contrast, while an account of profits can be claimed in respect of income made by infringement of intellectual property rights, there is some authority for saying that damages in the form of a licence fee or royalty could not be. It is difficult to find a principled explanation for these divergent rules.

The only type of intellectual property recognized by the common law is goodwill, exploitation of which is the subject of the head of tort liability called "passing off". There can be liability for passing off even if D did not intend to take advantage of P's goodwill and was not negligent in doing so. Unlike infringement of intellectual property rights, however, passing off is not actionable *per se*. On the other hand, in contrast with the position in relation to other common law property rights, income made by passing off is recoverable by way of an account of profits in addition to compensatory damages. There is an ongoing debate about whether the common law ought to recognize other assets (such as a person's character or photographic image) as property. Underlying this debate are fundamental issues of economic and social policy. One of the chief functions of intellectual property rights is to encourage invention and innovation by protecting property owners from competition so that they can recover their investment. The obvious danger in creating such rights too readily and of defining them too widely is that monopolies will be granted to those who can afford to invest most in research and development or who succeed (perhaps by luck as much as skill or foresight) in getting an idea into commercial circulation first.

Attempts to persuade courts to create new common law intellectual property rights or to extend existing ones are typically undertaken in the form of an action for (tortious) infringement of the alleged right.[26] More often than not, English courts decline to extend the list or to expand the scope of common law intellectual rights on the ground that the creation of such rights is properly a job for the legislature, not the courts. This is a difficult argument to assess in the abstract because both the superior courts and the legislature have law-making powers in our system, and there is no clear line of demarcation between the law-making responsibilities of judges and legislators. After all, the judges recognized business goodwill as property; so why not other "trade values" as well? This issue about the proper scope of judicial law-making is a pervasive one throughout the law in general and the law of tort in particular.[27] For example, it has been said by judges in the highest courts that the protection of the financial interests of houseowners against shoddy builders (a form of "consumer protection") is a matter for the legislature, not the courts. The fact is that in the absence of some relevant legislative provision prohibiting the courts from deciding particular issues (which are rare), it is the judges themselves who must decide the scope of their own law-making powers; and the courts have not developed any coherent theory about the proper scope or operation of their law-making power.

The fact that much of the law of tort has always been judge-made means that the courts inevitably play, and will continue to play, an important and large law-making role in this area. But in relation to tort law, as indeed in relation to all other areas of the law, the law-making competence of the courts is shaped and limited by their constitutional position vis-a-vis the legislature. Tort law is a complex amalgam of rules and principles made by the judges and by legislators.

[26] In one sense, the question of whether a property right exists is not a question of tort law but one of property law. However, this point is of no relevance to the present discussion because it is clear that the courts have the power, as a matter of constitutional theory, to invent new property rights. Given the way that English law is categorized, it is impossible entirely to disentangle property law and tort law.

[27] See the general discussion at p. 19 above.

In some cases the courts extend the protections of tort law in ways which the legislature might never have done; in other areas the legislature may develop tort law in ways which the courts, left to themselves, would never have done. As law-makers, the courts and the legislature, for a variety of reasons, operate quite differently; and, of course, any law made by the courts can be overturned by statute. But in practice, tort law is a result of a legislative partnership between the courts and Parliament, albeit one not regulated by any precise division of labour.

Returning to the topic of common law intellectual property, we should note that while loss suffered as a result of exploitation of goodwill can be recovered in the tort of passing off, damage to goodwill without exploitation is actionable under the head of "malicious (or "injurious") falsehood". This is a form of defamation involving false statements reflecting on someone's business or commercial reputation as opposed to their personal reputation. However, liability depends on proof that D acted "maliciously" which means either that D did not honestly believe that the false statement was true, or that D acted out of some improper motive, that is some motive other than the protection of D's own legitimate interests. The typical case of malicious falsehood arises as between business competitors, and this probably explains why malice has to be proved: otherwise healthy competition might be unduly impeded. In the typical case, too, the tort is actionable *per se*: damage to business reputation need not be proved.

Tort Law and the Protection of Property Interests

A few words of summary might be helpful at this point. The foregoing account shows that tort law protects four important incidents of property: the right to possess, the right to control use and to exploit, the right to enjoy, and the right that property should not be damaged, destroyed or lost. The two most distinctive characteristics of tortious protection of property interests are actionability *per se* and strict liability. As we have seen, however, neither characteristic is universal. Damage is often the gist of tort actions arising out of interference with property interests; and where damage is the gist of the action, the standard of liability is usually negligence or even malice, as in the tort of injurious falsehood. Most types of actionable interference with property rights can only be committed by positive acts, and not by omissions. This may be explained as a trade-off against strict liability and actionability *per se*. So far as tort remedies are concerned, the hallmarks of protection of property are injunctions (and other non-monetary remedies such as orders for possession) and disgorgement remedies – damages and account of profits. Punitive damages are sometimes available, but not according to any rational pattern (because of the rule that such damages may only be awarded under heads of liability for which they had been held to be available before 1964).[28] The complexity of tort law in this area is a reflection of the complexity of our concept of property and of the numerous social functions which property performs. Tort law plays an important part not only in protecting people's interests in property but also in shaping and defining the social roles of property: property is valuable not only as a private resource but also as a social institution on which the edifice of the market economy is built.

Concerning defences to tort claims for interference with property rights, little has been said chiefly because there are few relevant defences to the typical tort claim in this area. Contributory negligence may, of course, provide a defence to a claim for negligent damage to property, as may assumption of risk and illegality. Apart from consent, the only possible defence to a claim for possession would be that D had a right to possession better than P's. Legal authority may provide an answer to a claim for taking possession of property, for entry to property and for nuisance, but is unlikely to be available in other types of case. As we have seen, mistake as to the existence of the plaintiff's property right is rarely an answer; nor can D normally plead that the interference was neither intended nor negligent. Consent is a pivotal idea throughout this area of the law. In many cases, lack of consent to the interference is an element of the claim: for instance, trespass *is* an act unconsented to by the landowner. An important exception is nuisance, where not only is lack of consent not an element of the claim but also it is no defence for D to say that the nuisance existed before P came into proximity with it. A possible explanation for this difference is that a landowner is entitled to control who comes onto the land, but a neighbour has no right to control, in advance, what a person does on their land.[29]

---

[28] See p. 115 above.

[29] Also, although the common law places on a purchaser of an interest in land the burden of discovering defects in it (*"caveat emptor"*), it does not expect a person to bear the burden of discovering problems caused by the use of neighbouring land. See also p. 61 above.

CONTRACTUAL INTERESTS

Contractual Rights

Third Party Interference

There are, essentially, two types of third party interference with contractual rights actionable in tort, namely inducing a party to a contract (C) not to perform it and disabling a party to a contract from
performing it.[30] The basic difference between these two types of
interference is that the former operates through the mind of C
whereas the latter does not. Actionable inducement may take the
form of persuasion (by pointing out advantages to the contracting
party in non-performance or disadvantages in performance) or
threatening the contracting party with adverse consequences if they
perform (intimidation). Damage to P is the gist of interference with
contract. Persuasion and threats are, by their very nature, deliberate
acts, whereas disablement may not, *per se*, be deliberate. However,
there can be no liability for interference with contractual rights unless
D knew (or, perhaps, ought to have known) of the existence of the
relevant contractual provisions. Whereas the basic rule of privity of
contract is that only a party to a contract may sue for loss caused by
breach of it, tort liability for loss caused by interference with contract
is not limited in this way. On the other hand, tort liability is limited
by the requirement of intention: P must prove that D intended to
injure P.

Persuading someone not to perform a contract may be tortious
even if the acts of persuasion are, in themselves (or "independently"),
neither actionable nor even unlawful. While popular morality no
doubt supports liability for breach of contract, it is less clear that it
supports liability for persuasion of breach of contract by conduct
which is not independently unlawful. One view is that if breach of
contract is wrong, inducing (or assisting) it must also be wrong. On
the other hand, a party to a contract is bound by it in a way that third
parties are not, and we might imagine a situation in which it would
not be thought wrong for D to persuade C not to perform a contract
with P which D genuinely considered immoral, even though breach
would be a legal wrong by C. We might think that there would need
to be some reason, over and above the breach induced, for making
inducement actionable.

---

[30] In this section I shall use the terms "non-performance" and "breach" synonymously;
but see p. 85 above.

In practice, liability for inducing breach of contract is most important in two contexts: as between market competitors and as between employers and employees. In the former context, liability for inducement is additionally based on the desirability of preserving the security of transactions. Without stability of contracts, markets could not operate properly; and stability of contracts can be undermined just as much by inducement of breach as by breach itself. We all benefit from healthy competition, and should not seek to undermine it without sound justification. If the law allowed as justification the mere fact that D would benefit in competition with P by persuading C to breach a contract with P, the whole market system would be undermined. In fact, the only sort of justification recognized by law for inducement of breach of contract by persuasion is that D did it to protect some legal right of D's or, possibly, some public interest, which the law considers to be "superior" to the contractual right of the innocent contracting party.

As between employers and employees, inducing breach of contract is, in legal terms, the prime method by which unions organize strikes and other forms of industrial action, and liability for such inducement is the main basis on which employers can legally attack strikes. The law in this area has, for the past century, been a complex amalgam of common law and statute, the former laying down the basic rule of liability for inducing breach of contract, and the latter defining an area of "immunity" from liability the size of which has varied from time to time according to changing political and social views about the desirable balance between the interests of "capital" on the one hand and of "labour" on the other. In this context more than any other, tort law has been at the forefront of bitter arguments about the (ab)use and control of economic power in society. Here, the link between the rights and obligations created by tort law to regulate interactions between individuals, and large economic and political questions about the sort of society we want to live in, could not be clearer.

In tort law, inducing someone not to perform a contract by threatening them is called "intimidation". The rule is that intimidation is actionable only if D's conduct was independently unlawful; and it will be independently unlawful only if that which was threatened was unlawful. Threatening to do something lawful is not itself unlawful in this context. This rule creates an ethically unfathomable distinction between persuasion and threats. The rule that D's conduct must have been independently unlawful also applies to interference with contract by disablement. It is unclear whether the unlawful conduct must also be independently actionable. In light of the fact that there can be liability for interference with contractual rights only if D intended to injure P by bringing about the breach of contract, it might be thought that the additional requirement of unlawfulness is an unnecessary protection for defendants, especially given the existence of the defence of justification. It is true, of course, that much perfectly legitimate market activity involves intentionally inflicting economic loss on another; and in this light, the requirement of unlawfulness may be seen as an additional protection for competitive activity. On the other hand, it is one thing to intend to force one's competitors out of business, but another to do so by inducing or causing others to breach their contracts with one's competitors.

In the industrial relations context, at least, the main remedy in practice for interference with contract is the injunction. As for monetary remedies, compensatory damages are certainly available. It is less clear whether disgorgement or punitive damages can be awarded; but as in other contexts, the law in this respect suffers from a dearth of principled discussion in the cases. From an ethical point of view, if cynical, gain-seeking conduct is ever thought to deserve the disapproval expressed by awards of disgorgement and punitive damages, there is no obvious reason why such damages should not be available, in appropriate cases, for interference with contract. Compensatory damages are calculated according to the rules applying to torts, not breaches of contract, and the latter may be more generous to the plaintiff than the former. To the extent that they are, it might be argued that since the underlying wrong here is breach of contract, D's liability should be calculated according to those rules. This approach is most attractive in cases where the plaintiff in an action for interference with contract is the innocent contracting party. It is less attractive in cases where the plaintiff is a third party. But even in cases of the former type, it might be argued that since tort liability for interference with contract depends on proof of intention to injure, the tort rules are appropriate even if they produce a larger quantum of damages.

A corollary of the requirement of intention for tort liability for interference with contract is that it is, generally,[31] not tortious negligently to cause a person injury by bringing about a breach of contract. In the context of productive market activity, this rule is

---

[31] Liability for private and public nuisance constitute exceptions: see *Tort Law and Economic Interests*, (above n.20), 128.

explicable on the basis that much legitimate market activity consists in inflicting foreseeable financial loss on others. But the rule also applies outside the market context. A common explanation for the rule is a vague concept of fairness: it is often the case that many people may have a financial interest in the performance of a contract to which they are not parties, and to impose liability in favour of such "incidental victims" would be to impose an "undue burden of liability".[32] Losses suffered by incidental victims of interference with contract are called "relational" because they arise by virtue of the victim's relationship with another. Tort law is generally unwilling to impose liability for such losses. The "fairness" of such denial of liability is consistent with cases which suggest that there might, exceptionally, be liability to incidental victims for interference with contract if there was a "special relationship of proximity" between the defendant and the third parties, or if the third parties formed a limited class whom the defendant ought to have had especially in mind as vulnerable to the effects of negligence on D's part. Other cases have taken a different line by suggesting that an incidental victim of a breach of contract should not be allowed to recover if it can be said that the victim ought to have taken steps to protect themselves from loss of the sort occasioned by the interference. The latter line of argument has a more satisfying ethical basis than the former. It seems likely that it will be applied more against business plaintiffs than against individuals; and that its operation will be restricted to financial loss (including, perhaps, physical damage to commercial property). Although the argument is, in essence, that P was contributorily negligent, if successful it leads to denial of liability, not apportionment of damages.

Tort Liability of Contracting Parties

Some breaches of contract are also actionable ("concurrently") as torts at the suit of the innocent party to the contract. This is because one and the same set of facts may contain the elements of more than one cause of action (or "head of legal liability"). A cause of action consists of a set of rules concerned with protected interests and sanctioned conduct. Not all breaches of contract are actionable as torts. The paradigm of a breach of contract actionable as a tort is negligent misfeasance causing physical or financial loss. Contractual nonfeasance is less likely to be actionable in tort because nonfeasance is, in

---

[32] But see p. 70, n. 6 above.

general, less likely to be actionable in tort than misfeasance. Non-negligent breach of contract is also less likely to be tortious because there are few relevant grounds of strict tort liability.

Attached to each cause of action is a set of rules concerning the remedy or remedies available to the plaintiff, including rules governing such matters as remoteness of damage and limitation periods. Ideally, such rules would reflect the interest(s) protected and the conduct sanctioned by the cause of action, so that if two different causes of action arising out of the same facts protected essentially the same interest(s) and sanctioned essentially the same conduct, the remedial rules attaching to the two causes of action would be the same. Only if the causes of action protect different interests or sanction different conduct should there be any difference between the remedial rules attaching to them. Suppose, for instance, that a solicitor causes a client financial loss by negligently drafting a document. Under current law, the client could sue the solicitor in tort for negligence or in contract for breach of a contractual duty of care: the client has "concurrent causes of action in contract and tort". The choice of cause of action is the plaintiff's. Moreover, under current law, by choosing one cause of action rather than the other, the plaintiff may be able to take advantage of a remedial rule (concerning limitation period, for instance) different from that which attaches to the other cause of action. My argument is that remedial rules should reflect the interests protected and the conduct sanctioned by different causes of action, and that they should not vary as between causes of action simply because one is an action "in tort" and another is an action "in contract" (for instance). Tying remedies to categories such as "contract" and "tort" rather than to interests and conduct is a hangover of the formulary way of thinking about law. I am not arguing that more than one cause of action should never arise out of the same set of facts, but only that where they do, any remedial differences between them should reflect differences between the interests protected and the conduct sanctioned by the various causes of action. For instance, in the solicitor example, it is hard to think of a reason why the limitation period for the client's action should differ according to whether the client sues in contract or tort. On the other hand, there may be a good reason to allow the client to bring the action in contract rather than tort in order to obtain the remedy of rescission of the contract (which is, obviously, only available for breach of contract) in addition to damages (which would be available either in contract or tort).

There is no need to examine in detail here the way in which the rules of tort law and the rules of contract law may produce different results in cases of concurrent liability. In practice, the most important area of difference is limitation of actions. The point to be made here is this: remedies and the rules which regulate their availability protect the interests and sanction the conduct which form the building blocks of causes of action in the law of obligations and should, there-fore, reflect those interests and that conduct. The categories of "tort", "contract" and so on are convenient for organizing causes of action and understanding the similarities and differences between them. But to relate remedial rules to such categories rather than to the interests protected and the conduct sanctioned by the various causes of action within the categories would be an example of formularism. It would invest organizational categories with a juridical significance they should not have. As we will see in Chapter 6, this point is of rele-vance throughout the law of obligations.

Contractual Expectancies

Contracts are an important legal vehicle for the mutually advanta-geous transfer of goods and services from one person to another, and they are basic legal form of market activity. A corollary of the import-ance of contract to the operation of a market economy is that people should be free to make what contracts they choose with whom they choose, or not to contract at all. The principle of freedom of contract lies at the heart of that part of contract law which is concerned with the creation (as opposed to the protection) of contractual rights. The principle is much modified by statutory provisions and, to a lesser extent, by common law rules. In order to protect weaker parties from abuse of contracting power ("freedom") by stronger parties, or in order to further social goals, certain sorts of contract are illegal; cer-tain sorts of contractual provisions are declared ineffective or unen-forceable; and contracting parties may be allowed to escape from their contractual commitments and they may be awarded appropri-ate monetary remedies. The law sometimes even requires people to make contracts. Such provisions and rules are treated as part of the law of contract.

The part tort law plays in relation to the exercise of contractual freedom is to provide remedies for two types of interference with its exercise. To prevent someone exercising their freedom to contract or, in other words, to deprive someone of opportunities to contract,

may be tortious.[33] Conversely, it may be tortious to induce someone
to exercise their freedom to contract or in other words, to take an
opportunity to contract. Opportunities to make contracts are what I
refer to by the term "contractual expectancies". In some of the cases,
depriving someone of an opportunity to contract is called "interference with trade".

Deprivation of Contractual Expectancies

Contract is the basic legal form of market activity, and the essence of
competition is interference with the contractual expectancies of
others by luring away their customers. Extensive tort liability for
depriving others of opportunities to contract could undermine competition to an unacceptable extent. In imposing such liability, one of
the functions of tort law is to give effect to ideas about what sorts of
competitive activities are fair and what sorts are unfair. The rules of
tort law about liability for deprivation of contracting opportunities,
when applied to competitive market activities, are, we might say, part
of the common law of unfair competition.[34] The other main practical area of operation of these rules is that of trade disputes between
employees and employers.

Three main heads of tort liability are relevant here: conspiracy,
intimidation and causing loss by unlawful means (or, as I will call it,
"unlawful interference with trade"). Under all of these heads, liability will only arise if D intended to cause damage to P[35] by depriving
P of opportunities to trade. A second conceptual device used to limit
the scope of these heads of liability is that of independent unlawfulness. As a general rule, it is not tortious to deprive another of opportunities to contract by conduct (or "means") not intrinsically
unlawful. The only type of intrinsically lawful conduct which can
definitely be said to be capable of attracting liability is "simple conspiracy". A conspiracy is, essentially, an agreement. There are two
forms of conspiracy actionable in tort: "simple conspiracy", which
does not involve the use of unlawful means, and "unlawful means
conspiracy" which does. The traditional view of conspiracy is that
the element of agreement or combination is important in justifying
the imposition of liability. This is why an agreement to do a lawful

[33] Note that loss of opportunities to contract may result from interference with property
or contractual interests, and damages for such loss may be recoverable in tort actions to protect such interests. Here we are concerned with loss of opportunities to contract which are
not consequential upon interference with some other protected interest.

[34] Another part is the doctrine of restraint of trade in contract law.

[35] Damage is the gist of all these heads of liability.

act with the intention of injuring another's trade may be tortious when such conduct by one person acting alone would not be. The traditional view would also be consistent with saying that the unlawful means need not be independently actionable in order for a conspiracy to use them to be actionable. By contrast, another view is that conspiracy is a form of "secondary liability";[36] and since there can be secondary liability only if there is also a primary liability, a conspiracy to use unlawful means could only be actionable if the unlawful means were independently actionable. Even on the traditional view, simple conspiracy is now widely thought to be anomalous; but it is doubly so under the "secondary liability" view. The requirement of unlawfulness is crucially important in preventing the legal concept of "unfair competition" getting too far out of step with non-legal ideas of commercial morality and unduly restricting competition.

A third device used to limit the scope of these torts is the defence of justification. The defence is most important in relation to simple conspiracy – in this context, commercial self-interest justifies agreements to injure another. Where the means used were unlawful, commercial self-interest would be unlikely to provide a defence. Indeed, in general, the use of unlawful means would typically be difficult to justify. The main remedies for interference with trade are injunctions and damages.

Besides common law heads of liability for deprivation of opportunities to contract, there are various important statutory grounds of liability. For example, one of the main aims of the Sex Discrimination Act 1975 and the Race Relations Act 1976 is to provide monetary remedies for being deprived of employment or other contracting opportunities on grounds of sex or race. In contrast to the position under the common law heads discussed above, liability is strict; but there are a few statutory grounds of justification. The strictness of the liability is explicable in terms of the definition of the sanctioned conduct. At common law, the concept of "interference with trade" is so wide that it needs to be narrowed; and this is partly done by the requirement that the interference be aimed at injuring another. By contrast, the conduct proscribed by these statutes is much more narrowly defined with a view to its elimination; hence, strict liability.

There are statutory causes of action directed at anti-competitive practices in various sectors of the economy involving refusals to contract with certain individuals or refusals to contract except on

---

[36] D.J. Cooper, *Secondary Liability for Civil Wrongs*, Unpublished Ph.D. thesis, Cambridge, 1995.

onerous terms.[37] On the whole, however, the common law and statutory causes of action in tort play only a very minor part in protecting market participants from unfair practices by other participants.
Because of the large-scale nature of much anti-competitive activity,
government regulation and the criminal law are thought to be more
effective than individual tort actions in controlling such activity. For
the same reason, individual tort actions in this area would often pose
large economic questions about the operation of the market which
courts think better and more properly dealt with by non-judicial
governmental bodies. Because individuals are part of society, disputes
between them often have wide implications for large numbers of
people. If the courts feel incompetent or ill-equipped to assess such
implications, they may react by refusing to provide a remedy, thus
leaving it to aggrieved citizens to seek redress through other chan-
nels. In this way, the courts may attempt to place issues with which
they feel uncomfortable onto the political agenda; or, at least, to get
them into government in-trays. In this way, institutional issues about
the role of judges and courts in the processes of public decision-
making may have an impact on the substance of tort law. Tort law is
certainly a set of ethical principles of individual responsibility, but it
is not a self-contained or closed system of reasoning based solely on
principles of personal ethics. The principles of responsibility it consists of are based on and influenced by a complex mixture of individ-
ualistic, social and institutional concerns.

Finally, we should note that as a matter of common law, negligent
interference with opportunities to contract is not, as a general rule,[38]
actionable in tort. In competitive contexts, this rule is designed to
preserve competition which, by its very nature, often involves such
conduct. In other contexts, the rule is probably based on the idea that
people should take steps to protect themselves from negligent, non-
competitive interference with their trading interests. Trading interests, it might be thought, deserve less legal protection than certain
other types of interest.

Inducement of Contracting

In this context, the essence of the sanctioned conduct is inducing a
person to enter a contract by making a false statement about how

---

[37] For details see *Tort Law and Economic Interests*, (above n.20), 160–5.

[38] The exceptions to the rule arise out of liability for private and public nuisance. In relation to private nuisance, the explanation of the exception is probably that the loss of opportunities to contract is seen as consequential on interference with a property interest. The
public nuisance exception is harder to explain.

financially beneficial the contract is likely to be to that person. The contract may, but need not, be with the maker of the statement. There are two common law heads of tort liability: deceit and negligent misstatement. There is no strict common law tort liability for false statements except for defamatory statements. Deceit (or "fraud") involves making a false statement knowing it to be false or not caring whether it is true or false, with the intention of inducing a person to rely on it to their detriment. Liability for negligent misstatement arises only if D "assumed responsibility" to P for the truth of the statement. This opaque concept is designed to mark out those cases in which it is reasonable to allow a person to rely on the accuracy of another's statement without taking independent advice. In cases where the maker of the statement is the other party to the contract, the law will treat the former as having assumed responsibility. In other cases, there is no general principle which determines when someone will be held to have assumed responsibility for their statements. However, it has been held, for instance, that an auditor who makes negligent misstatements about the financial position of a company is not liable in tort to purchasers of shares in the company who rely on the auditor's report.[39] Also, the maker of a statement would not be held to have assumed responsibility for its accuracy if the statement was such that, or it was made in circumstances where, it was not, objectively judged, reasonable for P to rely on it.

The concept of assumption of responsibility exploits a distinction between obligations imposed on a person by law and obligations voluntarily undertaken by that person. There is a strong underlying assumption in much discussion of tort law that whereas it is perfectly acceptable for the law to impose on people obligations in respect of physical injuries to persons and property regardless of their will, in respect of purely financial injuries[40] the law should only (re-)enforce obligations which people have, in some sense, taken upon themselves by deliberate conduct (such as making a contract or agreeing to be (or acting like) a trustee). In general, we expect people to look after their own purely financial interests to a greater extent than we expect them to look after their "physical" interests. However, the words "in general" are of very great significance. For instance, the law of tort imposes important obligations designed to protect financial interests in property. Unauthorized exploitation of another's property may be actionable not because of any obligation undertaken by D but

---

[39] *Caparo Plc v. Dickman* [1990] 2 AC 605.

[40] That is, financial injuries which are not consequential upon physical injury.

because, on the contrary, D did not contract with P for the use of the property. Moreover, in the law of contract and trusts, there are a variety of grounds on which legal obligations may be imposed on a person in the absence of any deliberate conduct on the part of that person acknowledging the existence of an obligation. Imposed obligations are of essentially the same nature whether they are thought of as being part of the law of contract, trusts, tort, or anything else. The important question, regardless of the legal category in which it arises, is whether the law ought to impose an obligation or whether it should only reinforce an obligation already witnessed or acknowledged or undertaken by deliberate action. The fact is that the concept of "assumption of responsibility" as it is used in tort law normally signals the imposition and not the reinforcement of an obligation. The crucial difference between obligations imposed by tort law and those imposed by contract law or the law of trusts is that in the latter case, obligations are imposed as an adjunct or an addition to obligations arising from deliberate conduct, whereas in tort law they may be imposed in the absence of any relevant deliberate "obliging conduct".

A false statement which induces a person to enter a contract may also be a term of the contract; and if the maker of the statement was the other party to the contract, the plaintiff may have rights of action in contract as well as in tort in relation to the statement. Moreover, in addition to the common law heads of tort liability already mentioned, there are various statutory heads of tort liability for negligent misstatement under statutes such as the Misrepresentation Act 1967 (s. 2(1)) and the Financial Services Act 1986. The main remedy for tortious misstatement is compensatory damages. Neither disgorgement nor punitive damages are available in a common law action for negligence, and it is unclear whether they are available in a deceit action. Restitutionary remedies are available in certain circumstances under the Financial Services Act, but not under the Misrepresentation Act.

NON-CONTRACTUAL EXPECTANCIES

The next interest to be considered is the opportunity to secure financial gains by means other than the making of an advantageous contract. One example of this interest is that of a intended beneficiary under a will. If, as a result of negligence on the part of a lawyer, an intended beneficiary fails to receive a legacy, the lawyer may be liable to the disappointed beneficiary for the value of the expected gift. The technical explanation of the liability is that the lawyer assumes responsibility to the beneficiary, despite the fact that the lawyer may never have had any contact with the beneficiary and even if, at the time of the alleged negligence, the beneficiary knew nothing either of the testator, the will or the lawyer. Underlying this technicality is the idea that since the testator has died, nothing can be done to perfect the beneficiary's intended claim on the testator's estate; and since the beneficiary could not reasonably have been expected to do anything to protect his or her own financial interest, as between the beneficiary and the negligent lawyer, the latter should pay. By contrast, in a case in which a lawyer negligently failed to draft an *inter vivos* deed of gift, allowing the donor time to change his mind, the lawyer was held not liable. In terms of either the donees' interests or the lawyers' conduct, this difference of outcome is difficult to justify even though it might be widely accepted as intuitively fair.

In practice, the most important source of protection for non-contractual expectancies in tort law is the Fatal Accidents Act 1976. If a person's death was a result of the tort, a "fatal accident" claim may be brought under the Act on behalf of any "dependants" of the deceased. The prime purpose of such a claim is to compensate intimates of the deceased for loss of (actual and) expected financial support as a result of the death. Damages for non-pecuniary loss are limited to a small fixed amount for "bereavement" and are recoverable only by a small sub-class of eligible claimants. Most wrongful death actions are based on negligent conduct, and for this reason, such actions represent the major exception to the unwillingness of tort law to compensate for negligent interference with relational interests. Actions by which employers could recover damages for loss of the services of injured employees, and by which husbands could recover damages for loss of the services and "consortium" of injured wives (which had a long history) fell into disfavour and disuse in the course of the 20th century, and were finally abolished by statute in 1981 because they were inconsistent with contemporary ideas about individual autonomy: the implication of such actions was that the plaintiff in some sense "owned" the services of the injured person. In general, tort law does not compensate a person for financial loss flowing from injuries to another (as opposed to the other's death). There is, however, one head of tort damages for personal injury which effectively compensates one person for financial loss resulting from injury to another. If A gratuitously cares for P, P can recover from D damages representing the "reasonable value" of A's services, and P must pay the damages over to A.

The law's relative unwillingness to compensate one person for financial loss resulting from injury to or the death of another is often said to arise from a fear of floods of actions by people with a more or less remote financial stake in the other's activities. This fear typically rests on a perceived danger of clogging the legal system with claims and of imposing on tortfeasors unfair burdens of liability.[41] The latter concern could be rephrased in terms of personal responsibility. In modern society, the autonomy and separate identity of each individual is highly-prized. If I injure someone, my responsibility is to that person above all, and to those members of the person's immediate family who are most closely affected. The web of financial interdependencies in society is large and complex, but once we get beyond the centre of the web, people must take steps to protect their own financial interests. The classes of claimant listed in the Fatal Accidents Act represent the law's attempt to describe what is meant by "the centre of the web", and the head of damages for loss of income in the lost years is designed to benefit the same classes of person. In practice, most gratuitous carers also fall within one of the FA Act classes. In personal injury tort law, a concept of family intimacy represents the law's attempt to place acceptable bounds on the responsibility of tortfeasors for losses resulting from the tort but suffered by people other than the personal injury victim. Those not in the family circle must look after themselves. The reason why tort law protects the relational interests of intimates in cases of death but not of non-fatal injury is that in the latter type of case, the interests of the intimates can be protected through the injured person's claim. This reasoning is reflected in the head of damages for loss of income in the lost years.

TRADE VALUES

The term "trade values" refers to a person's interest in exploiting the fruits of his or her skill and effort for financial gain. One way in which the law protects trade values is by creating property rights in them (thus creating "intellectual property"). A person may also be able to protect their trade values by contract – franchising and "character merchandising" are common examples. For the "creator", one of the main advantages of the property technique over the contractual is that property rights can be enforced against people generally

---

[41] But see p. 70, n. 6 above.

whereas contractual rights can only be enforced against those who have made contracts for the exploitation of the trade value. A third legal technique for protecting trade values is to create rights of action which, in effect, establish obligations not to engage in conduct which exploits a person's trade values. There are various statutes which create such rights which can be enforced by means of an action for breach of statutory duty. The normal civil remedies for breach of statutory duty are injunctions and compensatory damages. Some of the statutes provide for other remedies, such as delivery up of illicit recordings of musical performances or an account of profits.

Apart from these statutory causes of action, it is often suggested that the common law should recognize a general principle of liability for unauthorized exploitation of trade values – or in a long-established pithy phrase, for "reaping without sowing". English courts have always resisted the adoption of so general a principle of liability for "unfair competition", essentially on the ground that in the modern world, it is a job best left to the legislature to decide how far and by what means the law should protect the interests of creators in exploiting their creative powers for financial gain. The only important judicial activity in this area is found in the law of passing off. The essence of passing off as developed in the nineteenth century was causing loss to another by misrepresenting one's own goods or services to be those of the other and thus confusing consumers into buying one's own goods or services instead of the other person's. The courts are constantly being asked to extend passing off to cases involving neither misrepresentation or confusion, and they have made moves in this direction in recent years. However, the tort of passing off is still a long way from embodying the principle that one must not reap without sowing; and recent changes in the statutory law of trademarks make it less likely that the common law will develop in this direction. Once again, then, we find the substance of tort law being moulded and affected by considerations of institutional competence.

INFLICTION OF FINANCIAL LOSS

Finally, we must examine cases in which the form of the complaint is simply that as a result of D's conduct, P is financially worse off or, in other words, that P has suffered financial loss. Some grounds of liability for intentional conduct such as malicious prosecution or abuse of legal process and liability for "misfeasance in a public office" may provide a platform for such a complaint. A claim that as a result of a misstatement by D (whether fraudulent of negligent) P gave money away to C would fall into this category. Relational losses may also be considered here. Relational losses (it will be recalled) are losses suffered by P as a result of injury to another (A). Cases of relational losses arising out of a contractual relationship between P and A were considered earlier.[42] A person may also suffer non-contractual relational losses as where, for instance, a parent pays the medical expenses of an injured child or where a citizen suffers financial loss as a result of closure of a bridge owned by a public body after it is damaged by negligent navigation of a vessel by D. In the former case, the parent's losses would be taken into account in assessing the child's damages. In the latter type of case, the rules governing D's liability are similar to those dealing with liability for contractual relational losses.

Another important type of case to be discussed in this context is one where P receives a substandard service from D, or acquires premises or goods which are defective as a result of D's unintentional conduct, having paid more for the services or the premises or the goods than they are worth. To the extent that P suffers personal injury or physical damage to tangible property as a result of D's conduct, P's remedy will depend on rules we have already examined concerning tort liability for these types of injury. Our concern here is with purely financial loss, that is financial loss not consequential upon physical injury to person or property. Such loss may consist of the amount by which the services provided or the premises or goods acquired were, by virtue of their substandard or defective nature, worth less than what P paid for them; or of financial loss consequential upon that substandard or defective nature, such as loss of profits or the cost of hiring a substitute while defective goods are repaired.

The general rule of common law is that purely financial loss flowing from the acquisition of defective premises, goods or services is recoverable in a tort action for negligence only if D assumed responsibility to P for the quality of the thing acquired. We have already observed the opaqueness of this criterion of liability, and it is necessary to say a little more about when a defendant might be held to have assumed responsibility. In the first place, it seems that the negligent provider of a financial service is more likely to be held to have assumed responsibility than the negligent builder of premises or producer of goods. Indeed, there is a strong body of authority for the

42 See p. 153 above.

proposition that under normal circumstances, builders and manufacturers do not assume responsibility to purchasers of their output for the quality of that output and so are not normally liable to them in tort for purely economic loss flowing from the defectiveness of the output. Secondly, whether an assumption of responsibility will be found depends partly on a judgement of the court about whether it would be reasonable to expect P to protect his or her own financial interests in some way. In one case, for example, it was held that a ship surveyor who negligently certified for the owner that a ship was seaworthy was not liable in tort to the owner of cargo being carried on the ship for financial loss suffered when it sank. The underlying rationale of the decision appears to be that it was reasonable to expect the cargo owner, which was a commercial entity, to protect itself from such financial loss by taking out insurance, for instance.

This last example also raises two other interesting and important points. The first arises from the fact that although the injury suffered by the cargo owner consisted of physical loss of its property, the court effectively treated its loss as purely economic. This might suggest that in tort law, interests in commercial property receive less protection than interests in non-commercial property, and that the rules discussed above about liability for physical damage to and loss of tangible property may not always apply to commercial property which is viewed by its owner purely as a financial asset. So far as physical damage is concerned, tort law has traditionally given tangible property a status and protection similar to that accorded to a person's body. This attitude dates from a time when tangible property was by far the most common form of wealth. Moreover, people often form emotional attachments to tangible property. Now that intangible property is just as, if not more, important as a form of wealth, we have come to realize that tangible property is often nothing more than a form of wealth, and so there may be no reason to treat damage to or loss of tangible property as anything more than a loss of wealth.

The second point concerns the nature of the surveyor's responsibility for the loss of the cargo. The surveyor was not the immediate cause of the loss of the cargo. The immediate cause was the putting to sea of an unseaworthy ship. The surveyor's negligent act merely failed to prevent the loss of the cargo. Thus it could be said that the person primarily responsible for maintaining the ship in a seaworthy condition and for the decision to put to sea was the shipowner; and that the surveyor was only secondarily responsible for the condition of the ship and the decision to sail. Courts are less willing to hold that a party who was secondarily responsible in a causal sense has "assumed responsibility" for economic loss than to hold that a primarily responsible party has.

A final point about assumption of responsibility follows from this one. Courts are extremely unwilling to impose tort liability on a defendant for failure to protect another from purely financial loss, unless the defendant has been paid to provide protection. Moreover, even if there is a contract between P and D, liability for failure to protect a person from financial loss may only be imposed if the contract expressly requires D to provide protection. Put another way, the most the law will normally do is to reinforce an undertaking to provide protection based on deliberate conduct of D creating the undertaking.

If tort liability is imposed for purely financial loss resulting from acquisition of substandard services or defective premises or goods, the only remedy available will be compensatory damages.

There are some statutory grounds of liability relevant to the present discussion. Worthy of note is the Defective Premises Act 1972 which creates a statutory cause of action primarily directed towards purely financial loss, in particular the cost of repair. The cause of action only relates to "dwellings". This reflects the idea that commercial building owners can reasonably be expected to protect their financial interests to a greater extent that owners of dwellings. This idea also finds expression in the regime of liability for defective products under the Consumer Protection Act 1987 which allows recovery for physical damage to tangible property but only if the property was not being used commercially. Under both Acts, the only remedy available is compensatory damages.

It is, finally, worth observing again that whereas the sanction for contributory negligence is reduction of damages, the sanction for failing to take reasonable steps to protect one's own financial interests or for unreasonably relying on the statement of another without checking it is total denial of liability. The preference for the latter approach in relation to purely financial loss is, no doubt, another expression of the idea that financial interests may deserve less protection than physical interests unless they are bolstered by contract or are hallowed with the status of property.

CAUSALITY

Under some heads of tort liability, the sanctioned conduct is defined simply as some act, such as unauthorized entry onto land or refusing someone a job on grounds of sex. Typically in such cases, liability is strict; in other words, it attaches if the specified act was done, full stop. Strict liability for specified conduct is never imposed in the law of tort in respect of nonfeasance. Under other heads of tort liability, the sanctioned conduct is defined as some act or omission plus some consequence of the act or omission, typically injury, harm, loss or damage of some sort suffered by the plaintiff.[43] Under such heads, the consequence is said to be the "gist" of the plaintiff's claim. Such liability for conduct-plus-consequences may be strict but, in tort law, it is usually fault-based.

Under heads of liability for conduct-plus-consequences, the consequences form part of the description of the interest protected by the head of liability; and a crucial factor in linking P's protected interest to D's sanctioned conduct is the concept of causation. The defendant's conduct is related to the plaintiff's interest in a way which justifies the law in sanctioning it only if the conduct caused the consequences which are part of the description of the protected interest of the plaintiff. Even under heads of liability which sanction conduct without reference to its consequences, causation is a vital link in cases where P seeks to recover in respect of some consequence of the sanctioned conduct (such as damage to buildings caused by an unauthorized entrant). Causation is also relevant in cases where P, having established D's liability (whether or not under a head of liability defined in terms of conduct-plus-consequences), claims disgorgement damages. In such a case, P must prove that D's gain was causally related to the tort. The purpose of the first part of this section is to discuss the concept of causation. The second part examines the doctrine of "remoteness of damage". Rules of remoteness modify the basic principle that a tortfeasor is liable for all, but only, the harm caused by the tort.

Causation

In a tort action where P complains of some consequence of D's tortious conduct, the causal question is not, what was the cause of the consequence? but rather, did D's conduct cause the consequence? In tort law, the main criterion used for answering this question is

---

[43] Doing harm is the central form of causality in tort law. But there are other forms which may attract tort liability, such as failing to prevent harm occurring (omission), providing the opportunity for the commission of a tort (as in *Stansbie* v. *Troman* [1948] 2 KB 48), and authorizing, inducing or assisting the commission of a tort (secondary liability). See further p. 168 below.

necessity: was D's conduct a necessary condition of the occurrence of the consequence of which P complains? This criterion is often expressed in terms of the "but-for" test: can we say that the consequence would not have occurred but for D's tortious conduct? In other words, would the consequence have happened if D had acted non-tortiously rather than tortiously? There are some circumstances, however, in which the this test produces counter-intuitive results. Suppose D1 negligently collides with P's car and causes it damage which could only be repaired by replacing a door. Before the repair is done, D2 negligently collides with P's car and causes damage which could only be repaired by replacing the same door. For the purposes of tort law, the conduct of D1 and that of D2 have resulted in the same damage to P (the cost of having the door replaced); and applying the but-for test, neither D1's negligence nor D2's negligence was a necessary condition of the damage occurring. On the contrary, each act of negligence was sufficient by itself to necessitate the replacing of the door. So according to the necessity criterion, neither D1 nor D2 caused the damage to P's car! This defect in the necessity test can be overcome by combining it with the criterion of sufficiency so that D's conduct will count as a cause if it was a necessary element in a set of conditions which together were sufficient to bring about the complained-of consequence. This has been called the "NESS test".[44] Under the NESS test, both the conduct of D1 and that of D2 in the above example would count as causes of the damage.

Both the but-for test and the NESS test are more or less capable of explaining various different types of causal link encountered in tort law. The simplest type of causal link is illustrated by a case where D injures P by hitting P with his hand. Slightly more complex is where, for instance, D injures P by shooting him from a distance with a gun – here the injury is caused through the medium of the gun and the bullet. A similar type of case occurs where, for example, D injures P by pushing C against him. Several complex forms of causality can be illustrated by reference to liability for interference with contract. Such liability may be based on the disabling of another from performing the contract. By contrast, interference by inducement and threats both involve influencing another person's mental processes. The same is true of the making of a false statement – a statement will result in loss only if someone's mental state is affected by it (for instance, by coming to think the worse of P as a result of the making

---

[44] R. Wright, "Causation in Tort Law" (1985) 73 *California LR* 1741.

of a defamatory statement) or if someone does something in reliance on it (such as entering a contract). Other forms of causality which may attract tort liability are assisting another to commit a tort, and providing the opportunity for another to do so (the latter is important in vicarious liability).

Omissions may, at first glance, seem problematic in terms of causation: it may be thought odd to say that an omission can be a cause. But a failure to act may satisfy both the but-for test and the NESS test. Our unease about calling an omission a cause is partly a result of viewing the world as "a matrix into which, by our movements . . . we introduce changes".[45] However, the main source of worry about holding a person responsible for inaction is related not to causation but rather to the morality of imposing duties of positive action. In tort law, this issue is dealt with in terms of the concept of "duty of care".

Because of the way the causal question is posed in a tort action (did D's tortious conduct cause the consequence of which P complains?), the concept of necessity (whether or not supplemented by the concept of sufficiency) is often adequate to answer it. This is so even though necessity is a very indiscriminate criterion of causation by reason of the fact that for every event in the world there is an indefinite number of necessary conditions, and the necessity test gives them all equal significance. When human conduct occurring at a particular time combines with surrounding circumstances (other necessary conditions) to produce a particular consequence at that time or not too much later, we tend, at least for the purposes of tort law, to treat the human conduct as the "operative" or "effective" cause. Only if there was something quite abnormal in the surrounding circumstances might we treat it, rather than the human conduct, as the cause. But it is important to realize that even in straightforward cases, in treating the human agent as the cause we are doing more than just applying the necessity test, because even in the simplest case, the human conduct in question will be only one of a very large number of causal factors which satisfy the necessity criterion. The fact that a causal factor (A) satisfies this criterion in relation to an outcome (B) is not, by itself, the basis on which we might say that A "caused" B. For instance, there can be no fire without oxygen; but in most situations we would not say that oxygen "causes" fires.

---

[45] T. Honoré, "Are Omissions Less Culpable?" in P. Cane and J. Stapleton (eds), *Essays for Patrick Atiyah*, 31, 41.

However, the only type of situation which causes significant practical problems in applying the necessity test in tort law is one in which the complained-of consequence can be traced to two (or more) torts each of which was sufficient by itself to bring about the consequence. As noted earlier, in this type of case the but-for test produces the answer that neither tortfeasor is a cause, whereas the NESS test produces the answer that both of the tortfeasors are causes. Where the torts operate contemporaneously, English tort law treats them both as causes. Where they are separated in time, the first is treated as the cause and the latter is relieved of liability on the basis that a tortfeasor may "take the victim as found", and by the time the second tort had produced its consequence, the first had already brought exactly that consequence about.[46] This approach also applies where D's tort produces for P a consequence which a non-tortious cause had already produced: the tortfeasor escapes liability. The take-victim-as-found rule may seem hard to explain in terms of ethical notions of personal responsibility: surely the prior condition of the victim is just a matter of chance, outside the tortfeasor's control, which does not affect the culpability of the tortious conduct. However, on reflection we can see that this argument proves too much because the whole idea of causation in tort law is open to the same objection: it may be a matter of luck whether or not a person's risky conduct causes injury and, consequently, whether or not it attracts liability. People engage in risky conduct all the time without causing injury and, consequently, without incurring tort liability. This observation helps to explain the result in a case where a tortfeasor's conduct caused P to suffer a bad back. Some time later, P developed a natural condition which would have given him an equally bad back even if D's tort had not occurred. D was held liable for P's bad back only up until the time that P's later condition developed. A tortfeasor would probably also escape liability if the tort operated contemporaneously with a natural causal factor sufficient to cause the complained-of consequence. By the rules of causation, tort law gives some of the benefit of chance to victims, and some to tortfeasors. In this respect, as in others, tort law seeks to reflect and, perhaps, to supplement, commonly-held notions of personal responsibility and to strike a fair balance between the interests of victims and the interests of injurers.

---

[46] This result can be expressed in causal terms by saying that a person cannot cause a consequence which has already occurred: T. Honoré, "Necessary and Sufficient Conditions in Tort Law" in D.G. Owen (ed), *Philosophical Foundations of Tort Law*, (Oxford, 1995), 363.

Burden of Proof

When causation is an issue in a tort action, the plaintiff must normally prove that D's tortious conduct caused P's loss (or D's gain) (in the sense of satisfying the but-for or NESS test) "on the balance of probabilities". This means that P's claim will succeed only if it is more probable than not that D's conduct was the cause. In numerical terms, P must prove that D's conduct increased the risk of the complained-of consequence by more than 50 percent. The balance-of-probabilities test operates in an all-or-nothing way: if it is satisfied, P is entitled to a remedy for the consequences attributed to D's conduct; and if it is not satisfied, D escapes liability entirely. An implication of this rule about burden of proof is that as a matter of tort law, D's conduct may be held to be the cause of the complained-of consequence even though, in fact, D's conduct was not the cause. In criminal law, the burden of proof is much higher – "beyond reasonable doubt". This difference is usually said to reflect the greater social stigma and the potentially more serious penalties which attach to criminal as contrasted with civil liability. We are willing to hold a person civilly liable on weaker grounds than we require for the imposition of criminal liability.[47] Not only are notions of criminal responsibility different from those used in civil law,[48] but also we demand more evidence of personal responsibility in criminal than in civil law. One result of this is that if a person's conduct constitutes at one and the same time a tort and a criminal offence, the person may be acquitted of criminal liability but held liable in tort.[49]

In some types of case it may be very difficult for the plaintiff to discharge the balance-of-probabilities burden of proof. This is particularly so in cases of medical negligence and where the plaintiff's injury is an illness or a disease as opposed to a traumatic injury (such as a broken leg). For example, suppose that P is negligently denied a medical procedure with a high, but less than even, chance of success. Or suppose that P contracts a disease which has a number of possible causes, one of which is D's negligence, in circumstances where is it not possible to say on the balance of probabilities which of the causes was operative in P's case. Or suppose that P is negligently injured by

[47] This illustrates the importance of the sanction attached to particular conduct to ideas about personal responsibility for that conduct.

[48] For instance, a reprehensible mental state is much more often a requirement for criminal than for civil liability.

[49] This may be controversial: J. Stapleton, "Duty of Care: Peripheral Parties and Alternative Opportunities for Deterrence" (1995) 111 *LQR* 301, 326-7.

taking a drug of a type produced by a number of manufacturers in circumstances where it is not possible to prove on the balance of probabilities who manufactured the particular doses which P took. In such cases, P may be able to prove that D's negligence increased the risk of P's injury, but not that D's negligence increased the risk by more than 50 percent. This may appear to be a problem if compensating injured persons in circumstances such as these is thought to be a proper or desirable function for tort law to perform.

Two different approaches have been tried in attempts to overcome the problem. The first is to say that it is enough, in some cases at least, for P to prove that D's tortious conduct significantly increased the risk of P's injury, even though the increase was 50 percent or less. In cases where the increase in risk can be arithmetically quantified (say, 25 percent), a second approach is to argue that P should be able to succeed by proving, on the balance of probabilities, that as a result of D's conduct, P lost a 25 percent chance of avoiding the injury. The first approach involves modifying the burden of proof, while the second involves redefining the loss which P must prove (on the balance of probabilities) that D's conduct caused: P's loss is not the injury but the (25 percent) chance of avoiding the injury. Under this second approach, P's damages would be assessed as a proportion (25 percent) of what they would be if the loss had been the injury itself. Unlike the first approach and the balance-of- probabilities test, which are all-or-nothing rules, this second approach contemplates liability "proportional to risk".

Both the all-or-nothing and the proportional approaches have advantages for plaintiffs and defendants respectively, and corresponding disadvantages for defendants and plaintiffs respectively. The proportional approach makes it easier for the plaintiff to recover something, but reduces the risk that the defendant will have to pay out in full. On the other hand, the all-or-nothing, balance-of-probabilities approach makes it harder for P to establish liability, but once this is done, recovery follows according to the generous full compensation principle. It is by no means clear that either approach is ethically preferable to the other. In contrast, lowering the standard of proof below balance-of-probabilities under the all-or-nothing approach disadvantages defendants without offering them any compensating advantage and so, it might be argued, fails to strike a fair balance between the interests of plaintiffs and defendants.

The House of Lords has rejected the approach which involves lowering the standard of proof under the all-or-nothing rule.[50] The second (proportional) approach is followed in some cases. For example, if a solicitor negligently fails to begin a tort action in time so that the plaintiff fails to win any damages, the plaintiff may be able to sue the solicitor for loss of the chance of winning damages. If P can prove, on the balance of probabilities, that if the solicitor had not been negligent the action would have gone ahead with a significant chance of success, P's damages against the solicitor will be assessed as a percentage of what P would have recovered if the action which was never started had been successful, depending on the estimated chance that that action would have succeeded. In one case, however, the House of Lords refused to allow a plaintiff to recover damages proportional to the (25 percent) chance that a medical procedure which he had been negligently denied would have been successful and would have prevented him developing a medical condition.[51] The court did not address the question of whether "loss of a chance" can form the subject of an award of damages in a tort action but interpreted the claim as being that D had increased the risk of the condition which P developed by 25 percent; and since P could not prove that D had increased the risk by more than 50 percent, the claim failed.

These two different attitudes to awarding damages proportional to risk may be explicable by reference to a factual difference between the two examples.[52] In a tort action the causal issue always involves a hypothetical (or "counterfactual") question: what would have happened if D had acted non-tortiously rather than tortiously? Often this question requires the decision-maker to draw on knowledge and understanding of physical processes. This was so in the medical example given above. By contrast, sometimes answering the hypothetical causal question requires speculation about how someone other than the defendant would have acted. Thus, in the failed action case, the causal link between the solicitor's negligence and the plaintiff's loss had to be traced through the hypothetical decision of the court. It may, of course, be very difficult to answer the counterfactual causal question in relation to physical events as well as mental processes. However, it might be argued that there is a qualitative difference, based on the uniqueness of human consciousness, between speculating about what would happen in the natural world and speculating about what a person would do.

---

[50] *Wilsher* v. *Essex AHA* [1988] AC 1074.
[51] *Hotson* v. *East Berks HA* [1987] AC 750.
[52] See *Allied Maples Group Ltd* v. *Simmons & Simmons* [1995] 1 WLR 1602.

There are several difficulties with this explanation. First, in tort law the proportional approach to causation is adopted in speculating about future (as opposed to past) events whether or not the speculation concerns human conduct. As we saw in Chapter 4,[53] speculation about the future is a central feature of the process of assessing damages for losses which P will not suffer until after the date of assessment: the quantum of damages depends on determining what losses will flow from the tort in the future. Secondly, while the proportional approach is applied to speculation about what persons other than P and D would have done in the past if D had not acted tortiously, it is not applied to speculation about what P would have done if D had not committed the tort. An example will illustrate this difference. Suppose that P suffers financial loss as a result of receiving from D negligent advice about P's rights under a contract between P and C. If D had not given negligent advice, P could have attempted to persuade C to accept a renegotiation of the contract, and if C had agreed, P would not have suffered the loss. In this case, answering the counterfactual causal question requires speculation about what P would have done and about what C would have done. The present law appears to be that in relation to what P would have done (would P have attempted to renegotiate?), the test applied is all-or-nothing balance-of-probabilities, whereas in relation to what C would have done, the correct approach is to assess the chance that C would have agreed to the new terms suggested by P, and to award P damages proportional to the chance (providing it is significant) that C would have agreed. The third problem with the explanation is that it does not explain why the response to the need to speculate about human conduct should lead to an abandonment of the all-or-nothing approach rather than adherence to it accompanied by a lowering of the standard of proof below balance of probabilities.

The easiest of these problems to resolve is the different treatment of speculation about third party conduct on the one hand and plaintiff's conduct on the other. It can be argued that it is not unreasonable to expect the plaintiff to satisfy the court about what P would, more probably than not, have done, because information relevant to answering this question is peculiarly within P's knowledge in a way that knowledge about what other people would have done is not. Concerning the use of the proportional approach in assessing damages, the answer may well be that this approach to the assessment of

[53] See p. 106 above.

damages offsets perceived unfairness in the all-or-nothing rule of causation. If this is correct, then the third problem may not give cause for concern: in practice, the distinction between the proportional approach to causation on the one hand, and the all-or-nothing approach to causation coupled with a proportional approach to the assessment of damages on the other, would entail no difference provided that in cases where the proportional approach to causation was adopted, the chance that P might have suffered the loss even if the tort had not occurred was ignored in assessing damages. Moreover, the fact that the proportional approach applies to the assessment of damages perhaps lessens the force of any objection there might be to lowering the standard of proof under the all-or-nothing approach.

If these explanations are accepted, the next obvious question is why the basic rule of liability is an all-or-nothing one rather than a test of proportionality to risk. A practical answer to this question may be that a thoroughgoing system of liability proportional to risk would be exceedingly difficult to operate because in very many cases, the statistical evidence which would be necessary to calculate risks in a mathematically accurate way would not be available. At a theoretical level, the key to answering the question is, I believe, to suggest that tort law, and our non-legal concepts of personal responsibility, seek to strike a fair balance between the interest of the plaintiff in not being interfered with and the interest of the defendant in freedom of action. The rule of no-liability below a threshold and full liability above it is a rough but not obviously unfair compromise between the competing interests of the two parties, especially given that the proportional approach is adopted in the assessment of damages for future loss. On this basis, the only theoretical difference between the proportional approach to causation and the all-or-nothing approach coupled with the proportional approach to assessment of damages lies in the treatment of past losses: under the all-or-nothing approach, these are not assessed proportionally.

The final question which deserves an answer is why the standard of proof under the all-or-nothing approach is set at the balance of probabilities. Earlier we noted the traditional argument in favour of having a lower threshold in civil than in criminal law. But why choose balance of probabilities? The best answer may simply be that the balance-of-probabilities standard is intuitively attractive as a minimum; that it would be difficult to describe clearly in words any particular threshold higher than balance of probabilities and lower than beyond reasonable doubt; and that to use a figure (such as 75 percent) would be pointless given that the statistical information necessary to arrive at such a figure would rarely, if ever, be available. Furthermore, in practice, because reliable statistical evidence will usually be lacking, what matters is not whether the balance-of-probabilities threshold has been reached but whether the court is satisfied that it has. This means that in order to meet the burden of proof, a litigant can do none other than bring before the court all the evidence they have supporting their case and hope that it will satisfy the court that the threshold has been reached.

Remoteness

Rules of remoteness deal with two types of situation. The first is where the harm caused to P by D's tort is of an "unforeseeable" or "unexpected" kind. The basic rule is that D may be liable for harm caused by the tort even if it comes about in an unforeseeable way or is unforeseeably severe, provided only that it is of a foreseeable "kind". In one case, for example, as a result of the negligence of his employer, a farmworker contracted a rare disease, which usually resulted from rat bites, by being exposed to rats' urine. The court held that the harm suffered was of an unforeseeable kind.[54] As this case illustrates, the classification of injuries into "kinds" is by no means unproblematic. The important point to note, however, is that the requirement of foreseeability may relieve D of liability for harm which, according to the principles discussed in the first part of this section, was caused by D's tort.

The second type of situation with which rules of remoteness deal involves "ulterior harm". This term refers to harm which results from the intervention of some independent causal factor (i.e. some factor outside D's control) between D's tort and some harm of which P complains. Suppose, for instance, that D negligently injures P in a road accident. Some weeks later, on the way home from hospital, the taxi in which P is travelling is involved in an accident as a result of the negligence of the driver (C), and P is injured again. Or suppose that D negligently injures P; P requires medical treatment, which is negligently administered by C, causing P further injury. Is D liable for the further injury caused by C as well as for the initial injury? In these examples, D's tort, C's conduct and P's harm are on the same causal chain in the sense that D's tort created the opportunity or the necessity for the conduct of C which harmed P. In each of these

54 *Tremain v. Pike* [1969] 3 All ER 1303.

cases, we would probably treat D's tort as the cause of the "initial harm" suffered by P, but not as the cause of the ulterior harm flowing from C's conduct. The same would be true in cases where the intervening causal factor was some conduct of P or some non-human event. Nevertheless, in some cases, the law may hold D liable for ulterior harm. For example, D would probably be liable for harm resulting from the negligent medical treatment in the second case; and D may be held liable for ulterior harm resulting from conduct of P, provided P's conduct was not "unreasonable". But D would probably not be held liable for the ulterior harm in the taxi case. Moreover, liability for ulterior harm (and, indeed, for initial harm) is more likely to be imposed under some heads of liability than others. For instance, whereas liability for negligent conduct only extends to consequences of a foreseeable kind, liability for fraud extends to "direct" consequences, even if these are of an unforeseeable kind.

What are we to make of this jumble of rules – of the fact that a tortfeasor may not be held liable for initial harm caused by the tort (as in the rat disease case), but may be held liable for ulterior harm not caused by the tort (as in the case of negligent medical treatment); and of the fact that liability for consequences is more extensive under some heads of liability (such as fraud) than under others? I think that the key to understanding what is going on here lies in the relationship between ideas of personal responsibility and the phenomenon of "luck". In this context, "luck" refers to factors outside the tortfeasor's control. As noted earlier,[55] it is often a matter of luck whether or not tortious conduct causes harm and, consequently, attracts liability. Tort law often imposes liability for events and consequences which were in some respect(s) beyond the tortfeasor's control. Elsewhere, I have explained why I believe tort law does this and why, despite appearances, it is not unfair.[56] Nevertheless, control is important to our ideas of personal responsibility, and both within the law and outside it, a person may escape responsibility for events and consequences which were, in some respect(s), beyond their control. The fact is that control influences but does not determine judgements of responsibility. There is an important line to be drawn between factors beyond an agent's control for which the agent may be held

[55] See p. 170 above.
[56] P. Cane, "Retribution, Proportionality and Moral Luck in Tort Law" in P. Cane and J. Stapleton (eds), *The Comparative Law of Torts: Essays in Honour of John G. Fleming* (Oxford, forthcoming, 1998).

responsible and such factors for which the agent will not be held responsible.

In tort law, this line is drawn in terms of the foreseeable and the unforeseeable, the normal and the abnormal, the reasonable and the unreasonable. Thus, an agent's conduct may not be treated as the cause of an event if it operated against a background containing an abnormal causal factor. Similarly, a tortfeasor may not be held liable for ulterior harm resulting from a coincidence (as in the taxi example) or from unreasonable conduct of the plaintiff, but may be held liable for ulterior harm resulting from events within the bounds of "normality" (such as negligent medical treatment). Again, a tortfeasor may not be held liable for unforeseeable initial harm. On the other hand, the more culpable the tortfeasor, the more extensive the liability for consequences beyond the tortfeasor's control – hence the remoteness rule of directness in the tort of deceit as opposed to foreseeability in the tort of negligence. Viewed in this way, the rules of remoteness supplement the rules of causation as a mechanism for drawing the line between factors beyond the tortfeasor's control for which liability may be imposed and those for which D is not expected to answer. The basic underlying idea is that human agents must take as they find it the world in which their conduct occurs and takes effect (including other human agents and their conduct), except to the extent that the world exhibits features which are considered unforeseeable, abnormal or unreasonable. Taking account of the role of luck in human life and in our ideas of personal responsibility is crucial to understanding this and many other aspects of tort law.

Causation and Victim's Conduct

Finally, a few points need to be made about the role of causation in relation to the conduct of the victim. Take defences first. A defence of contributory negligence will succeed only if the plaintiff's negligent conduct contributed (in a but-for or NESS sense) to the losses for which damages are to be awarded which will be the subject of apportionment. A defence of illegality will succeed only if the plaintiff's illegal conduct contributed to P's losses not just in a but-for or NESS sense, but also "directly" (not just "coincidentally").

Secondly, the denial of liability on the basis that the plaintiff ought to have taken steps to protect his or her own interests, or that P relied unreasonably on a statement made by D, rests on the assumption that P's loss was caused by that failure to take protective steps or by the act of reliance. Indeed, the only significance of reliance as a criterion of liability in tort law is causal.

Thirdly, we should note the "doctrine of mitigation". Under this doctrine a defendant will not be held responsible for loss flowing from the tort if the plaintiff could reasonably be expected to have taken some action to prevent the loss occurring. For example, in a personal injury case, a defendant will not be held liable for loss caused by unreasonable refusal by the plaintiff to undergo medical treatment. The doctrine of mitigation, coupled with the doctrine of intervening causation, express the plaintiff's responsibility for losses resulting from P's reactions to the tort, whether acts or omissions.

This brief survey of the various ways in which conduct of the plaintiff is relevant to tort liability prompts the following observation: whereas tort law is more wary of imposing on defendants liability for nonfeasance than liability for misfeasance, no such wariness seems to apply to the attribution of responsibility to plaintiffs for the losses they suffer. Plaintiffs are expected to take reasonable care for themselves even if this requires positive steps. The explanation for this difference in the treatment of plaintiffs and defendants seems grounded on a widely held ethical principle of self-reliance to the effect that people who do not take care of themselves cannot expect others to bear the cost of their lack of care.[57] The main context in tort law in which this principle is not given effect to is that of protecting property from misappropriation and exploitation.[58]

CONCLUSION

In this chapter I have attempted to map the structure of tort law by showing how the components discussed in previous chapters are put together. I have not done this in very great detail, but even so, it is clear that the structure is extremely complex, as is the relationship of tort law with other areas of the law, such as the law of contract and of property. The picture which emerges gives a much sharper account of the ethical foundations of tort law than does the traditional analysis of tort law. It is clear that although tort law rests on ideas of personal responsibility and freedom, these broad ideas find

---

[57] The role of this principle in social welfare systems which do not rest on ideas of personal responsibility is controversial. Witness current debates about whether expensive NHS medical procedures should be made available to smokers and users of other drugs of dependence.

[58] See p. 60 above.

expression in a large variety of more detailed principles and precepts. The question which inevitably arises, and to which I turn in the next chapter, is what, if anything, makes tort law as it is normally understood, a distinctive area of the law. This question raises issues not only about the types of interests which tort law protects, the types of conduct it sanctions and the sanctions it uses, but also about how tort law relates to other parts of the law of obligations.

6. THE DISTINCTIVENESS
OF TORT LAW

THE ARGUMENT SO FAR

I HAVE argued that the best way to understand tort law is as a set of ethical rules and principles of personal responsibility. The three basic elements of the anatomy of tort law are protected interests, sanctioned conduct and sanctions. Heads of tort liability consist of elements relating to protected interests and to sanctioned conduct, and to each head of tort liability attaches a set of remedial rules which reflect (and partly define) the interest(s) protected and the conduct sanctioned by the head of liability. We have examined the component parts of these three elements of tort law. They form the building blocks of tort liability, and in Chapter 5 I discussed the way the building blocks are put together in various combinations in accordance with the principle of correlativity. The aim of this chapter is to discover in what ways, if any, tort law is distinctively different from other departments of the law of obligations (which, of course, also have a correlative structure); and whether there is any unifying principle which can be said to underlie the heads of liability which are included under the rubric of "the law of tort". Putting the basic question crudely, does the law of tort have any conceptual or juridical coherence or is it no more than a "loose federation of causes of action"?[1] I will argue that the main source of the distinctiveness of tort law lies in the interests (assets and resources) which it protects; but also that as a legal category, tort law lacks conceptual unity and should be used, if at all, only for expository purposes. In deciding, in concrete cases, whether liability ought to be imposed, it is best to proceed by way of an analysis in terms of protected interests and sanctioned conduct.

The best first step towards these conclusions is to locate tort law within the wider field of the law of obligations.

[1] P. Cane, *Tort Law and Economic Interests*, 2nd edn (Oxford, 1996), 447.

THE PLACE OF TORT LAW IN THE LAW OF OBLIGATIONS

The law of obligations is normally divided into the categories of tort, contract, restitution and equitable obligations (including trusts). These categories provide a convenient way of grouping together causes of action which are related to each other in some way. However, the normative heart of the law of obligations is to be found in the interests it protects, the conduct it sanctions and the remedies triggered by various causes of action. In this book, I have analyzed the law of tort in terms of these concepts, but the whole of the law of obligations can be analyzed in the same way. The normative heart of all of the departments of the law of obligations is to be found in protected interests, sanctioned conduct and sanctions. The way these elements are put together to form causes of action embodies the state-backed principles of personal responsibility which constitute the law of obligations in general and the law of tort in particular.

It is beyond the scope of this book to provide a detailed analysis of the whole of the law of obligations in terms of protected interests, sanctioned conduct and sanctions. The question which underlies this chapter is the following: if it be accepted that the normative heart of the law of obligations resides in protected interests, sanctioned conduct and sanctions, what use, if any, are the organizational categories of contract, tort, equity and so on? Do these categories help us to understand the normative principles underlying the various causes of action which fall within them or do they just encourage a sort of formularistic thinking which invests the organizational categories with a normative significance they do not have? The question whether the category of tort law has any distinctiveness and unity in terms of ethical principles could be asked of all of the organizational categories of the law of obligations. The way I will seek to answer this question in this chapter is, in very general terms, by examining the extent to which the categories of the law of obligations other than tort law utilize building blocks of liability which are not found in the law of tort. For instance, does the law of contract protect any interests which the law of tort does not, or does it refuse protection to any interests which tort law protects? Does contract law sanction any conduct which the law of tort does not, or does it refuse to sanction any conduct which tort law sanctions? Does contract law provide any remedies which the law of tort does not, or does it refuse any remedies which tort law provides? If the answers to all of these questions were negative, it would be difficult to say that the law of contract was dis-

tinct from the law of tort in any way which would justify maintaining its separate existence or allowing a litigant to choose between
suing in tort and suing in contract. But to the extent that contract law
uses different building blocks of liability from those used by the law
of tort or recognizes different heads of liability from those recognized
by tort law, to that extent the two bodies of law are distinct from one
another in ways which would justify maintaining their separate existence for analytical purposes. I am using tort law as the baseline (as it
were) for the following discussion not because I assume that tort law
is in some way more important or fundamental than other categories
of the law of obligations but only because, having analyzed the building blocks of tort law in detail, it provides us with the most convenient starting point.

Having determined in what ways and to what extent the various
departments of the law of obligations are distinct in the ways just
explained, we will then be in a position to start the task of understanding the ethical principles of responsibility and freedom embodied in the rules and principles of those various departments. In broad
terms, the issue addressed in the following discussion concerns the
extent to which the various departments of the law of obligations
embody and give effect to different ethical principles of personal
responsibility (and freedom). My argument is that because the normative heart of the law of obligations resides in principles of personal
responsibility understood in terms of protected interests, sanctioned
conduct and sanctions, organizational distinctions within the law of
obligations are only valid and useful if and to the extent that they
reflect relevantly different principles of personal responsibility.

Tort Law and Contract Law

The law of contract protects financial interests in the nature of contractual rights and contractual expectancies (in the latter case by providing remedies for misrepresentation, for instance). It protects
against personal injury and death, psychological injury and, in certain
circumstances, anxiety and inconvenience. It also protects against
physical damage to tangible property. The standards of liability recognized in contract law are negligence and liability without fault.
Contract law does not recognize intentional conduct as an independent trigger of liability. Remedies available include injunctions and
compensatory damages, but not aggravated or exemplary damages or
(disgorgement) damages representing gains made by breach of contract which do not correspond to losses suffered by the plaintiff.

A contract is a technique by which people can bind themselves to act (or refrain from acting) in certain ways in the future. One of the functions of contract law is to police agreements about future conduct. It is because of this that contract law makes available certain distinctive remedies, notably specific performance, rescission and termination, by which obligations to behave in certain ways can be enforced, or cancelled either prospectively or retrospectively. Tort law, by contrast, is mainly concerned to deal with the consequences of momentary interactions between individuals.

An order for specific performance requires a party to a contract to perform his or her obligations under the contract. If this obligation is to pay a sum of money, the plaintiff's claim will take the form of a "debt action"; an order to pay a contractual debt is, in effect, an order for "monetary specific performance". Termination is a remedy which brings the contract to an end as from the date of termination. From that date the parties are relieved of future obligations under the contract. Rescission goes one step further by declaring that the contract should be treated as never having existed. Termination is a remedy for serious breaches of contract, whereas rescission is a remedy for misrepresentation, duress and other factors which affect the making rather than the performance of the contract. Rescission is available as a remedy only if the plaintiff can substantially restore to the defendant benefits received from the defendant under the terms of the contract; and in return, the defendant must return what D received from P under the terms of the contract. This is called "*restitutio in integrum*". In the case of property, it involves the return of the actual property received. In the case of money, it involves a monetary payment. *Restitutio in integrum* is not itself a remedy but rather a precondition of rescission. In addition to restoration of benefits received, the defendant is required to "indemnify" the plaintiff for (the value of) benefits transferred by the plaintiff to third parties in accordance with the terms of the contract. The measure of indemnification is different from that of compensatory damages because it is limited to losses incurred in performance of a contract; it does not extend to losses suffered by action in reliance on the contract. In cases of non-fraudulent misrepresentation, damages may be awarded *in lieu* of rescission under section 2(2) of the Misrepresentation Act 1967. The discretion to award such damages is designed to prevent injustice to the defendant, and in this sense they are analogous to damages *in lieu* of an injunction. It is not clear what the measure of damages is under this provision. One suggestion pitches it at the difference between the value of what D received from P and what D gave to P under the contract; and this suggestion is appealing because such a measure would achieve a similar result in terms of money to that achieved by *restitutio in integrum* following rescission. There is no provision for damages *in lieu* of rescission in cases of duress, undue influence and so on.

Perhaps a more important distinctive feature of the law of contract than its remedies is that it recognizes strict liability for nonfeasance. The common law of tort, as we have seen, sometimes imposes strict liability for misfeasance, but never strict liability for nonfeasance.[2] Another way of putting this is to say that in the law of contract, but not in the law of tort, a person may be liable for failing to bring about a specified state of affairs even though the failure was not the result of faulty conduct on the part of that person. In the law of contract a person may be liable simply because a state of affairs does not materialize, full stop. Such liability will be imposed only if the contract placed on the defendant the risk that the state of affairs would not materialize; and it is reflected in the measure of damages referred to as "the expectation measure" or, more accurately, the "entitled result measure".[3] Only a contract can create a right to sue another if a promised state of affairs does not materialize. Not all contractual rights are of this nature – some are merely rights that another should take care in relation to the materialization of a state of affairs. It is rights of this latter sort which may, under current law, be actionable in tort as well as in contract.

We have also seen that the law of tort is sometimes unwilling to impose liability for negligent nonfeasance or, in other words, negligent failure to prevent injury or loss occurring (as opposed to causing injury or loss). By contrast, a contract is a means by which a legally enforceable obligation to take care to protect another from injury or loss may be created. However, the courts have shown themselves very unwilling to imply such obligations into contracts when they are not expressly stated. To do so would be tantamount to imposing such an obligation.

Thus the main distinguishing feature of the law of contract, compared with the law of tort, is a greater willingness to impose strict and

---

[2] The only way in which strict tort liability for nonfeasance may arise is if a strict statutory duty of positive action is held actionable in the tort of breach of statutory duty: e.g. *Thornton* v. *Kirklees MBC* [1979] 1 QB 626.

[3] J. Stapleton, "The Normal Expectancies Measure in Tort Damages" (1997) 113 *LQR* 257.

negligence-based liability for nonfeasance. In other words, contract provides a technique for creating legally enforceable obligations of positive action, both strict obligations and obligations to take care. It is beyond the scope of this book to analyze the conditions for the existence of contractual rights. Suffice it to say that the central features of the paradigm contract are conduct (statements or acts) by one person directed to another which could reasonably be interpreted by the latter as an expression of willingness to act or to refrain from acting in a particular way; and some *quid pro quo* given by the latter in return for the former's expression of willingness. However, obligations which are contractual may arise even in the absence of one (but probably not both) of these features. The paradigm contractual relationship is bilateral, and as a general rule, the contract creates rights and obligations only as between the two parties to the relationship. This is part of the explanation of why liability for third party interference with contract has traditionally been conceptualized as tortious rather than contractual.

One way of explaining the relationship between tort law and contract law is to say that tort law provides a basic measure of legal protection for a wide range of interests. If a party seeks legal protection for an interest which tort law does not protect, or protection (for an interest which tort law does protect) greater than that provided by tort law, contract may provide a technique for securing such protection. Conversely, contract provides a technique (subject to significant statutory limitation) for excluding or limiting the protection afforded by tort law. However, this picture of the role of contract law is misleading to the extent that it suggests that the institution of contracting is essentially protective. The possibility, by contract, of creating strict obligations of positive action is what makes it the prime legal mechanism for wealth creation and the productive exchange of resources. The law of contract, as traditionally defined, contains both a set of rules for the creation of rights and a set of rules for the protection of those rights. This distinction between what I earlier called the "constitutive" and the "protective" aspects of contract law is, as I will explain later in this chapter, one of the keys to understanding the structure and distinctiveness of tort law.

Tort Law and Equity

Historically there was a deep chasm between the common law (developed by the common law courts) of which the law of tort was a part, and the law of trusts and equitable obligations (developed by the courts of Chancery, or "Equity"). The chasm was institutional rather than substantive; and since the distinction, based on divided jurisdiction, between common law and equity was rendered obsolete in the late nineteenth century, there is no reason why the two bodies of law should not be integrated into one. This has happened to all intents and purposes in relation to the remedies developed by the courts of Equity (such as injunction and account of profits). Even though such remedies may still be spoken of as "equitable", their jurisdictional origin is generally no longer seen as relevant to their availability or to the scope of their application. The availability of any remedy is now decided by consideration of the interest for which protection is sought and the conduct to be sanctioned.

Integration of equity and common law would not, however, result in absorption of one into the other, because the Chancery courts developed certain juristic concepts which the common law courts did not make use of. Four stand out as of great importance: the notion of "equitable property"; the ideas of "fiduciary obligation" and "unconscionability"; and the concept of "proprietary remedies".

Equitable Property Interests

The term "equitable property" describes the interest of the beneficiary under a trust. The trust is a technique by which obligations can be imposed on the owner of (tangible or intangible) property (the "trustee") to use that property for the benefit of another ("the beneficiary"). The basic reason why the interest of the beneficiary under a trust is conceptualized as proprietary is that the beneficiary's rights in relation to the use of the property are enforceable not only against the trustee but also against (certain) third parties who acquire the trust property. Moreover, under certain circumstances the beneficiary may be free to transform his or her beneficial interest into a full ownership interest.

The basic juristic function of equitable property rights is different from the function of what may be called "common law" property rights (that is, in the trust context, the rights of the owner/trustee over the trust property). The basic juristic function of the latter is to allocate assets to individuals; that is, to create a legally enforceable pattern of distribution of resources in society. By contrast, the basic juristic function of equitable property rights is to create obligations enforceable by one person as to the use of assets allocated to another. The holder of common law property rights who is not a trustee of the property may (subject to specific legal limitations) exercise those rights (that is, may use the property) for his or her own benefit. However, if the common-law property-right holder is a trustee, that person must exercise his or her rights over the property for the benefit of the beneficiary of the trust. Moreover, whereas legal liability (in tort) for misappropriation of, interference with and exploitation of common law property rights is, as a general rule, strict, the liability of parties, other than the trustee, to the beneficiary for misappropriation of trust property or its exploitation otherwise than for the benefit of the beneficiary is generally not. A third party who pays for trust property will not be liable to the beneficiary for having received the property unless he or she knew of the beneficiary's interest in the property (although a recipient who does not pay for it may be); and a third party exploiter of trust property will be liable only if he or she knew of the beneficiary's interest in the property or was consciously indifferent to its existence. The liability of a third party for interference with the rights of a beneficiary is more akin to liability for interference with contract than to liability for interference with common law property rights. Put another way, the interest of the beneficiary under a trust is a hybrid of property and contract.

Traditionally, whereas liability for interference with common law property rights was conceptualized as common law tort liability, liability for interference with equitable property rights was conceptualized as equitable liability. In other words, whereas the law of tort was the main source of legal protection for common law property rights, it was not a source of protection for equitable property rights. This was a result of the jurisdictional divide between the common law and the equity courts. Nevertheless, most of the building blocks of equitable liability for breach of trust by trustees and for interference with trust (or "involvement in breach of trust") by third parties are present in tort law. Depending on the nature of the breach, a trustee's liability is either strict or negligence-based; and when it is negligence based, the standard of reasonable conduct is in some circumstances "ordinary negligence" and in others "extraordinary negligence".[4] The liability of third parties is similarly based on the concepts of deliberate, intentional and reckless conduct which are also used in tort law. In fact, the distinctiveness of equitable liability for breach of or interference with trust rests not in the notions of sanctioned conduct it utilizes but in the types of interest it protects. The trust is a means of creating interests in the use of property different from those

---

[4] For the meaning of these terms, see p. 41 above.

attaching to common law ownership. Contract provides another technique for creating interests in the use of property. Trust and contract differ in two important respects: the conditions which have to be fulfilled to create a contractual obligation as to the use of property are different from the conditions which have to be fulfilled to create a trust obligation. Nevertheless, as between the person who provides the trust property and the trustee, a trust shares many of the characteristics of a contract. The second important difference between a contract and a trust is that as a general rule, the former creates rights and obligations only between the parties to the contract, whereas a trust creates rights and obligations which may be enforceable by the beneficiary against persons other than the trustee.

Although both tangible and intangible property may form the subject-matter of a trust, all equitable property rights are purely financial interests. In this respect, the range of interests protected by the law of trusts is narrower than that protected either by contract law or tort law.

Fiduciary Obligations

The essential idea underlying the trust institution is that one person (the trustee) must act, in relation to the trust property, for the benefit of another and not for his or her own benefit. This same idea underlies the second of the distinctive features of equity law, namely fiduciary obligations. Trustees are fiduciaries, but not all fiduciaries are trustees. A person may be under an obligation to act for the benefit of another (the "principal") even if the former owns no property in which the latter has an interest. For instance, a solicitor is in a fiduciary relationship with his or her client.[5] In the capacity of solicitor vis-a-vis the client, the solicitor must act for the benefit of the client and not for his or her own benefit.[6] If a fiduciary makes a gain by improperly exploiting his or her position as such, the fiduciary must disgorge that gain to the person for whose benefit the fiduciary ought to have acted. The fiduciary's obligation is strict and is designed to prevent the exploitation of conflicts of interest, even if innocent. Fiduciary obligations are different from any obligation imposed by tort law. As a general rule, tort law does not require people to act for the benefit of others and to ignore their own interests, but only to

---

[5] It is beyond the scope of this book to explain in what circumstances fiduciary obligations arise.

[6] "The principal is entitled to the single-minded loyalty of [the] fiduciary": *Bristol & West Building Society* v. *Mothew* [1996] 4 All ER 698, 712 *per* Millett LJ.

avoid causing "disbenefit" to others. In some cases, through the medium of punitive damages, tort law does, it is true, impose liability for deliberate gain-seeking. The closest analogy in equity to such liability is third party liability to disgorge gains made by involvement in a breach of trust. The only basis on which tort law imposes strict liability for gains is exploitation of another's property without consent. The liability of a trustee to a beneficiary for exploiting trust property for his or her own benefit is analogous to this type of tort liability. However, the idea of fiduciary obligation can be used to impose property-independent obligations to act for the benefit of another. Strict, property-independent obligations to act for the benefit of another are a distinctive product of equity jurisprudence. Such obligations mark a distinctively "equitable" notion of personal responsibility.

Of course, a strict, property-independent obligation to do something for the benefit of another may be created by contract. The difference between a contractual obligation to benefit another and an equitable fiduciary obligation is that so long as a contracting party provides the contractual benefit, he or she is free to exploit the contract for gain. Indeed, mutual self-seeking is of the essence of contractual transactions. By contrast, fiduciary relationships are one-sided – the fiduciary must make no improper gain out of the relationship: any such gain from the relationship must go to the "beneficiary" of the relationship. This does not mean, however, that fiduciary and contractual obligations may not exist side-by-side. For example, the fact that a solicitor is a fiduciary vis-a-vis the client does not prevent the solicitor charging the client reasonable professional fees in accordance with the contract between them. The compatibility of self-seeking behaviour with contractual obligation is demonstrated by the basic rule that there is no obligation to disgorge gains made by breach of contract which do not correspond to a loss suffered by the other party. Some argue that this rule should be reversed so far as deliberate (or "flagrant") breaches of contract; but no-one appears to favour a general principle of liability for gains made by breach of contract precisely because contract is an institution designed to facilitate mutually self-seeking behaviour. A person must not harm another by breaching a contract with that other, but beyond that should normally be allowed to keep gains resulting from the interaction.

Unconscionable Conduct

The Chancery courts, it is commonly said, were "courts of con-
science". This did not mean that equitable liability was always based
on unconscionable conduct. Indeed, as we have seen, the equitable
liability of trustees and fiduciaries may be strict. What it did mean was
that Chancery courts were sometimes prepared to give remedies for
types of "shady" conduct which were not sanctioned by the common
law. For instance, whereas the common law courts would not hold a
person to a contract which they had entered in response to a threat
by the other contracting party to injure them or damage their property (for instance), the equity courts would go further and allow a
person to escape a contract made as a result of "undue influence"
exerted by another. Again, whereas tort law sanctions conduct which
is fraudulent in the narrow sense of knowingly making a false statement with the intention that another should rely on it, equity would
sanction conduct which was "fraudulent" in a much broader sense
captured by the term "unconscionability". "Unconscionability", like
"negligence", is a standard of conduct rather than a frame of mind.
But whereas negligence is failure to take reasonable care not to harm
others, unconscionability involves the promotion of one's own interests at the unreasonable expense of another. Unconscionability bears
a similar relationship to the strict liability of a fiduciary (discussed in
the previous section) as negligence does to strict liability in tort. In
general, tort does no more than require people not to harm others;
whereas equity will go further and require people not to advance
their own interests at the expense of others; or, in other words, not
to take unfair advantage of others.

These two different moral injunctions (do not harm others and
do not take advantage of others) are, in English law, identified with
two different bodies of law: common law and equity respectively.
In the late 20th century, throughout the English-speaking world,
courts and lawyers are attempting to integrate common law and
equity and to work out an acceptable relationship between legitimate self-seekingness (limited by a duty not to harm) and the proper
demands of altruism (expressed in the idea that one should not take
unfair advantage of others). This process finds expression, for
instance, in calls for the creation of a general tort of "unfair competition" or for a general duty to conduct contractual negotiations
"in good faith". In English law, the effects of the jurisdictional division between law and equity have made it harder than it need be

for courts and lawyers to grapple with these basic underlying moral issues.

Proprietary Remedies

So far as remedies are concerned, equity uses some of the same building blocks as tort: monetary compensation and orders for the transfer of property, for instance. Equity does not award punitive damages. This is surprising given the strict attitude which it takes to self-seeking conduct. So far as disgorgement damages are concerned, whereas the measure of disgorgement in tort is more commonly expense saved than profit realized, the typical measure in equity is profit realized. This is consistent with the fact that the basis of equitable liability is the prohibition of self-seeking behaviour. The most distinctive feature of the equitable law of remedies are the so-called "proprietary remedies". The concept of a proprietary remedy is best explained by reference to the effects of the award of a proprietary remedy. But before getting to that, a couple of preliminary points must be made. First, despite their name, proprietary remedies do not relate to specific items of (tangible) property. Whereas in a tort action for conversion of chattels, an order may be made for the return of the chattels which were converted, no equitable remedy relates to items of tangible property even if the sanctioned conduct involved some dealing with tangible property. All equitable proprietary remedies are monetary. Secondly, a proprietary remedy must be distinguished from what I shall call a "proprietary claim". A claim in tort for conversion of a chattel is a proprietary claim because chattels which have been converted remain the property of their owner even after the conversion. If the remedy awarded in a conversion action is damages, one effect of the payment of those damages by the defendant is that the defendant becomes the owner of the converted chattel by authority of the court. A proprietary claim is a claim based on an allegation that property in D's hands belongs to P. The importance of the distinction between proprietary claims and proprietary remedies resides in the fact that a proprietary remedy may not be available even if P's claim is proprietary. Remedies which are not proprietary are called "personal".

A proprietary remedy has two effects which no personal remedy has. The first concerns the rights of the plaintiff if the defendant is bankrupt or insolvent: whereas the beneficiary of a personal remedy ranks only as an unsecured creditor, the beneficiary of a proprietary remedy ranks as a secured creditor. Ranking as a secured creditor increases the creditor's chance of being paid the full amount owed by the bankrupt or insolvent. The second effect of a proprietary remedy relates to the amount of money recoverable by the plaintiff. All equitable proprietary remedies relate to something received by the defendant. Suppose that the defendant receives a bundle of shares worth £X in respect of which the plaintiff is awarded a proprietary remedy; and that between the time of receipt and the awarding of the remedy, the shares increase in value to £X+Y. The quantum of P's proprietary remedy will not be £X but £X+Y. An equitable proprietary remedy relates to something received by D, and if that thing has increased in value since D received it, P is entitled to that increase in value. The question of when equitable proprietary remedies should be awarded is hotly debated; but the basis on which all equitable proprietary remedies are awarded is that P is entitled to the property to which the remedy relates. By contrast, personal monetary remedies are awarded on the basis that D owes P a sum of money, not on the basis that D has something belonging to P. Equitable proprietary remedies may have very harsh effects on third parties, and for this reason many would argue that they should be available only in cases where the interest the remedy protects is a very highly valued one. In deciding whether to award such a remedy, the court has to take account not only of the seriousness of the sanctioned conduct but also of the interests of third parties who may be adversely affected by the remedy.

Equitable proprietary remedies (unlike other remedies developed by the courts of Chancery, such as the injunction) have only ever been available to protect equitable property rights. There is only one context in which proprietary remedies are available in aid of common law rights, and that is in the admiralty jurisdiction. In this context, proprietary remedies (such as arrest of ships and liens over ships) are not awarded on the basis that P is entitled to the property to which the remedy relates but rather as security for the payment of (compensatory) damages. For instance, in a tort action in respect of damage done by a ship brought in an admiralty court, the plaintiff may arrest the ship and may be awarded a lien over the ship in order to provide security for the payment of any damages awarded against the owner of the ship in respect of loss suffered by P. The "personal" equivalent of such proprietary "security remedies" is the so-called "*Mareva* injunction" which orders D not to dispose of assets pending the resolution of a claim made by P against D.

Our examination of the law of trusts and equitable obligations has added significantly to our range of building blocks in terms of protected interests (equitable property rights), sanctioned conduct (non-deliberate self-seekingness) and sanctions (proprietary reme-dies). But many of the building blocks of the law of trusts and equi-table obligations are the same as those utilized in the law of tort. And some equitable heads of liability (such as that of a trustee for loss suf-fered by the beneficiary as a result of negligent investment decisions by the trustee) are indistinguishable from tortious heads of liability. I will explore the implications of these conclusions later in this chapter.

Tort Law and the Law of Restitution

The law of restitution is concerned with liability for gains received by D as opposed to losses suffered by P. There is a large debate about the scope of the law of restitution, but the arguments need not be rehearsed here because my only concern is to attempt to identify building blocks used in the law of restitution which have not yet been discussed in our surveys of the law of tort and contract and the law of equitable obligations. There are, in fact, two such building blocks. The first is a matter of sanctions. All remedies in the law of restitu-tion are monetary. In the areas of law we have so far surveyed, mon-etary remedies either relate to loss suffered by P regardless of whether it corresponds to any gain made by D (compensation); or to gain made by D regardless of whether it corresponds to any loss suffered by P (disgorgement) or to neither (punishment). In some contexts, however, the monetary remedy to which P is entitled is measured by and limited to such gain made by D as corresponds to loss suffered by P as a result of the event which gave rise to the liability in question. This measure I shall refer to as "restoration". Restoration is con-cerned with reversing transfers of assets from one person to another.

It will be recalled that in Chapter 4 I argued that the remedies express the balance struck by the various heads of liability between the positions of the two parties to the cause of action. Viewed in this way, the remedy of restoration damages might be seen as imposing the least onerous obligation on the defendant consistent with recog-nizing that the plaintiff has a legitimate claim against the defendant. An obligation to restore relates to loss suffered by P, but only to the extent that the loss corresponds to a gain received by D; and it relates to gain received by D, but only to the extent that the gain corre-sponds to a loss suffered by P. In all of the areas of law we have so far considered, obligations to restore have no independent role to play because any head of liability in tort, contract or equity carries with it an obligation to compensate for any loss suffered by P regardless of whether it corresponds to a gain made by D. Conversely, all the heads of civil liability which give rise to common law obligations to disgorge[7] are heads of liability either in the law of tort or in the law of trusts and equitable obligations. The ground covered by the law of restitution which we have so far not traversed is covered by heads of liability which give rise to obligations to restore and only to restore.

The paradigm case which gives rise to liability to restore is that of receipt by D of a payment made as a result of mistake on the part of P that the payment was owed, in circumstances where the mistake was not induced by anything said or done by D. Suppose, for instance, that unbeknownst to D, P mistakenly makes an electronic transfer of funds to D's bank account. In this type of case, the trigger of the obligation to restore would appear not to be the receipt of the payment by D: D was not in any sense responsible for the making of the payment and it could not even be said that D could have done anything to prevent the payment being made. If D is to be required to restore the payment it can only be on the basis that once D knows that the payment was made by mistake, it would be unfair of D to retain it, unless D has "changed position" since receiving the payment in such a way as to make it unfair to require restoration.

In other cases where restoration seems the appropriate remedy, it can be said that D was responsible for the making of the payment, but that nevertheless D's liability should only be to restore the mistaken payment. Take misrepresentation, for instance. A misrepresentation is a false statement of fact made by A to B which induces B to enter a contract with A. Actionable misrepresentations may be fraudulent, negligent or innocent (that is, neither fraudulent nor negligent). Both fraudulent and negligent misrepresentations may give rise to tort liability to compensate; but an innocent misrepresentation is not actionable in tort. However, any type of actionable misrepresentation, whether fraudulent, negligent or innocent, may entitle the induced party to rescind the contract. As we noted in Chapter 5, a precondition of rescission is that the parties should restore to each other money or property transferred to them by the other party in accordance with the terms of the contract. Thus, innocent misrepresentation is a ground of liability to restore but not of liability to compensate. Liability to restore may also arise when a contract is

---

[7] Statutory provisions for forfeiture of the proceeds of crime effectively impose obligations of disgorgement.

terminated for frustration or, in certain cases, when a contract is illegal. Even in cases where D was, in some sense, responsible for the fact that P transferred the money or property to D, the basis of the liability to restore is not the receipt of the payment but the judgement that it would be unfair or undesirable to allow D to retain it in the light of the circumstances in which it was made or which have occurred since it was made. Liability to restore is not based on notions of personal responsibility for gains received but rather on the idea of unfair retention. In cases where the basis of liability for gains received by D is that D is rightly held responsible in law to P for their receipt, the law goes beyond imposing liability to restore and imposes liability to disgorge. Liability to restore is imposed where the basis of the liability is retention rather than receipt.

Thus the law of restitution utilizes two important building blocks unknown in the law of tort, namely the remedy of restoration, and retention of property received as a form of sanctioned conduct. The law of restitution also utilizes one defence not used in the law of tort, namely change of position. This defence is consistent with the fact that liability to restore is based on retention, not receipt, because it allows a recipient to escape liability in circumstances where it would be unfair not to allow D to retain the gain.[8] Change of position could not be pleaded in answer to liability based on unfair receipt as opposed to unfair retention of gains; and it follows that it could not be pleaded in answer to a claim for which the remedy was disgorgement rather than restoration.

THE DISTINCTIVENESS OF TORT LAW

So far in this chapter I have treated tort law as a sort of background against which to view other departments of the law of obligations and to discern their distinctiveness. By doing this, we have added to our list of juristic building blocks in relation to each of the three elements of protected interests, sanctioned conduct and sanctions. We are now in a position to analyze the distinctiveness of tort law. Negatively, we can say, of course, that tort law is distinct in that it does not make use of certain juristic building blocks which other departments of the law utilize. But are there any building blocks which are peculiar to tort law? So far as sanctioned conduct is concerned, the only respect in which tort law is distinctive is that in some cases there can be no tort

---

[8] Concerning the relevance of post-receipt alterations in the financial position of P to the fairness of the retention see *Kleinwort Benson Ltd* v. *Birmingham CC* [1996] 3 WLR 1139.

liability unless the sanctioned conduct was independently unlawful. However, the distinctiveness of tort law lies most in the interests which it protects. The law of tort is the predominant source of legal protection for interests in the person. Tort law is also the main source of legal protection for common law (as opposed to equitable) property interests, for contractual expectancies and for reputation.[9] It is, of course, true, that all of these interests can be protected by contract; but tort law protects these interests in their own right and for their own sake, and not because the plaintiff is entitled under a contract to the protection of the interest by another. So far as sanctions are concerned, it is in protecting property interests that tort law utilizes the only non-statutory remedies unique to it, namely orders for specific return of chattels and for possession of real property. These remedies are a reflection of the concentration of the judge-made law of tort on tangible property. Greater recognition of the central role of tort law in protecting property is one of the most important products of the mode of analysis adopted in this book.

THE UNITY OF TORT LAW

It is often asserted that tort law is different from the law of contract or the law of trusts in that there is no unifying principle which underlies all the heads of tort liability. One form of this argument says that what we have is a law of *torts*, not of *tort*. In Chapter 1 I explained why I thought this approach was unhelpful and anachronistic, and in Chapters 2 to 5 I suggested a different way of looking at tort law which does not involve dividing it up into discrete torts. Another form of the argument says that tort law is something like what I myself have elsewhere called "a loose federation" of heads of liability serving a plethora of different juristic and social functions. By contrast, in the law of contract, for instance, there is only one head of liability, namely breach of contract. To some extent this contrast is misleading because the law of contract also serves a plethora of juristic and social functions. Moreover, there are various grounds of recovery which are traditionally included in expositions of the law of contract which are not based on breach of contract but on concepts such as mistake, illegality and frustration.

[9] But a claim for loss of "business reputation" may arise in contract if, for instance, a bank wrongfully dishonours its customer's cheque: *Kpohraror* v. *Woolwich Building Society* [1996] 4 All ER 119.

Nevertheless, the observation that the law of tort is more internally heterogeneous than the law of contract, for example, seems to contain more than a grain of truth. I believe that the approach I have taken in this book explains why this is so. The first point to make is that classifications in the law, such as contract, tort and equity, are lawyers' inventions designed to make it easier to understand, expound and teach the law, and to make it more user-friendly for lawyers seeking to solve real-life problems for clients. Classifications, we might say, perform a useful "expository" function, facilitating access to and understanding of the law. However, under the influence of the formulary way of thinking about law, classifications tend to take on a life of their own. We talk about causes of action "in tort" or "in contract"; and, more importantly, criteria of success and failure in legal actions may come to turn on such classifications. When this happens, classifications take on what we might call a "dispositive" role. For instance, the rules about limitation of actions or remoteness of damage vary according to whether the action is brought "in tort" or "in contract" regardless of whether there is any good reason why the difference of classification should be reflected in a difference in outcome of the action. It is very important that lawyers should remain the masters of their own categories and not become servants of such conceptualism.

The second point to make is to reiterate the distinction I have used earlier in this book between constitutive rules and protective rules. In the context of this book, constitutive rules are rules which lay down the conditions for the creation of legal interests such as property rights, contractual rights and rights under trusts. Protective rules are rules which state the ways in which such interests are protected. Not all of the interests protected by the law are the product of constitutive rules. For example, our interest in health and safety or in freedom of action exists simply by virtue of our humanity. These interests are recognized by law, but they are not a product of the law in the way that contractual interests, for instance, are. The basic point to make, however, is that fundamental to our understanding of the law of obligations is a distinction between legally protected interests and the forms of legal protection (which are a function of the various concepts of sanctioned conduct and the various remedies provided by law).

This brings me to the main point. Once we analyze the law of tort and contract, for instance, in terms of protected interests, sanctioned conduct and sanctions it becomes clear why the law of contract appears to have a degree of internal homogeneity lacking in the law of tort. The reason is that the law of contract protects only one, or at the most two, interests, namely contractual rights and, to a much lesser extent, contractual expectancies. Tort law, by contrast, protects a large number of very different interests. In this respect, it can also be contrasted with the law of equitable obligations, which protects a relatively small number of interests. If we concentrated on that part of the law of tort which is concerned with the protection of common law property interests, we would find that it had probably as much internal unity as the law of contract. Moreover, if we reclassified that part of the law of tort which protects common law property interests as part of the law of property, the law of property would have a structure very similar to that of the law of contract. The law of contract is a mixture of constitutive rules and protective rules. By contrast, in relation to common law property, the constitutive rules are classified as part of the law of property, while the protective rules are classified as part of the law of tort.

My argument, then, is that what gives the law of contract a unity which the law of tort clearly lacks is that its scope in terms of protected interests is much narrower than that of the law of tort. There is simply no point in looking for this sort of unity within tort law, and theorists who have done so tend to be able to explain only a segment of tort law. The segment they most commonly explain is that concerned with personal health and safety. The question which this conclusion raises is whether having a legal category called "tort law" covering the large field which it presently covers serves any useful purpose. In answering this question, we should bear in mind the distinction I drew earlier between the expository and the dispositive uses of legal classifications. My answer to the question is that while it may be useful to recognize the category of tort law for expository purposes, neither it nor the other categories of the law of obligations should, as such, be used for dispositive purposes to decide cases.

This assertion needs elaboration. For the purposes of applying it to concrete situations, the structure which I have suggested for analyzing the law of tort starts with a statement of the interests (in the sense of the assets and resources) it protects. The trigger of the law's protection is invasion of or interference with a protected interest by sanctioned conduct. The nature of the protection is defined by the available remedies and by a constellation of remedial rules which determine matters such as limitation periods, remoteness of damage, assessment of damages and so on. The nature of the protection provided in any particular case is and should be a function of the

interaction between the parties defined in terms of protected inter-
est(s) and sanctioned conduct. One effect of investing the category of
"tort" with a juristic significance which it does not have is that the
content of remedial rules may come to be determined by reference
to whether or not the plaintiff's claim is "in tort" rather than by
reference to the interaction between the parties defined in terms of
protected interest(s) and sanctioned conduct. This is precisely what
sometimes happens in cases of concurrent liability. Suppose that a
professional advisor causes financial loss to a client by giving negligently faulty investment advice. Such conduct may constitute both a
tort and a breach of contract, and the client is allowed to choose
whether to frame an action against the professional "in tort" or "in
contract". Different rules concerning matters such as limitation of
actions and remoteness of damage may apply to the case according to
how the action is framed, and may lead to different results despite the
fact that the interest protected and the conduct sanctioned are the
same however the action is framed. The practical point of concurrent
liability is often to allow litigants to take advantage of remedial rules
which are a function of legal categories (such as tort, contract and
trust)[10] rather than of the interaction between the parties defined in
terms of protected interest and sanctioned conduct.

I am not saying that we should draw *no* distinction between tort,
contract, trust and so on. Indeed, the whole point of this chapter has
been to identify the distinctiveness of each of these categories of the
law. My argument is that the categories in themselves ought not to
be given *dispositive* significance because they are no more than convenient *expository* devices for grouping together causes of action
which share common features in terms of protected interests, sanctioned conduct and sanctions. The fact that a particular ensemble of
protected interests and sanctioned conduct falls within more than one
of these expository categories, thus creating what are called "concurrent causes of action", tells us nothing about what remedial regime
should apply to that ensemble. All it tells us is that our expository categories overlap. Concurrency of causes of action, to the extent that
it allows different remedial regimes to apply to identical ensembles of
protected interest and sanctioned conduct, should be abolished.

---

[10] Regarding concurrency between the law of tort and the law of equitable obligations in
respect of liability for negligent professional services see *Bristol & West Building Society* v.
Mothew [1996] 4 All ER 698; and, to a quite different effect, J.D. Heydon, "The Negligent
Fiduciary" (1995) 111 *LQR* 1. For an illustration of the formulary approach to limitation
periods see *Nelson* v. *Rye* [1996] 1 WLR 1378.

MAPPING THE LAW OF OBLIGATIONS

This book is primarily about the law of tort. However, if the argument made in the last section, which is based on our examination of the law of tort and its relationship to the other categories of the law of obligations, is accepted, I believe that it has implications (going beyond the law of tort) for the way we understand the law of obligations. What are these implications? The first is that the content of remedial rules in the law of obligations ought to be a function of protected interests and sanctioned conduct. The second implication is that the categories of the law of obligations, namely tort, contract, equity and restitution, should be recognized for what they are, namely expository devices. They should not be given any dispositive significance.

Thirdly, however, I would also argue that while "contract" and "trust" (and here I use this term to cover both the institution of the trust and the (fiduciary) principle against self-seeking behaviour) are coherent expository categories because they each concern the protection of only one interest or of a very small number of closely related interests, the categories of "tort" and "restitution", at least as they are presently understood, are much less coherent as expository tools. The lack of coherence within tort law is reflected in the fact that many of the standard works on the law of tort begin by admitting how difficult it is to define "a tort" or even concisely to explain the scope and boundaries of the law of tort. The best approach to the law of tort as an expository category is to treat it as an umbrella category sheltering bodies of law dealing with the protection of a diverse range of different interests. The four main categories of interest (in the sense of assets or resources) which tort law protects are: (1) interests in the person, physical, psychological and dignitary; (2) interests in property, both tangible and intangible; (3) contractual rights and expectancies; and (4) monetary wealth. I think that our understanding of tort law is much improved by recognizing this diversity within the expository category of tort law. Dividing tort law up in this way enables us to see that the distinctiveness of tort law resides in categories (1) and (4) and that category (2) is an adjunct of property law.

Category (3) presents an expository dilemma. To the extent that it is concerned with liability of one contracting party to the other for breach of contract, there seems no reason not to treat the category as part of contract law. If this were done, and if my argument were accepted that remedial rules should be a function of protected interest(s) and sanctioned conduct, there would be good reason not to allow breaches of contracts to be classified as torts. To the extent that category (3) is concerned with third party inducement or causation of breach of contract, there is as good an argument for treating it as an adjunct of contract law as for classifying it as part of tort law. But this expository choice should have no implications for the substance of the rules about third party liability for interference with contract. It should not matter to the substance of the law whether such liability is treated as part of the law of contract or as part of the law of tort. The same is true of liability for interference with contractual expectancies ("trade") – there is a case for treating the law about deprivation of or interference with advantageous contracting opportunities as an adjunct of contract law. But provided nothing is made to turn on the classification, there is no reason why it should not be dealt with under the rubric of tort. The basic point it that expository classification and dispositive classification serve quite different purposes. Dispositive classification should be based on analysis in terms of protected interest and sanctioned conduct because dispositive classification affects remedies. By contrast, the criteria of good expository classification are analytical elegance and economy, and facilitation of the teaching and learning of the law and of the process of finding out what the law is and of understanding what it means.[11] I can see no reason why expository classifications should not track dispositive classifications and relate to analysis of protected interests, sanctioned conduct and sanctions. But so long as the distinction between the two types of classification is understood and recognized, it does not matter much whether they do or not.

"Restitution" is also a difficult category. In understanding its structure, it seems to me that the most important distinction is that between liability to disgorge gains regardless of whether they correspond to any loss suffered by the plaintiff, and liability to restore gains which correspond to losses suffered by the plaintiff (or, in other words, to restore (the value of) assets transferred to D by P). All the triggers of obligations to disgorge presently recognized in the law are also triggers of liability to compensate for losses regardless of whether they correspond to gains made by D. This does not mean, of course,

---

[11] Classification also plays an important part in defining the roles of many academic lawyers in terms of the segment of the law in which they specialize. Practising lawyers (and some academics), by contrast, tend to define their roles in terms of "functional" legal categories, such as "commercial law" or "family law", which cut across conceptual classifications such as "contract" or "tort". "Criminal law", however, is both a conceptual and a functional category.

that liability to compensate will always accompany liability to disgorge because D may make a gain without P suffering a loss. But it
does mean that liability to disgorge will only be available as a remedy
under heads of liability in respect of which liability to compensate
would be available as a remedy for any loss suffered by the plaintiff.[12]

By contrast, triggers of liability to restore are, by definition,
neither triggers of liability to compensate nor liability to disgorge
because liability to restore is limited to corresponding gains and
losses. The distinctiveness of the "law of restitution" resides in such
liability to restore. The title "law of restitution" is an odd way of
referring to heads of liability to restore because unlike the terms
"tort", "contract" and "trust", the term "restitution" refers to the
remedy, not to the trigger of the remedy. In fact, the structure of
the law of restitution is rather like that of the law of tort. Several of
the triggers of liability to restore could just as well be classified as
adjuncts of the law of contract. Indeed, an old name for the "law of
restitution" was the "law of quasi-contract". But there are some triggers of liability to restore, such as uninduced mistake, which cannot
be convincingly treated as adjuncts of any other expository category.
In dispositive terms, however, the crucial point to understand and
observe is the difference between liability to restore on the one hand,
and liability to compensate and disgorge on the other. There are
some heads of liability which attract only an obligation to restore, and
however these are classified for the purposes of exposition, they must
be treated as distinct for dispositive purposes.

My argument in this section is, then, that however we divide the
law up for expository purposes, we should adopt for dispositive purposes classifications based on protected interests and sanctioned conduct of the sort I have started to develop in this book. The term "the
civil law of obligations" is misleading to the extent that it is most apt
to refer to sanctions or, perhaps, sanctioned conduct; it ignores protected interests. Equally misleading would be some phrase such as
"the civil law of protected interests" because it ignores sanctioned
conduct and, to an extent at least, sanctions as well. In fact, the basic
elements of the civil law constitute a complex web of causes of action
defined in terms of protected interests, sanctioned conduct and sanctions. The technique of analysis of tort law adopted in this book provides, I believe, a good tool for understanding all the strands of this
complex web and the way they fit together and relate to one another.

[12] See further P. Cane, "Exceptional Measures of Damages: A Search for Principles" in
P. Birks (ed), *Wrongs and Remedies in the Twenty-First Century* (Oxford, 1996), 312–323.

CONCLUSION

In this chapter I have argued that such distinctiveness as tort law has resides in the interests it protects. I have also argued that the legal category of tort law should only be used for expository and not for dispositive purposes. However, an even more iconoclastic conclusion to the discussion in this chapter might be suggested, namely that we should abandon entirely the division of the law of obligations into the law of tort, contract, restitution and equitable obligations and replace it with categories based on protected interests (assets and resources). If this conclusion were accepted, the whole project of writing a book on the law of tort would be, at best, suspect, and at worst, intellectually dishonest. On this basis alone, I shrink from propounding it, even though I find it compelling. I console myself with the thought that Canute found his watery project equally compelling!

7. ANATOMY, FUNCTIONS AND EFFECT

IN this book I have argued that the best way of understanding tort law is as a set of ethical rules and principles of personal responsibility organized under heads of liability defined in terms of protected interests, sanctioned conduct and sanctions. However, tort law is a human artefact, a social institution which exists not for its own sake but for the achievement of human goals and the performance of social functions. Such goals and functions will obviously be related to and will affect the structure of the institution of tort law, but they are identifiably separate from the rules and principles which constitute that institution. Identifiably separate from both the institution itself and the goals and functions it serves are the effects it has. Once again, the effects of an institution are obviously related to its goals, but the former may diverge from the latter to a greater or lesser degree. An institution may achieve the goals set for it more or less effectively; but an institution may have unintended effects quite unrelated to any goal or function which it is meant or expected to serve.

The purpose of this chapter is to examine the relationship between these three aspects of tort law: the ethical rules and principles of personal responsibility which constitute it, the goals which are set for it and the functions it is used to serve, and the effects it has. My basic arguments are that the functions and effects of tort law can only properly be understood in the light of its correlative structure and its nature as a set of principles of personal responsibility; and that tort law is justified partly by the extent to which it embodies sound ethical principles of personal responsibility and partly to the extent that it furthers desirable human and social goals. In the process of developing these arguments I examine, amongst other things, economic interpretations of tort law, and the idea that one of the functions of tort law is "loss-spreading".

THE FUNCTIONS OF TORT LAW

The functions of tort law are those purposes or ends which people seek to further or achieve through tort law.[1] The functions of tort law may be usefully divided into two groups: "intrinsic functions" and "extrinsic functions". Intrinsic functions I define as those which are implicit in ("intrinsic to") the idea of tort law as a set of ethical rules and principles of personal responsibility organized in terms of protected interests, sanctioned conduct and sanctions. The main intrinsic functions of tort law are to provide guidance to individuals about how they may and ought to behave in their interactions with others, to provide protection for certain interests of individuals, to express disapproval of and to sanction certain types of conduct, to provide a means of resolving disputes between individuals and in this way to maintain social order and promote social cohesion, and to supplement morality both by applying its general principles to particular circumstances and by providing socially acceptable and enforceable compromises between irreconcilably conflicting moral views.[2]

What I call the extrinsic functions of tort law are related to the particular interests which tort law protects, the particular types of conduct it sanctions, the particular sanctions it makes available, and the way these elements are combined in constructing particular heads of tort liability. These extrinsic functions can be divided into two groups: direct and indirect. Direct extrinsic functions relate to ends which are immediately served by the award of a remedy in a particular case, while indirect functions relate to wider social or economic goals (or "policies") to which decisions in individual cases may contribute. In other words, direct functions relate to the interaction between P and D which forms the subject of any particular "tort dispute", while indirect functions relate to the significance for third parties of the resolution of the dispute between P and D. Whereas direct extrinsic functions are only served by decisions to impose liability, some indirect extrinsic functions may be served equally by refusals to impose liability as by impositions of liability.

The direct extrinsic functions of tort law are closely tied to the available remedies: to compensate for losses, to secure disgorgement of gains, to express disapproval and to punish (and, conversely, to

---

[1] For a much more detailed discussion of many of these functions see P. Cane, *Tort Law and Economic Interests*, 2nd edn (Oxford, 1996), chs 5 and 10.
[2] On this last function see p. 26 above.

engender in P a sense of vindication or satisfaction), to secure that D acts in a particular way (such as returning chattels to P) or refrains or desists from acting in a particular way (as when an injunction is awarded in a nuisance action), and to deter D from engaging in the future in conduct similar to the conduct sanctioned by the remedy (this last function being commonly referred to as "deterrence").

The indirect extrinsic functions of tort law are multifarious and include the protection of property, deterring people other than D from engaging in the sort of conduct for which D was sanctioned ("general deterrence"), reinforcement of contract (by the imposition of liability for third-party interference), the preservation of competition (by the limitations on liability for causing economic loss to a competitor), loss spreading (*via* vicarious liability and as a result of interaction between tort liability and liability insurance), the protection of life and property (by, for instance, taking account of the fact that D acted in an emergency), law enforcement (by providing defences such as lawful arrest to claims for trespass to the person), the due administration of justice (by giving judges and advocates an immunity from tort liability in respect of their conduct in court), preserving the freedom of action of public authorities (by applying the test of extraordinary negligence[3] in negligence actions against them), and preserving freedom of contract (by allowing selective contracting-out of tort liability). Such functions often appear in judgments of the courts in the guise of "policy considerations".

Two related points should be made about indirect extrinsic functions. The first (noted above) is that such functions are as much a product of the limits of tort liability as of the triggers of tort liability. Thus, the concept of duty of care in the tort of negligence, which is used partly to define the limits of liability for negligent conduct, plays a very important part in establishing and advancing indirect extrinsic functions of tort law. The concept of protected interests also plays a central role in establishing the indirect extrinsic functions of tort law. This is because protected interests are typically defined in quite general terms which are apt to include certain broadly defined human activities within the protection of tort law and to exclude others from that protection. By contrast, the concept of sanctioned conduct tends to be defined much more by reference to the facts of individual cases in such a way as to reduce its relevance for parties other than those to the dispute in question.

[3] See p. 41 above.

Secondly, whereas the direct extrinsic functions of tort law are related to the remedies made available by the courts in individual cases, many of the indirect extrinsic functions of tort law are a product of statutory accretions to tort law. Putting this point another way, whereas the law of "tort remedies" is fundamentally the handiwork of the courts, many of the indirect functions of tort law have been ascribed to it by the legislature. Thus, heads of tort liability concerned with intellectual property rights are almost all statutory; the "anti-discrimination torts" are statutory, and there are many other statutes breach of the provisions of which can give rise to claims which are analogous to claims classified as part of tort law.

Tort law offers a set of remedial possibilities which can be used to protect many different interests against a relatively narrow range of types of sanctioned conduct. The various heads of tort liability are triggers of these various remedial possibilities. Some of these triggers have been created by the courts, and others have been created by legislation. The indirect extrinsic functions of tort law are related to the triggers of tort remedies, and its direct extrinsic functions are related to those remedies. Seen from the point of view of the "owners" of interests protected by tort law, being able to trigger tort liability is a valuable resource; and seen from the point of view of a person who interferes in some way with an interest of another, freedom from tort liability is a valuable resource. By creating triggers of tort liability, the courts and the legislature allocate valuable resources. When, in *Donoghue v. Stevenson*, the House of Lords held that a manufacturer could be held liable to a consumer for personal injury caused to the latter by a defect in the former's product, it gave consumers a valuable resource at the expense of manufacturers. The indirect extrinsic functions of tort law are related to the allocation of "tort resources" in society. It is by the creation of rights of action in tort or by the refusal to create such rights of action that the indirect extrinsic functions of tort law are defined and furthered.

THE RELATIONSHIP BETWEEN THE ANATOMY OF TORT LAW AND ITS FUNCTIONS AND EFFECTS

General Approach

So far in this book I have dealt mainly with the internal structure of tort law and its conceptual relationship to other departments of the law of obligations. I have not (explicitly, at least) been much concerned with the question of how tort law is to be justified. Rules and principles of tort law are not like rocks – rocks just exist, and we are not concerned to ask what justifies the existence of rocks, as opposed to what explains their existence. Law in general, and tort law in particular, is a different matter. Law is a human artefact, and it interesting and important to ask not only what explains the existence and content of tort law, but also what justifies its existence and content. Tort law is an ethical, normative system, and is itself amenable to examination and assessment in ethical, normative terms.

Perhaps the most fundamental issue debated by modern theorists interested in tort law concerns the best way to go about justifying tort law. On one side of the debate are those who say that the justifiability of tort law depends on whether the functions it performs (or is designed to perform) are desirable ones and, if so, how well tort law performs those functions. On the other side of the debate are those who say that instead of asking whether tort law is "a good thing" judged by its functions and its effects, as the "functionalist" or "consequentialist" approach to tort law does, the question we should ask is whether tort law gives effect to our ideas of what is "right". For want of a better term, I shall refer to this latter view as "essentialist". In philosophical jargon, essentialists assert the "priority of what is right over what is good", while functionalists equate the right with the good.

A leading exponent of the essentialist position is Ernest Weinrib.[4] Greatly simplifying his view, he believes that what justifies the existence and content of tort law is that it embodies the principle that people should not wrong others by their actions. This principle is said to be derived from the very idea of what it means to be a sentient moral human being. Weinrib also believes that the functions of tort law, whether intrinsic or extrinsic, can and should play no part in justifying tort law. As far as Weinrib is concerned, the existence and content of tort law are justified because, and only to the extent that, they embody the idea of responsibility of each person for their actions. To the extent that rules and principles which we classify as part of tort law do not embody this basic notion, they are not properly part of tort law. The "essence" of tort law is rooted in this idea of responsibility for human action, and by definition any element of what we call tort law which is inconsistent with this essence is not actually part of tort law. For Weinrib, tort law is as tort law

---

[4] *The Idea of Private Law* (Cambridge, Mass, 1995).

should be. Any aspect of tort law which should be otherwise is not tort law!

At the other extreme of this debate about the justification for tort law are those who have argued that tort law is properly understood as a means for achieving what is called "economic efficiency". The concept of "efficiency" is a very complex one, and for present purposes there is, fortunately, no need to examine it in detail. My interest is not in the substance of the "economic interpretation" of tort law but in the methodology of those who espouse it. They say that the existence and content of tort law is justified because, and only to the extent that, it serves the function of achieving economic efficiency which, in very general terms, means the allocation of scarce resources to their most productive use. In other words, according to these economic analysts of law, the sole function of tort law is to maximize wealth. Maximizing wealth is, according to some such theorists, not only a good thing but also the right thing to do. These theorists would not say that aspects of tort law which do not maximize wealth are not part of tort law, because their theory is not one about the "essence" of tort law. Rather, they would say that such aspects of tort law are not justified because they do not further the goal of wealth maximization.

In my view, both of these extreme positions are unattractive. I have defined tort law as a system of ethical rules and principles of personal responsibility. I have also said that I believe that tort law serves certain functions. I do not understand theorists who adopt either of the extreme positions outlined above to deny either of these propositions. The extreme nature of their positions lies rather in views about the relationship between the justifiability of tort law on the one hand and the ethical principles it embodies and the functions which it serves on the other. In my opinion, the best approach to justifying tort law is to take account of both of these aspects. In other words, the value of tort law lies to some extent in the principles of right conduct which it embodies and to some extent in the goodness of the functions which it serves. I do not believe that tort law has an essence such that ethically wrong rules and principles of tort law are, for that very reason, not part of tort law. Nor do I believe that tort law can be justified only by reference to whether it espouses or achieves certain goals. The public acknowledgement and enforcement of certain principles of personal responsibility can be valuable for no other reason than that of reinforcing those principles. On the other hand, tort law may not be the only way of reinforcing such principles, and if doing so through tort law serves no good social purpose beyond reinforcing the principles themselves, we may want to question whether tort law should not be abandoned in favour of some other method of reinforcement.

Once we abandon the idea, which seems to be implicit in the extreme essentialist approach, that tort law should be understood solely in terms of what it means to be a human being, we will want to ask whether the benefits of tort law, be it in terms of reinforcement of principles of personal responsibility or in terms of some other social function, are worth the costs of the tort system. Like all social institutions, tort law has costs. The system of publicly enforceable ethical principles of personal responsibility which tort law consists of requires money and human labour to administer. Because tort law is a human artefact, its value and its justifiability need to be assessed in the same way as we assess the value and justifiability of all other human products – namely by weighing its costs against its benefits.

In short, I think that tort law is justified partly by the extent to which it embodies sound ethical principles of personal responsibility and partly to the extent that it furthers desirable human and social goals. Moreover, justifiability is not a black and white thing but a matter of degree. This is obviously true as concerns the achievement of functions – a human artefact which is designed for certain purposes may achieve those purposes more or less well. Moreover, even if an artefact performs a particular function as well as that artefact can, we might still not approve of it if some other artefact could perform the function better at the same or less cost. By contrast, if we could imagine no such alternative artefact, we might consider the one we have to be acceptable even though it does not achieve its function as well as we would like. I believe that justifiability is also a matter of degree so far as the embodying of ethical principles of personal responsibility is concerned. This is because reasonable people may disagree about what are the correct principles of personal responsibility. In a society, such disagreements need to be managed if unacceptable and even destructive levels of social conflict are to be avoided. This is one of the functions of tort law. Reasonable people might disagree not only about the extent to which tort law embodies correct principles of personal responsibility, but also about the extent to which tort law embodies a defensible compromise between conflicting views about personal responsibility. To the extent that tort law serves the function of moderating between conflicting moral views, it may be judged more or less successful as a public set of ethical principles.

My general approach, therefore, to the relationship between the structure, the functions and the effects of tort law is that examination of functions and effects is necessary for a rounded assessment of its justifiability and acceptability as a social institution. My aim in this book is not to support a view one way or the other about the justifiability of the existence or current content of tort law. Rather, in previous chapters I have sought to give an account of the structure of tort law; and in this chapter my aim is to discuss the functions typically attributed to tort law and the extent to which tort law aids the realization of those functions. In this chapter I will also consider whether tort law has any side-effects relevant to an assessment of its acceptability. I leave it to the reader to decide whether the ethical principles of personal responsibility embodied in tort law are the correct ones and whether tort law embodies good compromises between conflicting moral views about personal responsibility. Similarly, I will leave it to the reader to decide whether the functions attributed to tort law are desirable ones for tort law to pursue and whether any side-effects of tort law make it more or less acceptable. To the extent that the side-effects of tort law are seen as being positive, they may add to its acceptability; and to the extent that they are judged to be negative, they may count as a cost of tort law which will need to be outweighed by countervailing advantages in order to ensure its acceptability.

One final general point needs to be made about the relationship between tort law and its functions. In my view, not only must we pay attention to both the structure and content of tort law and to its functions in order to make a rounded assessment of its justifiability, but I also believe that we cannot properly understand tort law and the way it works as a social institution without giving proper weight to both of these aspects. There are two reasons for this: first, as I have said before, tort law is a human artefact which exists not for its own sake but for the service of human goals and aspirations. Seeking to understand tort law without referring to its functions is rather like seeking to understand traffic lights without knowing what they are for. Secondly, the achievement by tort law of any and all of its functions is inevitably constrained by its structure and content. This is just as true of the intrinsic as of the extrinsic functions of tort law. We might say that one of the intrinsic functions of tort law is to protect valued human interests. But tort law only protects certain human interests. Similarly, we might say that one of the intrinsic functions of tort law is to sanction unacceptable human conduct. But tort law only sanctions certain types of unacceptable human conduct. Or consider the direct extrinsic function of compensation: we might say that a function of tort law is to compensate for harm caused by human conduct. But tort law only compensates for certain types of harm and only if it is caused by certain types of conduct. It does not further our understanding of tort law to attribute to it functions for which it is ill-adapted by reason of its structure and content without acknow ledging the mismatch. Of course, people may seek to use tort law to perform functions which it is not well-suited to performing, just as a homeless person might take up residence in an empty garage. Moreover, people might seek to adapt tort law to make it more suitable for performing certain functions by changing its structure or content, just as redundant churches are sometimes adapted as dwellings. A rounded understanding of either of these phenomena requires a recognition of the symbiotic relationship between the structure and content of tort law on the one hand, and its functions on the other.

Intrinsic Functions

There is obviously an intimate relationship between the intrinsic functions of tort law and its anatomy. Indeed, we may say that the intrinsic functions of tort law form part of the definition of what tort law is. It does not follow, however, that tort law will necessarily fulfil all of these functions equally well. For instance, the amount of guidance which tort law gives to people about how they should behave will depend on how clear and precise its rules are, and on the extent to which they are internally consistent. More generally, the precision, clarity and internal consistency of the rules and principles of tort law or their lack of these qualities are important determinants of how well tort law performs its intrinsic functions. But at the risk of tautology, we can say that unless tort law performed its intrinsic functions to some minimal extent, it would not be tort law. A blunt knife may still warrant the name "knife"; but a length of thin metal pipe would not. If a set of rules and principles was so lacking in precision, clarity and internal consistency that it provided those to whom it was addressed with no effective guidance as to how they should behave, we would not describe it as a system of ethics or personal responsibility.

Nevertheless, there is a distinction between tort law and its intrinsic functions. This distinction is implicit, for instance, in the idea that the rules of tort law might be "reformed" and improved. It is a legitimate criticism of a rule or principle of tort law as such that it is too vague to give any real guidance to those to whom it is addressed about how they should behave, or that it is inconsistent with another rule or principle of tort law which is thought to be a good one. Even if we believe that the main criterion of acceptability of tort law is the correctness of the ethical rules and principles it contains and the acceptability of the moral compromises it gives effect to, we might still want to say that tort law can be judged as better or worse according to how well or badly it serves the intrinsic functions listed above.

Direct Extrinsic Functions

Remedies in Individual Cases

As I said earlier, one of the intrinsic functions of tort law is to resolve disputes so as to maintain social order and promote social cohesion. Essential to the realization of this function is both the existence of adjudicative bodies, independent of the parties in dispute, which have power to resolve disputes authoritatively, and also a set of enforceable remedies. Tort law is not simply a system of ethical rules and principles of personal responsibility, but an ethical system enforceable with the assistance of the state. One of the most important factors which distinguishes the system of ethical principles of personal responsibility which we call "tort law" from the analogous system of ethical principles of responsibility which we call "morality" is that different sanctions attach to infringements of the two systems. If infringements of tort law could not trigger remedies enforceable with the assistance of the state, we would not recognize it as tort law. A system of independent adjudicative bodies and a set of enforceable remedies is intrinsic to our concept of tort law (and, indeed, of law generally).

However, this general point leaves many questions undecided about the nature of such independent adjudicative bodies and about the remedies available for infringements of tort law. For example, it has recently been suggested that medical negligence claims would be better dealt with by specialist tribunals rather than by traditional courts. As for remedies, there is a lively debate about whether punitive damages ought to be available at all in tort law. The general point also says nothing about the way individual tort claims are dealt with. In fact, the vast majority of tort claims are not resolved by independent adjudicators but are "settled" by agreement between the parties in dispute. In such cases, the dispute is directly resolved not by the award of an enforceable remedy but by a contractual agreement as to what the parties will do. Breach of such an agreement could, ultimately, attract an enforceable remedy, but only after the instigation of legal proceedings for breach of contract (not for the tort). Even though there may be disagreement about the best way to resolve tort disputes, or about the sort of remedies which ought to be available in tort law, we still think that what we are disagreeing about *is* tort law. Such disagreements are not intrinsic to our conception of tort law as a publicly enforceable set of ethical principles of personal responsibility. Also, the fact that a tort dispute is settled by agreement between the parties rather than by recourse to an independent adjudicator and the enforcement machinery of the state would not, by itself, cause us to say that the settlement did not involve an application of tort law. Putting this point slightly differently, the way tort law is applied and enforced in individual cases is not intrinsic to the idea of tort law. Tort law exists as an enforceable public set of ethical rules and principles independently of its operation in relation to individual disputes.

It is on this basis that I have distinguished between the intrinsic functions of tort law and its direct extrinsic functions. Tort law performs its direct extrinsic functions by the remedies available to resolve individual cases. The remedy awarded or obtained in any individual case is not intrinsic to our idea of tort law, and this is why I have called the functions performed by such remedies "extrinsic". It is intrinsic to our idea of tort law that it have a set of enforceable remedies; but the content of that set of remedies and the particular remedy or remedies awarded to resolve particular tort disputes are not intrinsic to our idea of tort law. Even though compensation for loss suffered by the plaintiff is available as a remedy for every tort, I do not think that compensation for loss is intrinsic to our idea of tort law. Compensation for losses suffered is not part of the idea of a publicly enforceable set of ethical rules and principles of personal responsibility. If this is true of this pervasive remedy, how much more must it be true of other less pervasive remedies, such as disgorgement of gains. In this sense, the functions performed by particular tort remedies are extrinsic to our idea of tort law.

The Effectiveness of Tort Remedies

At one level, how effectively, in individual cases, tort law performs the direct extrinsic functions of compensating, punishing, securing disgorgement and bringing it about that defendants act or refrain from acting in particular ways depends on how effectively the remedy awarded is enforced. If the defendant pays to the plaintiff any monetary award made by way of compensation, disgorgement or punishment, or complies with any order to act or to refrain from action, then tort law will have performed its relevant direct extrinsic function in that case. Moreover, if the defendant complies with any order to act or to refrain from acting, the direct function of deterring future tortious conduct by that defendant will also have been effectively performed.

In cases where the remedy is a monetary award, this deterrence function is much more problematic. In the first place, not all monetary remedies in tort cases can plausibly be said to have deterrence as one of their functions. For example, if a defendant is ordered to pay compensatory or disgorgement damages in respect of purely innocent conduct, it makes no sense to say that a function of such damages is to deter the defendant from similar innocent conduct in the future. The prime purpose of such remedies is to affirm the importance of a protected interest, not to deter the conduct of the defendant. It is meaningful to speak of deterrence as a direct extrinsic function of tort remedies only in cases where the conduct in question was intentional, reckless or negligent. Secondly, in cases where damages are awarded "*in lieu* of an injunction", it is certainly not a function of the award to deter the defendant from tortious conduct in the future. For instance, suppose that D commits an actionable nuisance against P and is ordered to pay damages *in lieu* of an injunction to restrain the nuisance. The fact that an injunction could have been awarded indicates that the courts believed that D would probably go on committing the tort of nuisance in the future. The purpose and legal effect of the award of damages *in lieu* is to legalize D's conduct: by paying damages, D acquires the legal right to continue with the conduct which has been held to constitute a nuisance. The message which the award of damages *in lieu* of an injunction gives is that D should not have interfered with the use and enjoyment by P of P's land *without compensating* P. The award gives no unconditional message that D should not have interfered with the use of the land by P. Furthermore, the law does not prevent a defendant against whom an injunction to restrain future tortious conduct is awarded from buying out the injunction by offering P a sum of money in return for being released from the obligation to comply with it.

We might be tempted to conclude from this latter example that even in respect of intentional, reckless or negligent conduct, the message implicit in an award of damages is not that conduct of the type for which D was responsible ought to be avoided but rather that *either* D should avoid such conduct in the future *or* D should pay damages in respect of such conduct if it inflicts loss on P or generates a gain for D. On this interpretation, people are free to choose between avoiding interference with the interests of another and paying damages in respect of such interference. Many would find this interpretation unacceptable, at least as a general approach. Few would be willing to accept that another should be allowed intentionally to inflict personal injury on them against their will provided only that the other was prepared to pay for the right to do so. Similarly, many people would be unwilling to accept that another should be allowed to take or use their property without their consent provided only that the other was willing to pay for the right to do so. Many would take the view that such an interpretation puts too high a value on the freedom of action and the autonomy of those who interfere with the interests of others and too low a value on the interests interfered with. Such people might say that in tort law, the freedom of action and the autonomy of defendants are recognized by limitations on the interests to which the law is prepared to extend its protection and by defining the sorts of conduct which it will sanction. Tort law does not protect all human interests against all human conduct. But it follows from the interpretation of tort law as a set of rules and principles of personal responsibility that conduct proscribed by tort law is conduct which is contrary to the ethical requirements of the law. Singling out certain conduct as worthy of sanction is intrinsic to tort law whereas ordering D to pay damages to P is not. The remedies of tort law are means of expressing the law's attitude to the conduct sanctioned by it. The rules and principles of tort law have an ethical status independent of and superior to the remedies of tort law. On this view, the remedies of tort law are (with only a few possible exceptions) not the price of interfering with the interests of another but a sanction for doing so. In general, the remedies of tort law are designed to sanction interferences with interests, not to licence them or create a market in them.

Is Tort Law an Effective Deterrent?

As a justification for the imposition of tort liability to pay damages, deterrence of future tortious conduct by defendants is problematic for two reasons. First, whereas the other direct extrinsic goals of tort remedies can typically be secured by state enforcement procedures, deterrence of future tortious conduct by D depends on how D reacts to the award of the remedy after the damages have been paid. There is no state machinery to ensure that the desired deterrent effect of monetary tort liability is realized. Secondly, we know relatively little about how effective tort remedies are in deterring tort defendants from future tortious conduct. This problem of proof is also relevant to consideration of deterrence as an indirect extrinsic function of tort law. Intuitively, one would expect the deterrent effect of tort law to be greatest in respect of people who have been held liable in tort and in respect of the sort of conduct for which they have been held liable. However, as far as I am aware, no empirical research has been done which would help us to confirm or deny the validity of this intuition. Such research as has been done into the deterrent effects of tort law has not systematically distinguished between people who have been held liable in tort and those who have not.

Deterrence Constrained by Structure and Content of Tort Law—In assessing the deterrent effect of tort law, it is extremely important to give adequate weight to a point made earlier, namely that the achievement by tort law of any of its supposed functions is constrained by the structure and content of tort law. Take, for example, cases of so-called "environmental harm". An important characteristic of such harm is that no individual sufferer can prove, on the balance of probabilities, that any given individual caused it. Because proof of causation on the balance of probabilities is a feature of tort law in most jurisdictions, it could be said that tort law is poor at deterring environmental harm. However, we should note that the reason why tort law can be said to be a poor deterrent of such harm is that tort law does not impose liability for such harm; it is not because, although tort law imposes liability for such harm, it has little effect in deterring the infliction of such harm. Faced with the weakness of tort law in deterring environmental harms, we could either attempt to alter the content or structure of tort law to bring environmental harms within its scope, or we could look to some other social institution than tort law as a means of deterring such harms. Which course of action we chose would depend on an assessment of the relative merits of a reformed tort law and of any alternative to it as a means of deterring such harms.

Deterrence and the Operation of the Tort System—Another very important point to take into account in assessing the deterrent effects of tort law is that tort law is used much more in some areas than in others as a means of resolving disputes and securing legal remedies. For instance, in relation to personal injuries, the vast majority of successful tort claims are made in relation to road and work accidents; very few are made in relation to accidents in the home, for instance. It follows that when considering deterrence as a direct extrinsic function, tort law is much more likely to be effective in relation to road and work accidents than in relation to home accidents. When considering deterrence as an indirect extrinsic function, patterns of successful tort claims are not so crucial because the very existence of tort law may have some deterrent effect even in the absence of successful tort claims. Even in this context, however, one would expect tort law to have more deterrent effect in areas where successful tort claims are common than in areas where they are not. The reasons why successful tort claims are more common in some contexts than in others are many, complex and not well understood. The point is that in assessing the efficacy of tort law as a deterrent, we need to take account not only of its structure and content but also of the way and the extent to which it is used in practice as a means of dealing with interferences with interests which, in theory, it protects by conduct which, in theory, it sanctions.

Not surprisingly, the bulk of the empirical research into the deterrent effect of tort law has concerned those events which give rise to most tort claims, such as road accidents, work accidents and medical accidents. The significance of this research cannot be properly understood without taking account of the existence of third party liability insurance. In the typical successful tort claim in respect of injuries and damage suffered in a road, work or medical accident, any damages awarded are not paid by the tortfeasor but by an insurance company which has agreed to cover the risk of the defendant being held liable in tort. Indeed, in many jurisdictions, it is compulsory for vehicle owners and employers to buy liability insurance to cover the risk of being held liable in tort to another road user or an employee. The effect, and the attractiveness, of liability insurance is that it spreads the impact of being held liable to pay damages across persons and across time. If an insured defendant is held liable to pay damages, those damages will be paid out of the pool of money which the insurer has built up out of the insurance premiums paid by all its customers; and the insured's contribution to that pool will be spread over the period of years during which the insured is a customer of that insurer. The typical psychological impact of this spreading effect of insurance is to lull the insured into feeling that someone else is paying the damages. This generates what insurers call "moral hazard" which means that parties who are insured against liability are likely, for that very reason, to take fewer precautions to avoid liability than they would if they were not insured but faced the prospect of paying any damages award personally. For the typical insured party, the incentive to avoid liability created by the need to pay a relatively small annual insurance premium is considerably less than the incentive which would be created by facing the risk of having to pay a large sum of damages.

Insurers adopt various techniques to combat moral hazard, all designed to create a direct correlation between the magnitude of the risk that the insured will incur liability and the likely amount of that liability on the one hand, and the size of the premium payable by the insured on the other. If the premium payable by the insured is properly and directly "related to the risk of liability", so the argument goes, then an insured party will have the same incentive to avoid liability as would an uninsured party, other things being equal. In other words, it is widely accepted that if insurance premiums are properly risk-related, liability insurance will not dilute any deterrent effect of tort liability, or at least it will dilute that effect only to the extent inevitably attributable to the spreading achieved by insurance.

In reality, liability insurance premiums are often not properly risk-related. This is partly because it is much more expensive for insurers to tailor premiums to the risk presented by each individual insured person than to charge a uniform premium to all insureds or to all insureds who fall within a category crudely defined in terms of factors thought to be relevant to risk (such as age). The main concern of commercial insurers is to make a profit, and so long as the total amount they receive in premiums is adequate for this purpose, they have no very strong incentive to ensure that each insured pays a properly risk-related premium, especially if this raises the company's costs and hence reduces its competitiveness in the insurance market. Of course, an insurer will lose business if its premiums are totally insensitive to risk; but beyond a certain point, the costs to the insurer of relating premiums to risk are greater than the benefits such risk-relatedness yields.

In respect of personal injuries, tort law only became an important source of compensation for victims with the development of liability insurance in the late 19th century. The tort system could not operate in the way it does as a provider of compensation for personal injury victims if liability insurance was not pervasive and, in some contexts, compulsory. This means that when we talk about the deterrent effect of tort law in this context, we are really talking about the deterrent effect of tort law coupled with liability insurance. We are not in a position to compare the deterrent effect of tort law by itself with that of tort law coupled with liability insurance. Furthermore, it is difficult to construct empirical research projects which tell us much about the deterrent effect of tort law coupled with liability insurance. In a recent comprehensive survey of the relevant literature,[5] the authors conclude in relation to medical accidents that it is "impossible", on the basis of available evidence, "to reach firm conclusions regarding the medical malpractice system as a mechanism for deterring accidents". The conclusion in relation to work accidents is similar.[6] In relation to road accidents, some research has been conducted in jurisdictions where the tort system has been totally or partially replaced by a non-tort, first-party insurance system of dealing with the consequences of such accidents. In this respect, the authors conclusion on the basis of the available evidence[7] is that the tort system and a non-tort system will have similar deterrent effects provided they contain similar incentives to take care in the form of risk-related insurance premiums. The fact of the matter is that we have insufficient evidence to enable us to say how effective or ineffective the tort system coupled with liability insurance is in reducing the incidence of tort-induced losses. For this reason, it would be unwise to pronounce the tort system either justified or unjustified in terms of its deterrence function.

Deterrence and Unitary Theories of Tort Law—In the light of this conclusion, it is important to bear in mind that deterrence is only one of the direct extrinsic functions of tort law (and only one of its indirect extrinsic functions). Even if it turned out that tort law had little or no discernible deterrent effect either through remedies awarded in individual cases or more generally, we might still think that tort law was a justified by its contribution to the achievement of other desirable goals.

However, some economic analysts of law see deterrence as the only function of tort law. For them, the only function of tort remedies is to provide incentives for the avoidance of economically

---

[5] D. Dewees, D. Duff and M. Trebilcock, *Exploring the Domain of Accident Law* (New York, 1996), 112.

[6] Ibid, 355.

[7] Ibid, 416.

inefficient behaviour. The aim of economic efficiency is the maximization of wealth in society regardless of how that wealth is distributed amongst the members of society. For this reason, there is no place in economic analysis of tort law for protected interests. For instance, economic analysts define negligent conduct as conduct the costs of which are greater than its benefits. Conduct which produces an excess of benefits over costs increases social wealth. By contrast, negligent conduct reduces social wealth. So in economic analysis, negligent infliction of personal injury is unacceptable not because everyone has a legitimate interest in bodily health and safety but only because negligent conduct reduces social wealth. In economic analysis, the only purpose of tort law is to ensure that the costs of inefficient behaviour are borne by the person engaging in the behaviour so as to give that person an incentive not to engage in such conduct in the future. The purpose of awarding damages to P is not to protect P's interest but to give an incentive to D not to engage in the future in inefficient conduct. For economic analysts, the only reason to require D to pay damages to P rather than to a charity (for instance) is to give injured parties an economic incentive to sue injurers and in this way to enable a court to give injurers incentives to avoid inefficient conduct.

The economic theory of tort law (which defines tortious conduct as inefficient conduct and says that the only function of tort law is to provide incentives for the avoidance of inefficient conduct) operates at three levels. At one level it presents itself as an explanation for the structure and content of tort law; at a second level it presents itself as a tool for predicting the outcome of tort cases; and at a third level, it presents itself as a criterion for judging whether particular rules and principles of tort law are acceptable or not. I leave it to the reader to decide whether tort law ought to be aiming to maximize social wealth and whether it ought to be changed to the extent that is does not further this goal. As an explanatory theory (to which the predictive role is an adjunct), economic analysis of tort law is unattractive for two related reasons. First, it fails to account for the fact that protected interests are just as important a component of the structure of tort law as sanctioned conduct. In economic analysis, defendants are centre-stage and plaintiffs mere functionaries; whereas the rules and principles of tort law are just as concerned with plaintiffs' interests as with defendants' conduct. In tort law, for instance, an injured plaintiff is entitled to receive damages, whereas in economic theory the only reason for paying the damages to the plaintiff is a secondary one of providing an incentive for the plaintiff to sue the defendant and, in this way, to enable the legal system to create the primary incentive for the avoidance of inefficient conduct by the defendant.

Secondly, economic analysts tend to concentrate on those parts of tort law which are concerned with sanctioned conduct, causation and remoteness of damage, and sanctions; and they tend to ignore equally important aspects of tort law, such as the concept of duty of care in negligence and the phenomenon of torts actionable *per se*. The reason why economic analysts ignore duty of care rules, for instance, is that such rules define the limits of the availability of remedies for negligent conduct. In terms of economic analysis, they define the limits of the availability of tort remedies for inefficient conduct. According to economic theory, all negligent conduct should be discouraged; but tort law does not do this. If we view the right to sue in tort and freedom from being sued in tort as valuable economic resources, the effect of a duty of care rule denying a right to sue in respect of negligent conduct is to distribute "tort resources" inconsistently with the dictates of efficiency. For instance, in English law a local authority which negligently causes economic loss to a houseowner by exercise of or failure to exercise statutory powers to enforce building regulations owes no duty of care to the houseowner. This is not because the local authority has not acted inefficiently – having acted negligently it has, by definition, acted inefficiently. Rather it is because the law wishes the costs of non-compliance with building regulations to be borne by builders, not enforcement authorities (and through them, the taxpayer). In order to achieve its desired distribution of the costs of shoddy building work, the law is prepared to forego the opportunity to give enforcement authorities incentives to avoid inefficient conduct.

The methodological weakness of the explanatory version of economic analysis of law is that it starts with a particular "unitary" theory of the function of tort law and works back from that to an examination of the structure and content of tort law. In doing this, it classifies as "mistaken" any aspect of its structure or content which is not consistent with the chosen function. Another explanatory theory of tort law which suffers from the same weakness is that which says that tort law is best understood in terms of "corrective justice". A leading exponent of this theory is Ernest Weinrib. In his view, the only purpose of tort law is to make good wrongful losses inflicted on one person by the positive conduct of another which unjustly intrudes on the autonomy of the former. In working out the implications of this theory, Weinrib classifies as mistakes, or as not really part of tort law, both liability for nonfeasance and strict liability. Like the economic analysts, Weinrib focuses on those aspects of tort law concerned with sanctioned conduct and ignores concepts such as duty of care. But whereas the economic analysts largely ignore the aspect of tort law which I have called "correlativity", Weinrib focuses on this aspect to the virtual exclusion of everything else. In contrast to both of these approaches, I have attempted both to give a rounded account of the structure and content of tort law and to examine the various functions which have been attributed to it. My account is, I believe, stronger as an explanation of tort law than either Weinrib's or that of the economic analysts. On the other hand, I have not, unlike these theorists, attempted to propound a normative vision of the function and purpose of tort law.

The reason why my explanatory account of tort law is not based on a single principle, and the reason why I have not attempted to propound a normative vision of tort law is partly that I take a certain view of human nature and of human morality which is different from that which I believe underlies theories such as those of Weinrib and the economic analysts. These theories assume that it is possible and desirable to discover a unifying explanatory idea or normative principle underlying institutions such as tort law. This approach seems to me to be based on an unrealistic view of human nature. It is typical of human beings that they pursue in their lives a large number of different goals, at least some of which conflict amongst themselves. Faced with such conflicts, people must choose to prefer one of the conflicting goals over the others. Typically, people make such choices not according to any unitary theory about the purpose of (their) life, but by assigning weights to the conflicting goals in the context of the particular conflict according to some value judgement which may, in another context, itself be in conflict with another of that person's goals. The process of resolving conflicts between our goals is one of constant readjustment in the light of circumstances rather than one of single-minded adherence to a unitary vision. If this is true of the way individuals approach difficult choices between conflicting goals (as I believe it to be), how much more is it likely to be true of the way goal conflicts are resolved in a social institution such as tort law. Tort law is infected with the same tendency to pursue multifarious and potentially conflicting goals as are other forms of human purposive activity. But it is even less likely than in the case of individuals that the life of a society will be informed by a unifying principle which could be brought to bear to resolve conflicts of goals within tort law. Here, as in the lives of individuals, conflicts of goals tend to be resolved by giving priority to one goal over another (or others) in the circumstances of individual cases according to value judgements which may themselves, in different circumstances, conflict with other social goals.

It might be argued that without a unifying principle, the choice between conflicting goals will be "arbitrary and indeterminate . . . unless there is some foundational norm that . . . at its deepest level is monistic rather than pluralistic".[8] I do not believe that human values and goals can be reduced in this way to a single principle. Indeed, inflexible adherence to a single goal is often taken as a sign of pathological obsessiveness and may even be considered a moral fault. Moreover, if we are to find a unifying principle "at the deepest level" it is unlikely to be much use in resolving the shallow conflicts which tort law has to deal with. But even if one accepted that a unifying principle could and should be found, it is unlikely that either economic efficiency or corrective justice would provide such a principle. It is undoubtedly true that increasing social wealth is a goal of individuals and of societies, but no individual or society pursues that goal to the exclusion of all others. And the same is true of corrective justice (at least as explained by Weinrib). As unifying explanatory concepts, both are inadequate because neither is "deep" or "abstract" enough. However, it also seems to me that even such highly abstract concepts as liberty or equality[9] are inadequate as unifying explanatory theories because although all individuals and societies value both liberty and equality, no-one values either to the total exclusion of the other or of many other valued ends. No single concept can explain tort law because no single concept can explain human motivation.

Because I believe that it is undesirable to seek and, indeed, impossible to find a unitary concept or principle to explain tort law, I also believe it to be undesirable to seek, and impossible to find, a unitary normative principle with which to evaluate and according to which to reform tort law. Plurality and indeterminacy in human life and social institutions is not only inevitable but also full of opportunity. If human life were ultimately governed by a single normative principle, the diversity, variety and infinite possibilities for which we value it would be destroyed, or at least seriously diminished.

[8] R. Wright, "Right, Justice and Tort Law" in D.G. Owen (ed), *Philosophical Foundations of Tort Law* (Oxford, 1995), 159, 160.
[9] The latter espoused by Wright.

Indirect Extrinsic Functions

Whereas the direct extrinsic functions of tort law are related to the resolution of individual tort disputes, the indirect extrinsic functions of tort law are related to the rules of tort law which have an impact beyond any individual tort dispute. Guiding and sanctioning conduct and protecting interests are intrinsic functions of tort law; and its indirect extrinsic functions are related to the particular guidance it gives, the sorts of conduct it sanctions and the interests it protects. The extrinsic functions of tort law may relate not only to rules about when tort liability may arise but also to rules about when it will not arise. For instance, a major goal of the courts in recent years in limiting liability for negligently caused purely economic loss has been to encourage people to seek protection in the market for certain of their economic interests. In one sense, the indirect extrinsic functions of tort law are more important than its direct extrinsic functions. In general, dispute avoidance is to be preferred to dispute resolution. The prime function of tort law is to establish a set of rules and principles of personal responsibility by which the lives of individuals in society can be regulated and coordinated. Dispute resolution is a secondary function of any body of law, even a body of law such as tort law which is protective rather than constitutive. Of course, the same set of rules and principles are implicated in the performance of both the direct and the indirect extrinsic functions of tort law. The direct functions relate to tort law as a dispute settlement mechanism and the indirect functions to tort law as a form of "applied morality". One of the things which distinguishes law from morality is exactly that the latter does not function as a social mechanism for resolving disputes because it lacks the institutional apparatus necessary for the performance of this function. What enables tort law to perform this function is not its structure and content as such but rather the system of public dispute-settling bodies which administer it.

It is not part of my aim in this book to spell out the indirect extrinsic functions served by the mass of rules and principles which make up tort law. Doing this would involve explaining what lawyers call the "policy justifications" for the multifarious rules of tort law. In other words, I use the term "indirect extrinsic functions" as a rough equivalent of the terms "policy considerations" or "policy justifications" or simply "policy", all of which are much used in tort law. These terms are most commonly used to refer to matters relevant to the function of tort law as applied public morality, as opposed to its function as a set of rules and principles for settling disputes. Because tort law performs both of these functions, and because the rules of tort law are generated in large part incidentally to the resolution of disputes between individuals, the courts must always have an eye on the role of tort law as public morality when resolving individual disputes. For this reason, it is unsatisfactory to view tort law solely or even predominantly in terms of the resolution of disputes between individuals because in doing this, courts must always have an eye to the impact on third parties of the way any particular dispute is resolved. It is considerations relevant to this wider impact which the courts refer to by the term "policy".

In some tort cases, this wider impact is all that is in issue before the court. Some of the most important tort cases in the last 70 years have been decided by a procedure involving the resolution of a "preliminary point of law". In these cases the issue has typically been whether the defendant owed the plaintiff a duty of care in the tort of negligence. The question before the court in such a case is not whether D has committed a tort against P but only whether, assuming D to have been guilty of sanctioned conduct, that conduct interfered with an interest of P which is protected by the law of tort. For example, in *Donoghue* v. *Stevenson* the only question before the court was whether a manufacturer owed a duty of care to persons, other than a purchaser of the manufacturer's product, injured by a defect in the product. Again, in *Dorset Yacht Co. Ltd* v. *Home Office*[10] the question before the court was, in effect, whether prison authorities owed a duty to owners of property near the prison to take care to prevent prisoners escaping and damaging the property. In such cases, the question is which of two groups in society should bear the risk of certain types of misfortune: should consumers or manufacturers bear the risk of injuries caused by defective products; and should prison authorities or property owners bear the risk that prisoners will escape and cause damage? Although the context in which such questions arise is a dispute between individuals, the answer to such questions is not directed solely or even primarily towards resolving that dispute. Indeed, courts confronted with such questions often complain that they are being asked to answer the question without knowing all the details of the dispute which gave rise to it; and the result of such a case is not to resolve the dispute between the parties but only to provide the parties with a legal rule relevant to resolving their dispute. More

[10] [1970] AC 1004.

importantly, such cases establish general rules which are added to the body of public morality which we call tort law.

Once again, it is extremely important to observe that the performance by tort law of its indirect extrinsic functions is constrained by its structure and content, especially when discussing the so-called function of "loss-spreading" or "loss-distribution". Loss-spreading, as the term indicates, refers to the phenomenon of the costs of tortious conduct (in terms of harm inflicted by sanctioned conduct) being spread widely and thinly amongst a group of individuals rather than being borne by the victim or the tortfeasor alone. The main instruments of loss-spreading are insurance and what might be called "passing-on". Insurance spreads losses amongst the members of the group of premium-payers who contribute to the pool of funds from which any insurance pay-out is made. Passing-on refers to the ability of producers of goods and services to spread their costs amongst their customers by increasing the prices of their goods and services, amongst their employees by adjustment of their wages, and amongst shareholders by adjustment of dividends. One of the direct functions of the imposition of tort liability to pay damages for loss caused is to shift that loss from the victim to the injurer (or, in other words, to compensate the victim); and conversely, one of the direct functions of a refusal to impose tort liability for loss caused is to leave that loss to lie where it fell, namely on the victim. If the party on whom the loss ultimately rests is insured against (liability for) that loss, or if that party is in a position to pass the loss on to a group of customers or employees, the loss may be spread. Spreading of losses is desirable because it prevents undue financial disruption and dislocation in the lives of individuals. The spreading of losses is also a practical precondition of the achievement of indirect extrinsic goals (such as compensation) of a system of legal liability under which defendants are regularly required to pay amounts of damages greater than the sum of their personal resources available for this purpose.[11]

The allocation of losses, either by shifting them from victim to injurer or by leaving them to lie where they fall, is clearly one of the direct extrinsic functions of tort law. Equally clearly, loss spreading is a function of insurance and of passing-on. But is the spreading of losses caused by conduct sanctioned by tort law a function of tort

---

[11] The whole system of legal liability would collapse if potential defendants were willing and able to make themselves "judgment-proof". For detailed and sophisticated consideration of this issue in the US context see L.M. LoPucki, "The Death of Liability" (1996) 106 *Yale LJ* 1.

law? At first sight, the answer to this question would apparently have to be negative because tort law cannot, by itself, achieve loss-spreading; and it is odd to suggest that people might seek to use a mechanism to perform a function which it is incapable, by reason of its structure and contents, of performing. On the other hand, if it were the case that some rule or rules of tort law governing the allocation of losses adopted, as a criterion of allocation, the ability of a party to pass the loss on, or the ability of a party to buy insurance against (liability for) the loss, we might be tempted to say that the function of that rule was to allocate loss in such a way as to facilitate its spreading by passing-on or insurance.

In fact, there are some rules of tort law which are open to such an interpretation. One is the principle that an employer is vicariously liable for the torts of its employees committed in the course of their employment. As noted in Chapter 3, vicarious liability is a form of strict, relationship-based liability.[12] One of the standard justifications given for the principle of vicarious liability is that the typical employer is better placed than the typical employee to insure against losses caused by employees' torts or to pass them on to customers and employees. Some people would say that a function of vicarious liability is to spread the costs of employees' torts.

A second example can be found in a recent House of Lords decision in a case called *The Nicholas H*.[13] In this case an inspector employed by what is called a "classification society" negligently certified that *The Nicholas H* was seaworthy following emergency repairs. The vessel set sail, but soon sank. The plaintiff's cargo was lost. P recovered damages for some of its loss from the shipowner; but the shipowner's liability was limited by an international convention, and P sued the classification society for damages representing the balance of its loss. The House of Lords held that the classification society owed no duty of care to the cargo owner. It was not argued that the inspector had not been negligent or that the negligence was not a cause of the plaintiff's loss. Rather, the majority based its decision on a variety of "policy" considerations including, "from the point of view of the cargo owners", that in a case such as this, the loss not recoverable from the shipowners was "under the existing system . . . readily insurable".[14]

---

[12] See p. 46 above.

[13] *Marc Rich & Co AG* v. *Bishop Rock Marine Co Ltd (The Nicholas H)* [1996] AC 211. See also P. Cane, "Classification Societies, Cargo Owners and the Basis of Tort Liability" [1995] *LMCLQ* 433.

[14] [1996] AC 211, 242.

It is on the basis of examples such as this that some people would argue that one of the indirect extrinsic functions of tort law is loss spreading. It is important to understand what this argument says and what it does not say. No-one argues that there is a rule of tort law to the effect that a person may be held liable in tort for loss suffered by another simply on the basis that the defendant was in a better position than the plaintiff to spread the loss; nor that there is a rule of tort law denying liability for loss suffered simply on the basis that the victim was in a better position than the defendant to spread the loss. The elements of every head of tort liability are protected interests and sanctioned conduct; and where P has suffered loss for which compensation is sought, there must be a causal connection between the loss and some conduct sanctioned by the law of tort. What some people do say, however, is that within the constraints of the structure of tort law, in deciding what conduct to sanction (in the case of vicarious liability, for instance) or what interests to protect (in the case of *The Nicholas H*, for instance), the courts sometimes take account of the loss-spreading abilities of the parties. To this extent, it is said, one of the functions of tort law is to ensure that losses are effectively spread.

A real problem with this argument lies in the qualification "within the constraints of the structure of tort law". The structure of tort law is that of a set of ethical principles of personal responsibility based on protected interests, sanctioned conduct, and sanctions. By contrast, the ability of a party to spread losses by insurance or passing-on is not the basis of a principle of personal responsibility. This means that even if a court purports to take loss spreading ability into account in constructing a rule of tort law, the need to justify the rule in terms of the structure of tort law as a system of principles of personal responsibility means that it will always be possible to rationalize a rule of tort law in terms of principles of personal responsibility (however contested), and that a court will typically provide such a rationalization even if it also rationalizes the decision in terms of loss spreading. So, for instance, one justification for vicarious liability is the principle of personal responsibility that one who stands to make a profit out of an activity should bear the risks associated with it;[15] and the decision in *The Nicholas H* might, perhaps, be justified in terms of personal responsibility by saying that the cargo owner ought to have taken precautions to protect itself as against the classification society. At any

---

[15] See J. Stapleton, *Product Liability* (London, 1994), ch. 8.

rate, Lord Steyn, speaking for the majority in that case thought that the decision in favour of the classification society was not only expedient in terms of loss spreading but also "just" as between the two parties.

Nevertheless, those who are responsible for building and maintaining an institution such as tort law and those who use it are free to utilize it to achieve what functions they choose. It is probably true that some people see loss spreading as a function of tort law and seek to use it to that end. The real difficulty is that tort law is, by reason of its structure, not well-designed to perform this function. It may be possible to adapt an institution structured around the concept of personal responsibility for conduct to perform the function of identifying the party best able to spread losses. The problem is that because of the way tort law is structured, the only loss spreaders available to the court as targets are the victim and the injurer. If the court were allowed to go beyond those two parties, it might identify a much better loss spreader than either of them.

Arguments for the Abolition of Tort Law

The conclusion of the last paragraph leads to a much more general point which has formed the basis, in the last 30 years or so, of many attacks on tort law and many calls for its "abolition", at least in certain areas. The general point is this: the effectiveness of tort law in achieving anything is constrained by its basic nature and structure as a set of ethical rules and principles of personal responsibility. This means that if we try to use tort law for some purpose unrelated to ideas of personal responsibility, it is bound to be more or less ineffective in achieving that purpose. People can use tort law for all sorts of ends, but the very nature and structure of tort law may make it an inadequate mechanism for securing some of those ends. However, if no other better tool is available, and if the existence of tort law is seen to stand in the way of the creation of some better tool, people may start to call for the abolition of tort law and its replacement by some other mechanism better adapted to achieving whatever end(s) they desire.

This has happened most obviously in relation to compensation for personal injuries. It is, of course, one of the functions of tort law to compensate victims of personal injuries. However, the rules of tort law establishing the conditions which a victim must meet in order to recover compensation exclude many victims of personal injuries from the protection of tort law. Moreover, even victims who can satisfy those conditions may face many practical difficulties, resulting from the way the tort system operates, in recovering any or all of the compensation to which the rules of tort law entitle them.

In the late 1950s a large number of pregnant women in Western countries took a drug called Thalidomide to combat morning sickness. The babies of many of these women were born with more or less serious physical disabilities. Tort claims for compensation made on behalf of these disabled children against the manufacturers of the drug turned out to be extremely problematic, and no manufacturer was ever found liable in tort to any of the disabled children. Even so, many people believed that whatever the legal position, the drug manufacturers were under a moral obligation to compensate the children (and significant sums of compensation were paid). This incident generated a great deal of dissatisfaction with the state of tort law. Many people came to think that whatever tort law said, the victims of the "Thalidomide tragedy" should have been legally entitled to compensation for their injuries. The main problems facing the Thalidomide claimants in establishing tort liability were the difficulty of proving that the drug manufacturers had been negligent and the difficulty of proving that the disabilities had been caused by the ingestion of the drug by the mothers. Similar difficulties in establishing that D acted tortiously, and in proving a causal connection between that conduct and injury suffered by P, continue to dog tort actions for so-called "environmental harms", such as cancers allegedly associated with living near nuclear installations or high-voltage electricity cables, as well as drug-related litigation. Tort law has proved to be an inadequate tool for meeting the demands for compensation and protection of victims of such "diffuse harms".

One consequence of the Thalidomide tragedy was the eventual adoption in many jurisdictions of stricter liability regimes in respect of injuries caused by defective products. Such regimes to a greater or lesser extent remove the requirement to prove negligence in product cases. However, they operate within the traditional structure of tort law, and so require P to prove a causal link between conduct of an identified individual (typically a manufacturer) and the injuries suffered. To overcome this problem (in addition to that of difficulty in proving negligence), many tort scholars began to advocate "no-fault" personal injury compensation schemes under which victims of (certain) personal injuries would be entitled to compensation without the need to prove that the injuries were caused by any identified or identifiable individual.

The aspect of these events which I want to focus on here is the methodology adopted by proponents of no-fault personal injury compensation schemes. They began by identifying the main functions of tort law as being compensation and deterrence. Next, they pointed out that there was very little evidence to suggest that tort law was very effective at reducing the incidence of tortiously caused personal injuries. They then observed that because of limitations in its coverage and of practical problems in its operation, the tort system left a large majority of the victims of personal injury uncompensated or, at least, undercompensated. They also observed that the costs of delivering tort compensation to victims, as a proportion of the amount of tort compensation paid, were very high (over 40 percent) and much higher than the administrative costs of the social security system, for instance (less than 15 percent of benefits paid). The conclusion drawn from these facts was that the tort system should be abolished as a mechanism for compensating the victims of personal injuries and replaced by a no-fault compensation fund. The job of reducing the incidence of personal injuries should be left to government health and safety regulators and the criminal law.

The emphasis on the compensation function of tort law was partly a response to the plight of victims such as the Thalidomide children. But it was also partly a response to the impact on tort law of the widespread availability of liability insurance. It was argued by some that because tort damages were typically not paid by tort defendants but by insurance companies, it made little sense to see tort law (as it operated in conjunction with liability insurance) as based on ideas of *personal* responsibility. Rather, because liability insurance was compulsory in relation to road and work accidents, it seemed more accurate to see the tort system (at least in these areas) as designed primarily to compensate victims or, in other words, to meet their *needs*. Viewed in this way, reformers in 1970s Britain found that tort law compared very unfavourably with the social security system, the motivating ideology of which was the meeting of needs. The social security system met more of the needs of more people more efficiently and cheaply than the tort system. It was true that social security benefits were generally smaller in amount than analogous tort damages; but this was seen as an acceptable price to pay for helping more people. The relatively large size of tort damage awards was also seen as creating an unjustified preference in favour of those personal injury victims who fell within the scope of tort law. In short, viewed as a compensation system for meeting the needs of personal injury victims, tort law was a miserable failure.

A quite different response to the impact of widespread liability insurance on personal injury tort law came to the fore in the US in the 1980s.[16] This grew out of the economic analysis of law which saw tort law as a sort of surrogate for the market. According to this approach, because, for practical reasons, it would be very difficult to organize a market in which road users (for instance) could sell protection from personal injury to, and buy it from, other road users, tort law steps in and allocates to road users those rights to personal safety which they would buy in the market if there was one. The essence of the market is that individuals decide for themselves what to buy and sell; and the moral underpinning of market activity is individual autonomy. In the 1980s, scholars who put a very high value on freedom of choice began to think that viewed as a system of insurance against personal injury, tort law coupled with liability insurance involved an undesirable intrusion on individual autonomy. This was because tort law effectively dictated to personal injury victims what losses they would be insured against and what benefits they would receive. Tort plaintiffs were forced to accept the insurance benefits which tort law provided (and indirectly to pay for those benefits) even if, left to themselves, they would not have bought those benefits or would have bought lower benefits. The conclusion was that tort law ought to be abolished, leaving people free to insure themselves against personal injury to the extent they chose.

Both of these responses to the impact on tort law of widespread liability insurance, the "needs approach" and the "choice approach", involved viewing tort law as a system for insuring against personal injury rather than as a set of rules and principles of personal responsibility. A rigorous pursuit of either approach inevitably leads to calls for the abolition of tort and its replacement by some other mechanism for dealing with personal injuries, because each is fundamentally inconsistent with the idea that personal injuries should be dealt with by a system of rules of personal responsibility. On the other hand, although the needs approach is often seen as based on a principle of *social* responsibility, while tort is based on principles of *individual* responsibility, the meeting of needs of others is as much a part of individual private morality as the idea of responsibility for one's actions. Respect for the autonomy and freedom of others is also an

[16] See J. Stapleton "Tort, Insurance and Ideology" (1995) 58 *MLR* 820, 833–43.

aspect of private morality. Morality is a complex mix of many principles and ideas, including responsibility for one's conduct, respect
for individual autonomy and freedom, and compassion for the needs
of others. The debates which have taken place in the past 30 years
about the best way to compensate victims of personal injury have
concerned the question of which moral principle(s) society ought to
adopt as the basis for dealing with personal injury.

In Chapter 1 I argued that tort law is a set of ethical principles of
personal responsibility which society finds acceptable as the basis for
state-sponsored dispute settlement and publicly enforceable sanctions. Social security and social welfare law is a set of rules and principles which society finds acceptable as the basis for social compassion
for the needs of the less well-off of its members. The complex web
of legal rules which support and regulate the market represent society's judgement about the proper bounds of individual autonomy and
freedom of choice in the economic sphere. Each of these bodies of
law is derived from, but is not necessarily coincident with, the moral
principles espoused by members of society as a basis for living those
parts of their lives which are beyond the purview of the law, and
which individuals may use as a basis for assessing and criticising the
Moreover, one of the functions of each of these bodies of law is
embody compromises between irreconcilable differences of moral
on amongst members of society about personal responsibility
the proper bounds of compassion and personal autonomy.

question of whether the basis of the social regime for dealing
claims of personal injuries should be personal responsibility,
individual choice is, at bottom, a political one. In fact, in
countries, "personal injuries law" is a complex amalgam of
principles, some based on ideas of personal responsibility,
of need, and some on the idea of freedom of choice.
instance, compensation for personal injuries is pro-
through tort law (based on principles of personal
and funded by liability insurance), partly through the
security system (based on the idea of need and funded by taxation), and partly through private insurance bought by victims
(expressing the idea of individual autonomy and the market). This is
not surprising because the law reflects morality, and the three ideas of
responsibility, compassion and autonomy, amongst others, jostle for
attention in the moral universe as much as in the legal.

Tort law is affected by the social context in which it operates. For
instance, in the 1960s and 1970s, the heyday of the Welfare State in

Britain, the bounds of tort liability were noticeably expanded in a variety of ways by stressing its compensation function and by strengthening concepts of responsibility at the expense of defendants. In the 1980s, however, a reaction set in under the influence of the enormous ideological shift associated with Thatcherism and Reaganomics. In various contexts, new emphasis was put on the value of individual choice; and in tort law this manifested itself in retrenchment of some of the expansion of the previous two decades and a stressing of the responsibility of victims of injury and damage to protect themselves. Nevertheless, many people still try to use the tort system to make good perceived defects in social provision for misfortunes of various sorts. Largely unsuccessful attempts to obtain tort damages for environmental harms, such as cancers allegedly associated with nuclear power generation or high-voltage electricity cables, provide obvious examples. Courts, however, are now less willing than they might have been twenty years ago to modify the rules and principles of tort law to provide compensation in such cases.

In the end, ideas of need and individual autonomy can only b[e] accommodated to a limited extent within the framework of tort la[w] built as it is around the idea of personal responsibility for o[ne's] actions. Compassion for others may override responsibility for t[heir] plight; and responsibility for another's misfortune has a moral f[orce] which is ultimately at odds with the individualist philosophy o[f the] market. The burning and unresolved political issue of tort law [is the] proper province of personal responsibility as the basis for leg[is]lation of social life and human interaction. Of course, re[asonable] people might disagree about how to resolve this issue; and [one of the] functions of lawmakers is to strike an acceptable c[ompromise] between such differing points of view. In the process of [trying] to organize social life through law, it is important to [respect the] nature of tort law and to avoid setting it tasks, and e[xpecting it to] perform functions and meet goals, which it is structu[rally unable to] achieve.

One final point deserves to be made relevant to the i[ssue of the] relationship between the structure of tort law and its functions. [The] debates of the past three decades about the fate of tort law have be[en] very largely concerned with one particular interest protected by tor[t] law, namely the interest in bodily safety (and, to a lesser extent[,] health).[17] Some have also argued that in some contexts, at least, tort

---

[17] On health see J. Stapleton, *Disease and the Compensation Debate* (Oxford, 1986).

liability for damage to or the destruction or loss of tangible property ought to be abolished leaving people free to make what arrangements they choose to protect their property. But no-one to my knowledge has argued, for instance, that tort liability for infringement of intellectual property rights or for defamation should be abolished, leaving people to purchase protection for such rights or for their reputation in the market, let alone in favour of some non-tort compensation scheme. The main reason for this concentration on bodily safety is, no doubt, that this interest is very highly valued, as witnessed by the statutory requirements for insurance against liability for road and work injuries. At any rate, the result is that discussion of personal injuries law has become a more or less self-contained part of the debate about the future tort law. It is true that tort liability for personal injuries caused by defective products has also developed as a quite distinct organizational category in the law, but as has been forcefully pointed out, the logic of this development is by no means clear.[18]

CONCLUSION

In this book I have given an account of tort law as a system of ethical rules and principles of personal responsibility. The account has stressed the correlative structure of causes of action in tort and rejected the traditional division of the law into "torts". Instead, I have dismantled tort law into its three basic components of protected interests, sanctioned conduct and sanctions, and then reconstructed tort law out of these components. In the process, fresh light has been thrown on many of the doctrines of tort law, and much has been learnt about the grounds and foundations of tort liability and about justifications for its imposition. In Chapter 6 I concluded that as a legal category, tort law should not be used for dispositive purposes but, at most, as a convenient expository tool. In this final chapter, I have explained the relationship between tort law viewed as a set of rules and principles of personal responsibility on the one hand, and its functions and effects on the other. Much can be learned by analyzing this relationship, and much misunderstanding has been generated by failure to do so. In short, the account of tort law offered in this book illuminates its internal structure, many of its central doctrines, its usefulness as a legal category, and its functions and effects. In my view,

[18] J. Stapleton, *Product Liability* (London, 1994), esp. Part 3.

the time has come to abandon the use of the categories of tort law and the law of obligations in an explanatory and certainly in a dispositive way. It may be that these categories still have some expository value. There may be no strong reason, for instance, to hive off the property torts into property law; and, no doubt, books on tort law will continue to be written. But we should cease to think of tort law as a category with juridical significance. Rather we should analyze private law causes of action in terms of protected interests, sanctioned conduct and sanctions.

INDEX

actionability *per se* 47, 89–90, 139, 148
  see also under damage as gist of action
acts and omissions 29, 63–4, 124, 125–9, 179
  see also under omissions *and* nonfeasance
assumption of responsibility 159–60, 164–6
autonomy 234–6

bailment 79
burden of proof 130, 171–6

categorization, legal 197ff, 201ff
  dispositive and expository 198ff
  restitution 202–3
causation 58, 90, 166ff
  but-for test 168–70, 178
  element of some heads of tort liability 48, 90
  intervening 176–7
  liability proportional to 171–6
  loss of chance 172–3
  necessity and sufficiency 168–70
  NESS test 168–70, 178
  omissions 169
  remoteness 176–8
  victim's conduct 178–9
causes of action 4, 29, 123, 153–5
Chancery courts 75, 187, 191
civil law 5, 11
civil law approach to tort law 3
Code Civil, Art. 1382 3
common law approach to tort law 3
compensation 46–7, 103ff, 136–7, 220–1, 231ff
  centrality of in tort law 104–5, 113
  full compensation principle 107–10
    criticisms of 110–112
    ethical basis of 111, 112, 116
    once-for-all rule 106–7
    100 percent principle 108–9
    standard of living principle 108, 109–110
  function of tort law 218–21, 231–7
concurrent liability 23–4, 81, 86, 153–5, 199–200
  categorization and 155, 182–3
  limitation of actions 23, 154–5, 200
conduct—*see under* sanctioned conduct
constitutive rules 10, 186, 198–9
contract
  see also under protected interests
  concurrent liability 23–4, 80–81, 86, 153–5
  exclusion of liability 93
  freedom of 87, 93, 155–6

good faith negotiations 191
contract law 10, 11, 80
  'classical law of contract' 6
  constitutive role of 10
  fiduciary obligations 190
  remedies 183–5
  tort law and 83–7, 153–5, 183–6, 198–9
  trusts and 84, 188–9
contribution between tortfeasors 110–11, 129
contributory negligence 14, 28, 42, 58–60, 131,
  149, 153, 166, 178
  apportionment of damages 110, 120–22, 153,
  166
corrective justice 17–18, 223–4
correlativity 1, 12ff, 15ff, 19, 42, 96, 116, 119,
  123, 139
courts, role of 16, 19–20
  see also under institutional competence
Criminal Injuries Compensation Scheme 14,
  102, 124
criminal law 9, 11, 52, 62–3, 100–1, 104–5, 124,
  158, 171, 175

damage as gist of action 48, 89–90, 167
  see also under actionability *per se*
debt actions 184
defective premises, goods and services 164–6
defences
  contributory negligence 14, 28, 42, 58–60,
  110, 120–2, 131, 149
  consent 42, 60–1, 120–2, 149
  defamation 35–6, 91, 135–6
  illegality 62–3, 120–22
  justification 92, 151, 157
  self-defence 92
deterrence 116, 119, 207, 217ff
discrimination 45, 53, 74, 87, 138, 157
distributive justice 17–18
duty of care 60, 64, 124–5, 128, 129

EC law 56–7
economic efficiency 210, 221–2
environmental harms 218, 232
equity
  courts 75, 101, 186–7
  fiduciary obligations 189–90
  tort law and 75–6, 186ff
  proprietary remedies 192–3
  unconscionable conduct 80, 191–2